7th Workshop on Balto-Slavic Natural Language Processing (BSNLP 2019)

Florence, Italy
2 August 2019

ISBN: 978-1-5108-9116-6

Printed by Curran Associates, Inc. (2019)

For permission requests, please contact the Association for Computational Linguistics
at the address below.

Association for Computational Linguistics
209 N. Eighth Street
Stroudsburg, Pennsylvania 18360

Phone: 1-570-476-8006
Fax: 1-570-476-0860

acl@aclweb.org

Additional copies of this publication are available from:

Curran Associates, Inc.
57 Morehouse Lane
Red Hook, NY 12571 USA
Phone: 845-758-0400
Fax: 845-758-2633
Email: curran@proceedings.com
Web: www.proceedings.com

BSNLP'2019

The 7th Workshop on
Balto-Slavic Natural Language Processing

Proceedings of the Workshop

BSNLP'2019
August 2, 2019
Florence, Italy

Preface

This volume contains the papers presented at BSNLP-2019: the Seventh Workshop on Balto-Slavic Natural Language Processing. The workshop is organized by ACL SIGSLAV—the Special Interest Group on NLP in Slavic Languages of the Association for Computational Linguistics.

The BSNLP workshops have been convening for over a decade, with a clear vision and purpose. On one hand, the languages from the Balto-Slavic group play an important role due to their widespread use and diverse cultural heritage. These languages are spoken by about one-third of all speakers of the official languages of the European Union, and by over 400 million speakers worldwide. The political and economic developments in Central and Eastern Europe place societies where Balto-Slavic languages are spoken at the center of rapid technological advancement and growing European consumer markets.

On the other hand, research on theoretical and applied NLP in some of these languages still lag behind the "major" languages, such as English and other Western European languages. In comparison to English, which has dominated the digital world since the advent of the Internet, many of these languages still lack resources, processing tools and applications—especially those with smaller speaker bases.

The Balto-Slavic languages pose a wealth of fascinating scientific challenges. The linguistic phenomena specific to the Balto-Slavic languages—complex morphology and free word order—present non-trivial problems for the construction of NLP tools, and require rich morphological and syntactic resources.

The BSNLP workshop aims to bring together researchers in NLP for Balto-Slavic languages from academia and industry. We aim to stimulate research, foster the creation of tools and dissemination of new results. The Workshop serves as a forum for the exchange of ideas and experience and for discussing shared problems. One fascinating aspect of Slavic and Baltic languages is their structural similarity, as well as an easily recognizable lexical and inflectional inventory spanning the groups, which—despite the lack of mutual intelligibility—creates a special environment in which researchers can fully appreciate the shared problems and solutions.

In order to stimulate research and collaboration further, we have organized the second BSNLP Challenge: a shared task on multilingual named entity recognition. We have built a new and significantly larger dataset than for the first shared task, organized in 2017. The data allows systems to be evaluated on recognizing mentions of named entities (NEs) in documents, lemmatization of NEs, and cross-lingual linking of NEs. This edition of the Challenge covers four Slavic languages—Bulgarian, Czech, Polish and Russian—and five named entity types, namely: persons, organizations, locations, events, and products.

We received 20 regular paper submissions, 11 of which were accepted for presentation.

The papers cover a range of topics. Two papers are related to lexical semantics, four to the development of linguistic resources, four to information filtering, information retrieval, and information extraction. Another group of four papers cover topics related to the processing of non-standard language or user-generated content. Finally, one paper describes the NE Challenge.

Sixteen teams expressed interest in participating in the NE Challenge, of which eight submitted results. Seven teams worked on NE recognition in all four languages. Five of the teams that participated in the shared task also submitted system description papers. They are included in this volume, and their work is discussed in the special session dedicated to the Challenge.

This Workshop's presentations—the regular Workshop papers and the Shared Task Challenge—cover at least nine Balto-Slavic languages: Bulgarian, Croatian, Czech, Polish, Russian, Slovak, Slovene, Serbian and Ukrainian.

This Workshop continues the proud tradition established by the earlier BSNLP workshops, which were held in conjunction with the following venues:

1. ACL 2007 Conference in Prague, Czech Republic;

2. IIS 2009: Intelligent Information Systems, in Kraków, Poland;

3. TSD 2011: 14th International Conference on Text, Speech and Dialogue in Plzeň, Czech Republic;

4. ACL 2013 Conference in Sofia, Bulgaria;

5. RANLP 2015 Conference in Hissar, Bulgaria;

6. EACL 2017 Conference in Valencia, Spain.

We sincerely hope that this work will help stimulate further growth of our rich and exciting field.

The BSNLP'2019 Organizers

Organizers:

Tomaž Erjavec, Jožef Stefan Institute, Slovenia
Michał Marcińczuk, Wroclaw University of Science and Technology, Poland
Preslav Nakov, Qatar Computing Research Institute, HBKU, Qatar
Jakub Piskorski, Joint Research Centre of the European Commission, Ispra, Italy
Lidia Pivovarova, University of Helsinki, Finland
Jan Šnajder, University of Zagreb, Croatia
Josef Steinberger, University of West Bohemia, Czech Republic
Roman Yangarber, University of Helsinki, Finland

Program Committee:

Željko Agić, Corti ApS, Copenhagen, Denmark
Senka Drobac, University of Helsinki, Finland
Tomaž Erjavec, Jožef Stefan Institute, Slovenia
Radovan Garabik, Comenius University in Bratislava, Slovakia
Goran Glavaš, University of Mannheim, Germany
Maxim Gubin, Facebook Inc., USA
Miloš Jakubíček, Masaryk University, Brno, Czech Republic / Lexical Computing, Brighton, UK
Tomas Krilavičius, Vytautas Magnus University, Kaunas, Lithuania
Cvetana Krstev, University of Belgrade, Serbia
Vladislav Kuboň, Charles University, Prague, Czech Republic
Nikola Ljubešić, Jožef Stefan Institute, Ljubljana, Slovenia
Olga Mitrofanova, St. Petersburg State University, Russia
Preslav Nakov, Qatar Computing Research Institute, HBKU, Qatar
Maciej Ogrodniczuk, Polish Academy of Sciences, Poland
Petya Osenova, Bulgarian Academy of Sciences, Bulgaria
Rūta Petrauskaitė, Vytautas Magnus University, Lithuania
Maciej Piasecki, Wroclaw University of Science and Technology, Poland
Jakub Piskorski, Joint Research Centre, Ispra, Italy/PAS, Warsaw, Poland
Lidia Pivovarova, University of Helsinki, Finland
Maja Popovic, Dublin City University, Ireland
Alexandr Rosen, Charles University, Prague
Tanja Samardžić, University of Geneva, Switzerland
Agata Savary, University of Tours, France
Kiril Simov, Bulgarian Academy of Sciences, Bulgaria
Inguna Skadiņa, University of Latvia, Latvia
Jan Šnajder, University of Zagreb, Croatia
Marko Robnik Šikonja, University of Ljubljana, Slovenia
Serge Sharoff, University of Leeds, UK
Josef Steinberger, University of West Bohemia, Czech Republic
Pavel Stranak, Charles University, Czech Republic
Stan Szpakowicz, University of Ottawa, Canada
Hristo Tanev, Joint Research Centre, Italy
Irina Temnikova, Sofia University Bulgaria
Andrius Utka Vytautas, Magnus University, Lithuania

Barbora Vidová Hladká, Charles University, Czech Republic
Roman Yangarber, University of Helsinki, Finland
Daniel Zeman, Charles University, Czech Republic

Invited Speaker:

Ivan Vulić, University of Cambridge, UK

Table of Contents

Workshop Program

Thursday, August 2, 2019

8:50–9:00   **Opening Remarks**

9:00–10:30 **Session I: Morphology**

9:00–9:25   *Unsupervised Induction of Ukrainian Morphological Paradigms for the New Lexicon: Extending Coverage for Named Entities and Neologisms using Inflection Tables and Unannotated Corpora*
Bogdan Babych

9:25–9:50   *Multiple Admissibility: Judging Grammaticality using Unlabeled Data in Language Learning*
Anisia Katinskaia and Sardana Ivanova

9:50–10:10 *Numbers Normalisation in the Inflected Languages: a Case Study of Polish*
Rafał Poświata and Michał Perełkiewicz

10:10–10:30 *What does Neural Bring? Analysing Improvements in Morphosyntactic Annotation and Lemmatisation of Slovenian, Croatian and Serbian*
Nikola Ljubešić and Kaja Dobrovoljc

10:30–11:00 **Coffee Break**

11:00–12:25 **Session II: Development of Linguistic Resources**

11:00–11:25 *AGRR 2019: Corpus for Gapping Resolution in Russian*
Maria Ponomareva, Kira Droganova, Ivan Smurov and Tatiana Shavrina

11:25–11:45 *Creating a Corpus for Russian Data-to-Text Generation Using Neural Machine Translation and Post-Editing*
Anastasia Shimorina, Elena Khasanova and Claire Gardent

11:45–12:05 *Data Set for Stance and Sentiment Analysis from User Comments on Croatian News*
Mihaela Bošnjak and Mladen Karan

12:05–12:25 *A Dataset for Noun Compositionality Detection for a Slavic Language*
Dmitry Puzyrev, Artem Shelmanov, Alexander Panchenko and Ekaterina Artemova

12:25–13:30   Lunch

13:30–14:30   Session III: Keynote

13:30–14:30   *Cross-Lingual Word Embeddings in (Less Than) 60 Minutes*
Ivan Vulić

14:30–15:30   Session IV: Shared Task – Part I

14:30–14:45   *The Second Cross-Lingual Challenge on Recognition, Normalization, Classification, and Linking of Named Entities across Slavic Languages*
Jakub Piskorski, Laska Laskova, Michał Marcińczuk, Lidia Pivovarova, Pavel Přibáň, Josef Steinberger and Roman Yangarber

14:45–15:00   *BSNLP2019 Shared Task Submission: Multisource Neural NER Transfer*
Tatiana Tsygankova, Stephen Mayhew and Dan Roth

15:00–15:15   *TLR at BSNLP2019: A Multilingual Named Entity Recognition System*
Jose G. Moreno, Elvys Linhares Pontes, Mickael Coustaty and Antoine Doucet

15:15–15:30   *Tuning Multilingual Transformers for Language-Specific Named Entity Recognition*
Mikhail Arkhipov, Maria Trofimova, Yuri Kuratov and Alexey Sorokin

15:30–16:00   Coffee Break

16:00–16:30   Session V: Shared Task – Part II

16:00–16:15   *Multilingual Named Entity Recognition Using Pretrained Embeddings, Attention Mechanism and NCRF*
Anton Emelyanov and Ekaterina Artemova

16:15–16:30   *JRC TMA-CC: Slavic Named Entity Recognition and Linking. Participation in the BSNLP-2019 shared task*
Guillaume Jacquet, Jakub Piskorski, Hristo Tanev and Ralf Steinberger

16:30–17:45   Session IV: Sentiment Analysis and Recommendation

16:30–16:55   *Building English-to-Serbian Machine Translation System for IMDb Movie Reviews*
Pintu Lohar, Maja Popović and Andy Way

16:55–17:15   *Improving Sentiment Classification in Slovak Language*
Samuel Pecar, Marian Simko and Maria Bielikova

17:15–17:35   *Sentiment Analysis for Multilingual Corpora*
Svitlana Galeshchuk, Ju Qiu and Julien Jourdan

17:35–17:45   Closing Remarks

Unsupervised Induction of Ukrainian Morphological Paradigms for the New Lexicon: Extending Coverage for Named Entities and Neologisms Using Inflection Tables and Unannotated Corpora

Bogdan Babych
Centre for Translation Studies
University of Leeds
UK
`b.babych@leeds.ac.uk`

Abstract

The paper presents an unsupervised method for quickly extending a Ukrainian lexicon by generating paradigms and morphological feature structures for new proper names and neologisms, which are not covered by existing static morphological resources. This approach addresses a practical problem of modelling paradigms for entities created by the dynamic processes in the lexicon: this problem is especially serious for highly-inflected languages in domains with specialised or quickly changing lexicon. The method uses an unannotated Ukrainian corpus and a small fixed set of inflection tables, which can be found in traditional grammar textbooks. The advantage of the proposed approach is that updating the morphological lexicon does not require training or linguistic annotation, allowing fast knowledge-light extension of an existing static lexicon to improve morphological coverage on a specific corpus. The method is implemented in an open-source package on a GitHub repository. It can be applied to other low-resourced inflectional languages which have internet corpora and linguistic descriptions of their inflection system, following the example of inflection tables for Ukrainian. Evaluation results show consistent improvements in coverage for Ukrainian corpora of different corpus types.

1   Introduction

> "Our language can be regarded as an
> ancient city: a maze of little streets
> and squares, of old and new houses,
> of houses with extensions from various
> periods, and all this surrounded by a
> multitude of new suburbs with straight
> and regular streets and uniform houses."
> (Wittgenstein, 2009)

This metaphor from Wittgenstein's 'Philosophical Investigations' may be applied to two aspects of the natural language lexicon, which so far have received little attention in computational linguistics. Firstly, like a city, the lexicon constantly evolves, reflecting political and technical changes in the society that take place very rapidly, so it may be insufficient to design static lexical resources and to expect that they would give the same high level of corpus coverage once and for all: the lexicon needs to be constantly updated to reflect live changes in the system. Secondly, even though there may be many irregularities in the lexicon, similar to 'a maze of little streets', this more often happens with an older lexical core, while new words typically follow more 'straight and regular' patterns, so the task of updating the lexicon for natural language applications may be facilitated by this tendency.

This paper investigates the extent of the new lexicon problem for different types of Ukrainian corpora and further proposes and evaluates a knowledge-light approach to extending lexical coverage of morphological resources to neologisms (new words, meanings or usages) and new single-word Named Entities (proper names) which follow regular inflectional patterns. The scripts and datasets which implement and evaluate the proposed methodology are available on Github (Babych, 2019).

Morphological annotation of the lexicon is an important component for many natural language processing pipelines, such as part-of-speech tagging, morphological disambiguation, parsing, semantic analysis, as well as for applications such as machine translation, information extraction, terminology detection, etc. For example, in part-of-speech tagging the morphological lexicon normally supplies lemmas and associated sets of possible parts-of-speech and values of morphological categories for each token (e.g., for Ukrainian this would be values for the grammatical case: nom-

1

Proceedings of the 7th Workshop on Balto-Slavic Natural Language Processing, pages 1–11,
Florence, Italy, 2 August 2019. ©2019 Association for Computational Linguistics

inative, genitive, dative, accusative, instrumental, locative, vocative; number: singular, plural; gender: masculine, feminine, neuter; person: 1st, 2nd, 3rd; mood: indicative, imperative, subjunctive; tense: past, present, future, etc.). The tagger then resolves any potential ambiguity using transition probabilities, trained neural networks, etc. For any language the creation of a morphological lexicon is difficult, because of a large number of lexical types needed to achieve good corpus coverage and also because of irregularities in word paradigms (systems of inflected word forms, lemmas and associated morphological features). For highly inflected Slavonic languages the creation of the morphological lexicon is even more challenging, since most words have complex morphological paradigms, which require fine-grained annotation of parts-of-speech and their grammatical subcategories. Creation of high-quality morphological resources for these languages often requires an extensive effort over many years.

Like the majority of other Slavonic languages, Ukrainian is a highly inflected language with the 'synthetic' grammar structure (where grammatical relations are predominantly marked within content word forms), so the task of morphological paradigm generation for it is not trivial. It is also more critical for the accuracy of related tasks, such as part-of-speech tagging, because of a larger potential number of combinations of possible morphological values: it is harder to guess the correct part-of-speech tag based on neighbouring tags in the case of a missing word form. Ukrainian paradigms for inflected parts of speech have between 7 and 28 distinct morphological feature combinations and associated word forms for a single lemma, and there is both regular and irregular ambiguity within and across different parts-of-speech and lexicogrammatical classes of words (i.e., animate vs. inanimate nouns, perfective vs. imperfective verbs). In Ukrainian, as in other highly-inflected languages most morphological information is supplied within the word rather than by the context, so lexical gaps are more detrimental for correct prediction of inflected word forms and their morphological characteristics.

For Ukrainian there exist wide-coverage lexical resources (see Section 2), however, extending them in a traditional rule-based way would involve continuous annotation effort requiring linguistic expertise and near-native knowledge of the language, making it hard to keep up with most recent lexical developments.

The approach proposed in this paper is designed for the scenario where for a highly-inflected language there exists a hand-crafted static morphological lexicon that covers potentially irregular and more frequent lexical core. For extending this lexicon to cover new regularly inflected entities I use an internet corpus and small inflection tables from grammar textbooks, e.g., (Hryshchenko et al., 1997), (Press and Pugh, 2015): such resources would often be available for other low-resourced languages, since the tasks that would require linguistic expertise (i.e., creating the core lexicon and inflection tables) need to be done only once, so paradigms for new entities can be automatically created whenever a new corpus becomes available. Core static morphological lexicons have been developed for several low-resourced languages, either as stand-alone resources or within shared frameworks, such as Universal Dependencies (Nivre et al., 2016), Apertium (Forcada et al., 2011) (in the context of Machine Translation) or Grammatical Framework (Ranta, 2011) (in limited subject domains). However, the task of extending morphological lexicon in response to dynamic processes in the lexical system, emergence of neologisms, new terminology or Named Entities has not been systematically addressed so far.

The paper is organised as follows. In Section 2 I review some of the previous work in the area, in Section 3 I describe the algorithm, datasets and an experiment on generating paradigms, in Section 4 I present experimental results on comparative evaluation of lexical coverage on different corpora for the baseline static morphological lexicon and for the extended paradigms which cover the new lexicon. Section 5 presents a discussion of examples of identified new entities and in Section 6 I summarise conclusion and ideas for future work.

2 Previous Work

Several projects have addressed the problem of developing the Ukrainian morphological lexicon and morphological disambiguation strategies: (Perebyjnis et al., 1989), (Gryaznukhina, 1999), (Rysin and Starko, 2019), (Kotsyba et al., 2009), (Kotsyba et al., 2010), (Babych and Sharoff, 2016). For the experiments presented in this paper I use the most complete morphological toolkit from (Rysin and Starko, 2019), which in its current

Corpus	No of words	No of sent
News	461,451,019	31,021,650
Wikipedia	185,645,357	15,786,948
Fiction	18,323,509	1,811,548
Law	578,988,264	29,208,302
Total	1,244,408,149	77,828,448

Table 1: Description of Ukrainian corpora from (Dyomkin et al., 2019).

implementation contains a wide-coverage lexicon: 366,846 Ukrainian lemmas, which are expanded into 5,690,688 word forms with corresponding morphological feature combinations.

We evaluate the coverage of this lexicon on large Ukrainian corpora collected in lang-uk project (Dyomkin et al., 2019), Table 1 is taken from this source, it describes these collections.

Detailed overviews of different approaches to developing morphological lexicons can be found in (Ahlberg et al., 2015), (Koskenniemi et al., 2018) and (Fam and Lepage, 2018). For our purposes the existing approaches can be characterised by their application scenarios and assumptions about available datasets. Interesting work has been done within the neural, supervised and semi-supervised frameworks, e.g., (Ahlberg et al., 2015), (Ahlberg et al., 2014), (Koskenniemi et al., 2018), (Silfverberg et al., 2018), (Wolf-Sonkin et al., 2018), (Kirov and Cotterell, 2018), (Faruqui et al., 2016), (Faruqui et al., 2015), (Aharoni and Goldberg, 2016), (Cotterell et al., 2017). Much of this work assumes availability of partially labelled data, such as word paradigms and/or clean datasets, such as lists of 'headwords' (lemmas) from which paradigms are generated. (Fam and Lepage, 2018) identify three main approaches to learning morphological inflection: the hand-engineered rule-based approach, which requires much cost and time for construction, the supervised approach, which relies on initial labelled datasets and the neural approach, which needs more training time and even more data. However, for low-resource scenarios more attention need to be given to unsupervised knowledge-light methods, which could make strong assumptions, e.g., based on compact linguistic descriptions of the inflection systems, but for the most part rely only unlabelled data or resources that would be typically available for low-resource languages.

A terminological note: in several papers, such as (Ahlberg et al., 2015), (Silfverberg et al., 2018), the term 'paradigm' is used to describe a generalised inflection pattern, which could apply to a class of words, while the term 'inflection table' characterises an individual system of inflection for a single word. This usage differs from the traditional understanding of the notion of a paradigm as a system of word forms for a given word, see e.g., (Spencer, 2001). In this paper I adhere to the traditional terminological usage for the term 'paradigm' as a system of word forms, and use the term 'inflection tables' referring only to tables of inflections, which may be attached to a class of stems.

The problem of characterising dynamic processes in the Ukrainian lexicon has been discussed in (Klymenko et al., 2008), (Karpilovs'ka et al., 2008), where these changes are attributed to political, cultural and technical developments in the society – the active 'social dynamics', which causes the active 'linguistic dynamics': renewal and additions to nominative and communicative resources of the language and changes in linguistic norms. While the grammar or phonology remain more conservative, the lexicon is very open to such changes. There is an ongoing work to record these lexical developments for Ukrainian and other languages, however, so far there is no systematic computational linguistic framework for modelling morphological features and inflections for neologisms and new Named Entities.

3 Algorithm Description

The proposed algorithm uses small set of inflection tables for inflected parts-of-speech which accepts new entities (i.e., nouns, adjectives and verbs, but not numerals or pronouns, which are closed class entities) and unannotated corpus (or a frequency list compiled from such a corpus). It attempts to split each token in the corpus into its stem and inflection using all inflections in all available inflection tables. When a split is successful, it generates a full hypothetical paradigm consistent with the split, using the identified stem and all other inflections for the given table. Then these hypotheses are checked against available word forms in the corpus: whether a sufficient number of forms can be found to confirm the hypothetical paradigm. In this approach for the paradigms to be generated reliably, the new entities need to have a sufficient morphological

```
Given: a list L= {t1 ... tN} // tokens from the corpus
       a set I={i1...iM} // inflection tables from grammar descriptions,
       where:
               iX = {fl1:mf1 ... flP:mfP} //inflections set mapped to m-features
for all tokens t in L do:
       for all tables i in I do:
               for all inflections fl in each iX do:
                       if token t = [stem] + inflection fl:
                               // generate paradigm expectations:
                               for all inflections fl in iX do:
                                       expectedToken = [stem] + flY and
                                       expectedToken=[stem]<distortion|+flY
                                       if expectedToken in list L: // corpus
                                               paradigmHypothesis(stem,iX)++
                               end
               end
       end
end
// generation of paradigms for paradigm hypotheses above a threshold:
for all paradigmHypothesis(stem,iX) > Threshold do: // stems + inflection sets
       for all inflections:morhFeatures fl:mf in iX do:
               wordForm = stem + fl : mf or
               wordForm = stem|distortion> + fl : mf
       end
end
```

Figure 1: Algorithm description.

diversity in the corpus: it has been experimentally established that at least 3 or 4 different word forms are needed to make a reasonably accurate prediction of a paradigm and its remaining unseen word forms. For confirmed paradigms the algorithm generates all remaining word forms, their lemma (as a designated 'dictionary' word form in the paradigm, e.g., the nominative singular form for nouns) and their sets of morphological category values associated with inflections, based on the expected structure of the paradigm. Multiple splits of a token are possible, so hypothetical paradigms are ranked by the number of confirmed word forms, and the paradigm with the highest number is selected among the competing paradigms. Figure 1 shows the general overview of the algorithm. Scripts are released on GitHub repository: https://github.com/bogdanbabych/ paralex4morphosyntax.

For a general case to cover less regular paradigms with stem alternations the algorithm may be complemented with a distortion model which modifies tested tokens and hypothetical word forms according to morphonological rules of the language, for Ukrainian this would cover historical alternations such as [o,e] -> [i] in 'newly closed' syllables, e.g., [kon'a] (horse.Gen.sing) -> [kin'] (horse.Nom.sing), [h, k, x] before [i] -> [z, ts, s], e.g., [ruka] (hand.Nom.sing) -> [rutsi] (hand.Dat.sing), etc.

The example in Figure 2 illustrates working of the algorithm. In this example I assume that the current token is рука (ruka = 'hand'), for which the algorithm will try to generate paradigms. In

this dataset I have inflection tables for the 'hard', 'soft', 'iotated' and 'mixed' groups of the 1st declination of nouns, taken from a Ukrainian grammar textbook (Hryshchenko et al., 1997): фабрика, робітниця, надія, площа (fabryka = 'factory', robitnyts'a = 'worker', nadija = 'hope', ploshcha = 'town square'): I use only inflection sets and morphological values from these tables (the stems in the inflection tables are only for illustration).

In the first stage the algorithm tries every inflection in every table to split the current token ('ruka'). A possible split is found in the inflection table for the 1st declination of nouns, for the 'hard' and 'mixed' groups illustrated by examples 'fabryka' and 'ploshcha'. The split separates the stem 'ruk' and the inflection 'a'.

In the second stage, trying the split for the 'hard' group, the word form hypotheses are generated from the inflection table: *ruk+y, ruk+u, ruk+oju, ruk-o, ruk, ruk+amy, ruk+ax* and with the distortion model: [k] /_[i] -> [ts] – *ruts+i*. For the split defined by the 'mixed' group inflection table, in addition two incorrect word forms will be generated *ruk+eju, *ruk-e, but the following three correct forms will not be generated: *ruk-y, ruk-oju, ruk-o*. Therefore, two paradigms for the split *rukla* will be competing with each other.

In the third stage, each of the competing paradigms will be verified against the corpus: in this example, for the 'hard' group the following four hypothesised word forms are actually found: *ruk, ruk+am, ruk+ax, ruk+y*, which, together with the 5th original form *ruk+a*, correspond to 7 morphological feature combinations, since *ruk+y* is ambiguous having three interpretations. While for the 'mixed' group only three hypothesised forms will be confirmed + initial *ruk+a* = 4, because the existing form *ruk+y* has not been predicted by the 'mixed' paradigm. As a result, the correct 'hard' paradigm will be ranked higher, with 5 confirmed word form hypotheses vs. 4 confirmed hypotheses for the wrong 'mixed' paradigm. When the corpus gets larger, more clues may differentiate such closely competing paradigms and more correct rankings may be produced.

In the fourth stage the top-ranking paradigm is confirmed and previously unseen word forms are generated, as well as possible part-of-speech code, lemma and all possible morphological feature combinations for both seen and unseen word

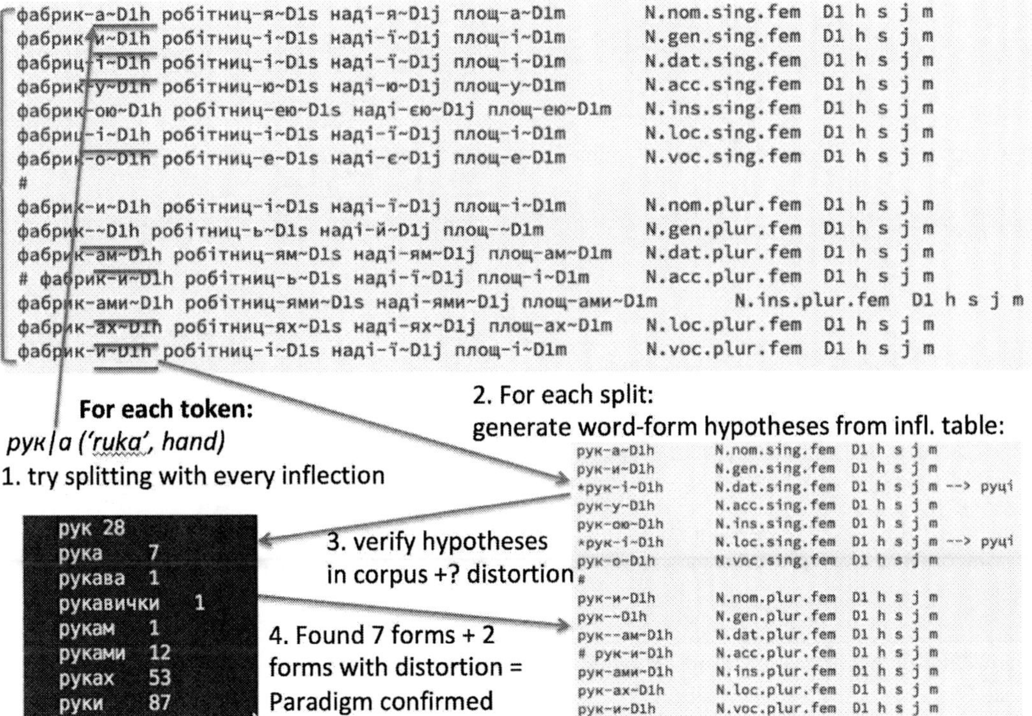

Figure 2: Illustration of the algorithm.

forms, such as values for case, number, gender, e.g., the unseen word form *ruk+u* will be generated with its morphological information *ruk-u : lem=ruka; PoS=N.acc.sing*, etc.

Note that for a single token it is not possible to clearly distinguish between a competing wrong paradigm and an alternative legitimate paradigm, which corresponds to a different reading of an ambiguous word form. For example, the word form *pryklady* belongs both to *PoS=N.nom.plur; lemma=pryklad* (*'example'*) and to *PoS=V.imper.pers2.sing; lemma=pryklasty/pryklad+u* (*'to attach'*). The limitation of the algorithm is that only one of these correct paradigms is confirmed for the given word form *pryklady*, depending on how many hypothesised word forms are found in corpus for each of the verbal or nominal paradigms. However, the same paradigm is confirmed via different routes, i.e., through splitting other word forms belonging to the same paradigm, e.g., in Figure 2 the paradigm for *lemma=ruka, PoS=N* will be also confirmed via splitting the corpus tokens *ruklam, ruklamy, ruklax*. This gives the proposed algorithm an advantage, compared to the approach described in (Ahlberg et al., 2015) for the case

of overlapping paradigms with ambiguous word forms: alternative readings will be confirmed by the tokens in corpus which are unique for each of the alternative paradigms, e.g., *pryklad+ut'* (*'they will attach'*) vs. *pryklad+om* (*'with an example'*). Interestingly, ambiguous word forms are not discarded: when unambiguous tokens are split for each of the overlapping paradigms, the ambiguous tokens will count in both cases to confirm both of the correct paradigms. This will not happen for competing wrong paradigms: their wrong word form predictions (such as **ruk+eju* in the example above) will simply not be found in corpus, so they will not initiate the process for the alternative paradigm.

For the purposes of this experiment I evaluate the coverage given by the algorithm without a distortion model, as such alternations are more typical for the older lexicon and often do not occur in recently borrowed items, e.g. [portu] (port.Gen.sing) - port (port.Nom.sing): [o] -> [i] alternation does not take place, as the word was borrowed after the phonological law of the 'open syllable' no longer worked in Ukrainian. However, in future the distortion models may be learnt from data or directly coded as explicit linguistic

Corpus	No of generated word forms
dict_uk	5,690,688
News	3,292,591
Wikipedia	3,765,774
Fiction	958,233
Law	1,788,288
All corpora	6,626,004

Table 2: Size of lexicon extracted from corpora.

knowledge, and in this way the older paradigms and live stem alternations may also be covered.

4 Evaluating Algorithm with Corpus Coverage

The algorithm is used for extending the Ukrainian morphological lexicon from four corpora: news, wikipedia, law and fiction, and from a combined corpus that merges these four corpora. Table 2 shows the number of word forms extracted from each of the corpora presented in Table 1.

We measure the coverage (in terms of lexical types) in four corpora and in the merged corpus, with gradually filtering out lower frequency ranges. The rationale for this evaluation method is that it is usually harder for the lexicon to cover low-frequent items, so I test this lexicons on a range of tasks of varying difficulty.

Another important aspect of evaluation would be the accuracy of the generated paradigms, e.g., the proportion of correctly generated entries, which in this paper is evaluated only indirectly, as the coverage on previously unseen corpus, as correctly generated paradigms should cover more types in the unseen corpora. Direct evaluation of accuracy will be a matter of future work, as it requires systematic sampling for different frequency ranges and more extensive manual annotation effort, which is beyond the scope of this paper.

Note that the accuracy evaluation for the algorithm would require a more complex potentially multidimensional metric, which would need to address the following aspects of accuracy: (a) correctness of the whole paradigm vs. correctness of individual forms and morphological codes, such as the case labels for animate vs. inanimate nouns that, e.g., may overlap in accusative and genitive or nominative, depending on this morphological category; (b) partial overlaps of sub-paradigms, e.g., soft, hard and mixed phonological groups, or the regular masculine vs. neuter overlap in sev-

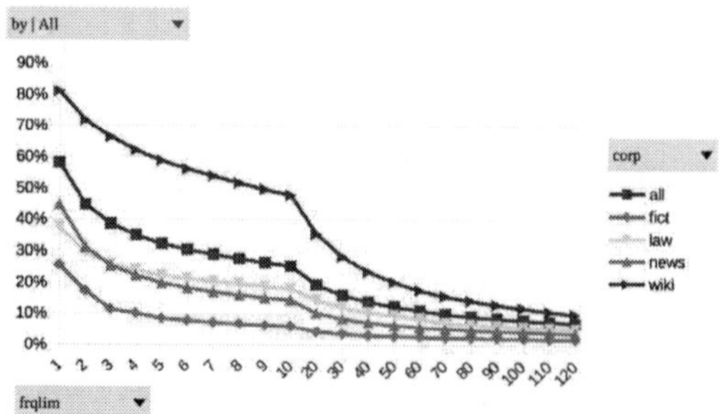

Figure 3: The baseline: Percent of non-covered types (y) in dict_uk lexicon, with filtered out lower frequencies, up to (x).

eral indirect case values in nominal and adjectival paradigms, etc.; (c) defective paradigms and potential word forms; (d) morphological variants in paradigms; (e) word forms determined by independent parameters but not by the paradigm-wide inflection class, e.g., vocative case in Ukrainian; (f) different impact of errors in paradigms, depending on syntagmatic frequency, which may be determined stylistically, grammatically or lexically (e.g., the imperative is less frequent in narrative texts, so imperative errors should be counted as less serious then errors in more common 3rd-person-singular forms).

Even though the accuracy evaluation would be important for understanding theoretical value of the proposed approach, it is less relevant for the practical scenario of updating the morphological lexicon for specialised domain, compared to the evaluation of coverage: incorrect (overgenerated) word forms in paradigms normally should not cause any additional errors compared to the baseline, as they would simply not match, the same as without the added lexicon.

As the baseline, Figure 3 shows the coverage of the existing static lexicon from the dict_uk project developed by (Rysin and Starko, 2019) (also characterised in the first row in Table 2). The horizontal axis indicates which frequency range has been filtered out. (Note the change of scale in the middle of the graph from 1 to 10 in one unit of length).

It can be seen from the figure that the Wikipedia corpus that contains many Named Entities and specialised terminology is the most problematic in terms of coverage: up to 80% of its types are not covered, which goes down only to around 50% if the frequency threshold is reduced to 10. At the same time a 'static' corpus of fiction texts is cov-

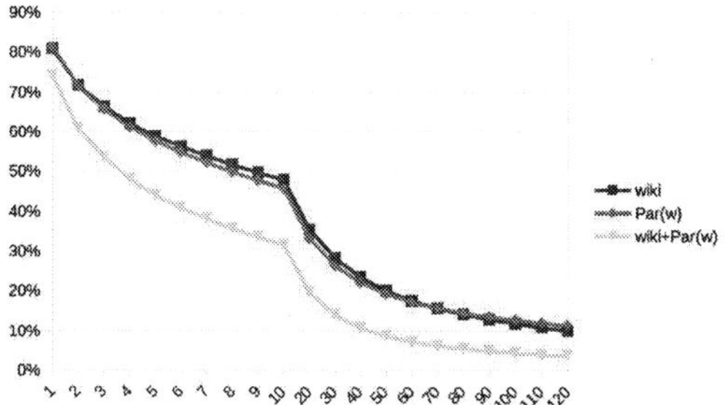

Figure 4: Percent of non-covered types (y) in Wiki corpus, with dict_uk ('wiki' line), with only proposed algorithm and paradigms generated from News corpus ('Par(w)' line), and with the two morphological lexicons combined (wiki+Par(w) line); filtered out lower frequencies, up to (x).

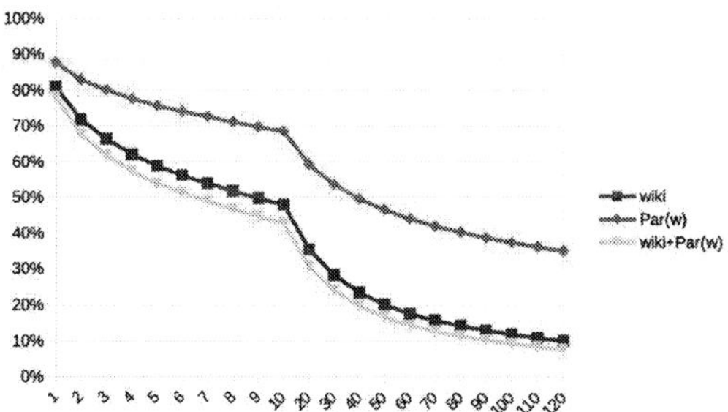

Figure 5: Percent of non-covered types (y) in Wiki corpus, with dict_uk ('wiki' line), with only proposed algorithm and paradigms generated from Law corpus ('Par(w)' line), and with the two morphological lexicons combined (wiki+Par(w) line); filtered out lower frequencies, up to (x).

ered the best by the existing morphological lexicon.

We evaluate the effect of the proposed algorithm via measuring improvements in coverage of lexical types across the frequency ranges for filtered out items. I use different corpora for the development and evaluation, so the following figures show the corpus coverage for these different combinations (lower lines indicate better results). Figure 4 and Figure 5 show coverage levels for the Wiki corpus with paradigms generated from the News and Law corpora respectively. Figure 6 and Figure 7 show coverage for the News corpus with paradigms developed from the Wiki and Law corpora. Finally, Figure 8 and Figure 9 show coverage for the Law corpus with paradigms developed from the Wiki and News corpora. In these figures the baseline graphs labelled 'wiki', 'news' and 'law' are the same as shown in Figure 3.

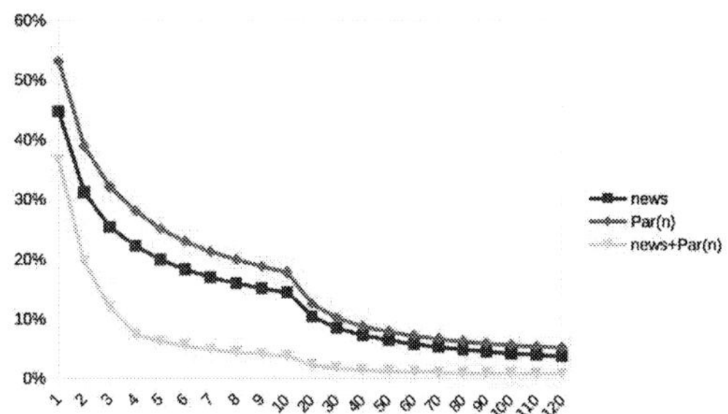

Figure 6: Percent of non-covered types (y) in News corpus, with dict_uk ('news' line), with only proposed algorithm and paradigms generated from Wiki corpus ('Par(n)' line), and with the two morphological lexicons combined (news+Par(n) line); filtered out lower frequencies, up to (x).

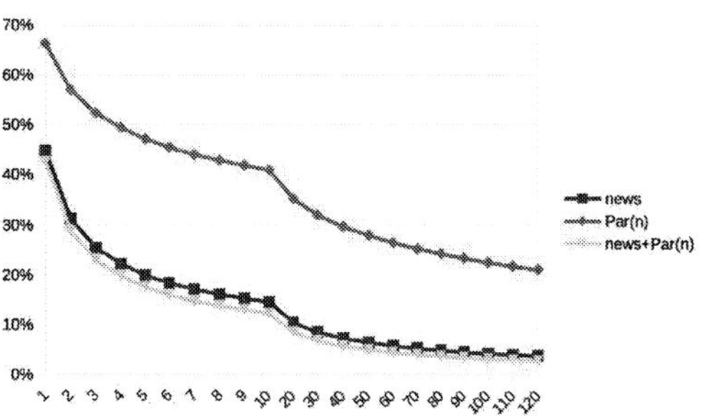

Figure 7: Percent of non-covered types (y) in News corpus, with dict_uk ('news' line), with only proposed algorithm and paradigms generated from Law corpus ('Par(n)' line), and with the two morphological lexicons combined (news+Par(n) line); filtered out lower frequencies, up to (x).

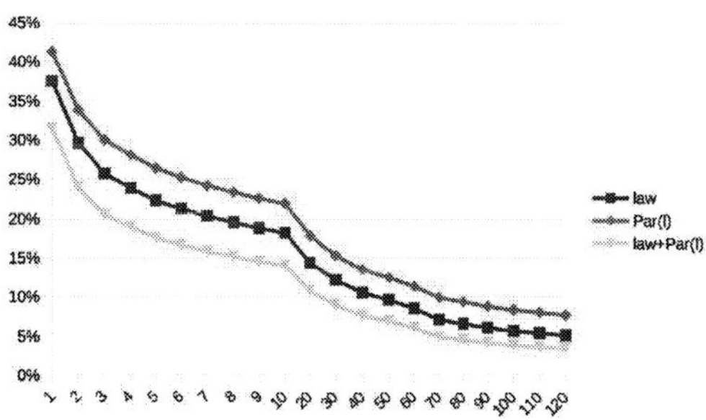

Figure 8: Percent of non-covered types (y) in Law corpus, with dict_uk ('law' line), with only proposed algorithm and paradigms generated from Wiki corpus ('Par(l)' line), and with the two morphological lexicons combined (law+Par(l) line); filtered out lower frequencies, up to (x).

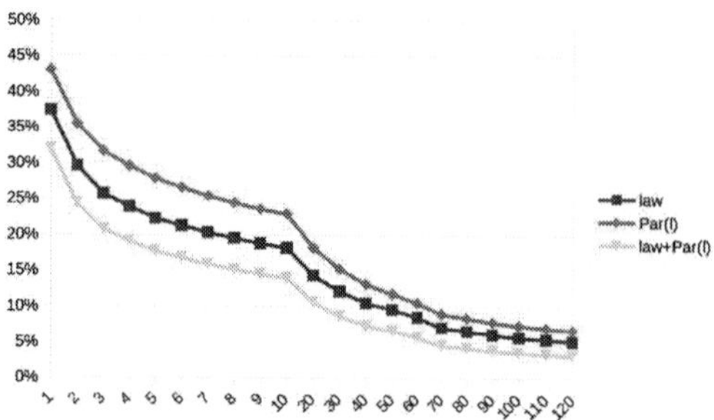

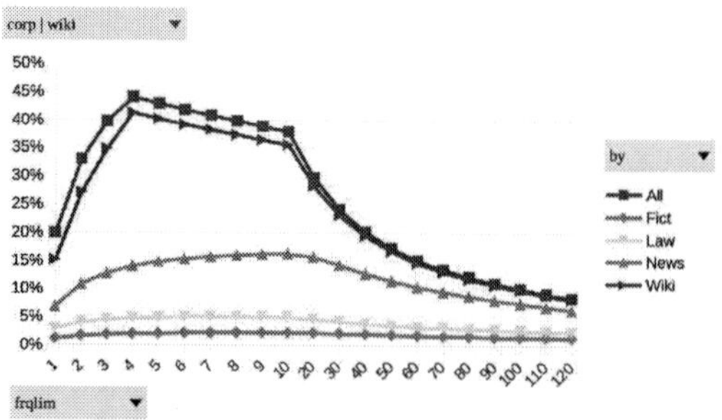

Figure 9: Percent of non-covered types (y) in Law corpus, with dict_uk ('law' line), with only proposed algorithm and paradigms generated from News corpus ('Par(l)' line), and with the two morphological lexicons combined (law+Par(l) line); filtered out lower frequencies, up to (x).

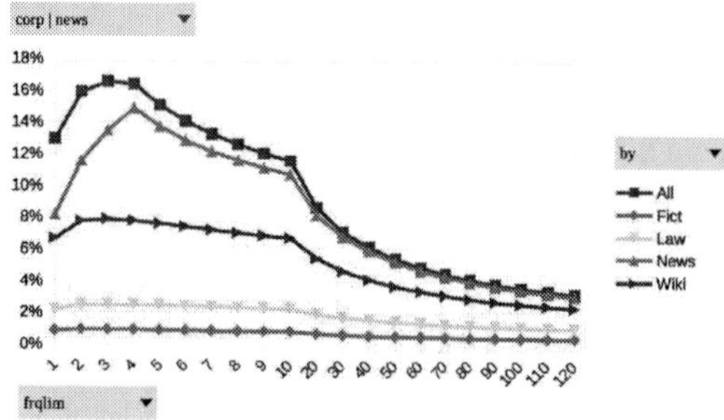

Figure 10: Improvement rates (y), of different corpora with the paradigms generated from New corpus; filtered out lower frequencies, up to (x).

Figure 11: Improvement rates (y), of different corpora with the paradigms generated from Wiki corpus; filtered out lower frequencies, up to (x).

which may be interpreted as improvement in reliability of paradigm prediction for more frequent items, and as an indication of a possible threshold for the minimal number of slots for predicting Ukrainian paradigms.

The results indicate that the proposed approach gives consistent improvements in coverage with paradigms generated from a lexically diverse corpora with sufficient number of neologisms and new proper names. The highest improvement rates across different corpora has been achieved for paradigms generated from the Wiki corpus used to test the News corpus – 16.3% for lexical items with frequencies 10 and higher.

5 Discussion

The algorithm proposed in this paper uses the fundamental idea that "the existence of a hypothetical lemma can be guessed if several different words found in the corpus are best interpreted as morphological variants of this lemma" (Clément et al., 2004). This idea has been developed for automated induction of morphological lexica for different languages and implemented in practical applications such as spell checking (e.g., ispell) and information retrieval systems: (Krovetz, 1993), (Grefenstette et al., 2002), (Segalovich, 2003), (Clément et al., 2004), (Oliver and Tadić, 2004), (Sagot, 2005); recent work in this area uses more accurate machine learning approaches: (Šnajder, 2013), (Ljubešić et al., 2015).

The approach proposed in this paper develops these ideas further by explicitly focussing on the following conceptual points:

(1) The extracted units are paradigms, and not lemmas or mappings from inflected word forms to lemmas or paradigms. The advantage of such

It can be seen from the figures that for the proposed algorithm the morphological and lexical diversity of the corpus are essential: the Law corpus has very little effect on the coverage of both News and Wikipedia corpora, while the News and Wikipedia consistently improve the coverage of all the corpora on which they are evaluated. This may be due to the small type/token ratio (i.e., small lexical diversity) of the Law corpus.

Finally, Figures 10 and 11 summarise improvement rates (i.e., the difference between the baseline and the proposed approach) for all the corpora using the News and Wiki corpora for generating paradigms.

It can be seen from these figures that the coverage of Fiction and Law corpora is harder to improve, while News and Wiki corpora are most complementary, improving each other well. Also an interesting effect can be observed when a corpus is used to improve itself: the improvement rate peaks at the value of filtered frequencies up to 4, approach is that inflected word forms in the corpus provide only indirect, latent justification for the existence of paradigms, so there is a separation between a form which initiates generation of hypotheses and those (possibly ambiguous) word forms that are used as evidence: they can independently justify the existence of several different paradigms, which avoids the artificial pressure to choose a single top-ranked paradigm and lemma for each inflected form, as it is the case in (Oliver and Tadić, 2004) or (Ahlberg et al., 2014). This latent paradigm induction is also more robust against potential noise in the corpus, since misspellings would not normally collect enough inflected forms.

(2) The proposed approach focusses only on the regular dynamic component of the lexicon, which enables a clean separation between the core method of the paradigm induction and the extensions or other methods needed to address historical or irregular features, such as stem alternations or suppletive forms, for which separate distortion models can be developed or learnt from corpora. Also the inflection tables for generating paradigms hypotheses are derived from comprehensive grammatical descriptions rather than from potentially noisy data. This reflects a typical scenario of morphological lexicon development for many under-resourced languages, which still have a smaller dictionary that covers most frequent items and comprehensive inflection tables in traditional grammars, but where it is hard to recruit language specialists on a recurrent basis to keep up with constant lexical developments in different subject domains of the language for which applications need to be developed or updated.

(3) Evaluation in the proposed approach is part of the development workflow: it focusses on the dynamics of corpus coverage with generated word forms for different maximum frequency thresholds. Such comprehensive automated evaluation indicates on the large scale where maximal improvement in coverage can be expected, so which frequencies can be used as cut-off points to filter out noisier and less reliable paradigms.

Most lexical items covered with the proposed paradigm generation algorithm are single-word Named Entities – names of organisations, geographical places or people, as well as technical terms, e.g.: мінохоронздоров'я ('The Ministry of Health') інтербізнесконсалтинг ('Internet business consulting'), кременчуккм'ясо ('The Meat of Kremenchuk' company), кривбасводопостачання ('Kryvbas Water Supply'), броваритепловодоенергія ('Brovary Heating, Water and Energy' company), могадішо ('Mogadishu') озоноруйнуючих . ('ozone-destroying').

However, the list also contains interesting political lexicon, such as йолка ('Christmas tree': the distorted ukrainized spelling of the Russian word, which became a symbol of the people's resistance to political violence during the Ukrainian revolution of dignity in 2013-2014) and проффесор (again, a distorted spelling of the word 'professor', which was used for mocking the fugitive pro-Russian president, who held this title, but allegedly misspelt it in an official document).

The appearance of this politically charged lexicon is in line with Karpilovs'ka et al.'s (2008) suggestion that lexical changes are driven by the social dynamics, especially at the times of major political developments. However, it can be also seen that this political lexicon is still much less frequent and less changeable compared to Named Entities, which dominate the new lexicon.

6 Conclusions and Future Work

The proposed algorithm complements static linguistic resources and increases corpus coverage for new entities, such as neologisms and proper names. The highest improvements are achieved for the corpus types that typically have many neologisms, specialised terminological lexicon and Named Entities: the Wikipedia and News. These corpora are not well covered by existing morphological resources. The advantage of the proposed approach is that it uses unlabelled corpora and small inflection tables for unsupervised induction of paradigms. However, its limitation is that in this stage it doesn't predict irregular paradigms.

Future work will involve the development of distortion models to cover less regular cases and a systematic evaluation of the accuracy of paradigm prediction for different frequency ranges: while for more frequent items such prediction is highly reliable, there is a need to experimentally establish frequency and coverage thresholds for different error rates on this task for less frequent items. Another area for future research is the use of contextual and syntactic features to verify predicted morphological properties.

References

Roee Aharoni and Yoav Goldberg. 2016. Morphological inflection generation with hard monotonic attention. *arXiv preprint arXiv:1611.01487.*

Malin Ahlberg, Markus Forsberg, and Mans Hulden. 2014. Semi-supervised learning of morphological paradigms and lexicons. In *Proceedings of the 14th Conference of the European Chapter of the Association for Computational Linguistics*, pages 569–578.

Malin Ahlberg, Markus Forsberg, and Mans Hulden. 2015. Paradigm classification in supervised learning of morphology. In *Proceedings of the 2015 Conference of the North American Chapter of the Association for Computational Linguistics: Human Language Technologies*, pages 1024–1029.

Bogdan Babych. 2019. Induction of morphological and syntactic models for under-resourced languages. *GitHub repository.* https://github.com/bogdanbabych/morphosyntax.

Bogdan Babych and Serge Sharoff. 2016. Ukrainian part-of-speech tagger for hybrid MT: Rapid induction of morphological disambiguation resources from a closely related language. In *Fifth Workshop on Hybrid Approaches to Translation (HyTra).* EAMT, Riga: June 1st 2016.

Lionel Clément, Bernard Lang, and Benoît Sagot. 2004. Morphology based automatic acquisition of large-coverage lexica. In *LREC 04*, pages 1841–1844.

Ryan Cotterell, Ekaterina Vylomova, Huda Khayrallah, Christo Kirov, and David Yarowsky. 2017. Paradigm completion for derivational morphology. *arXiv preprint arXiv:1708.09151.*

Vsevolod Dyomkin, Dmytro Chaplinskyi, Anatoliy Stegnii, Oleksandr Marikovskyi, Viacheslav Tykhonov, Oles Petriv, Serhii Shekhovtsov, Mykhailo Chalyi, Tetiana Kodliuk, Mykyta Pavliuchenko, Oksana Kunikevych, and Khrystyna Skopyk. 2019. lang-uk. *GitHub repository.* http://lang.org.ua/en/corpora/#anchor4.

Rashel Fam and Yves Lepage. 2018. IPS-WASEDA system at CoNLL-SIGMORPHON 2018 Shared Task on morphological inflection. *Proceedings of the CoNLL SIGMORPHON 2018 Shared Task: Universal Morphological Reinflection*, pages 33–42.

Manaal Faruqui, Ryan McDonald, and Radu Soricut. 2016. Morpho-syntactic lexicon generation using graph-based semi-supervised learning. *Transactions of the Association for Computational Linguistics*, 4:1–16.

Manaal Faruqui, Yulia Tsvetkov, Graham Neubig, and Chris Dyer. 2015. Morphological inflection generation using character sequence to sequence learning. *arXiv preprint arXiv:1512.06110.*

Mikel L Forcada, Mireia Ginestí-Rosell, Jacob Nordfalk, Jim O'Regan, Sergio Ortiz-Rojas, Juan Antonio Pérez-Ortiz, Felipe Sánchez-Martínez, Gema Ramírez-Sánchez, and Francis M Tyers. 2011. Apertium: a free/open-source platform for rule-based machine translation. *Machine translation*, 25(2):127–144.

Gregory Grefenstette, Yan Qu, and David Evans. 2002. Expanding lexicons by inducing paradigms and validating attested forms. In *LREC 2002.*

Tetiana O. Gryaznukhina, editor. 1999. *Syntactic analysis of scientific texts on computers. / Sintaksicheskiy analiz nauchnogo teksta na EVM.* Naukova Dumka, Kyiv, Ukraine.

Arnold P. Hryshchenko, Liubov I. Matsko, Mariya Ja. Pliushch, Nina I. Totska, and Ivanna M. Uzdyhan. 1997. *Modern Ukrainian Literary Langauge / Suchasna Ukrajins'ka Literaturna Mova.* Vyshcha Shkola, Kyiv.

Yevheniya A. Karpilovs'ka, Larysa P. Kysliuk, Nina F. Klymenko, Valentyna I. Kryts'ka, Tetiana K. Puzdyr'eva, and Yuliya V. Romaniuk. 2008. *Active resources of modern Ukranian nomination. Ideographic dictionary of the new lexicon / Aktyvni resursy suchasnoji Ukrajins'koji nominatsiji: Ideohrafichnyj slovnyk novoji leksyky.* KMM, Kyiv.

Christo Kirov and Ryan Cotterell. 2018. Recurrent neural networks in linguistic theory: Revisiting pinker and prince (1988) and the past tense debate. *Transactions of the Association for Computational Linguistics*, 6:651–665.

Nina F. Klymenko, Yevheniya A. Karpilovs'ka, and Larysa P. Kysliuk. 2008. *Dynamic processes in the modern Ukrainian lexicon / Dynamichni protsesy v suchasnomu ukrajins'komu leksykoni.* Vydavnychyi Dim Dmytra Burago.

Kimmo Matti Koskenniemi et al. 2018. Guessing lexicon entries using finite-state methods. In *Proceedings of the Fourth International Workshop on Computatinal Linguistics for Uralic Languages.* Association for Computational Linguistics.

Natalia Kotsyba, Andriy Mykulyaky, and Igor Shevchenko. 2009. UGTag: morphological analyzer and tagger for the Ukrainian language. In *Proceedings of the international conference Practical Applications in Language and Computers (PALC 2009).*

Natalia Kotsyba, Igor Shevchenko, Ivan Derzhanski, and Andriy Mykulyak. 2010. MULTEXT-East Morphosyntactic Specifications, version 4. 3.11 url: http://nl.ijs.si/ME/V4/msd/html/msd-uk.html.

Robert Krovetz. 1993. Viewing morphology as an inference process. In *Proceedings of the 16th annual international ACM SIGIR conference on Research and development in information retrieval*, pages 191–202. ACM.

Nikola Ljubešić, Miquel Espla-Gomis, Filip Klubička, and Nives Mikelić Preradović. 2015. Predicting inflectional paradigms and lemmata of unknown words for semi-automatic expansion of morphological lexicons. In *Proceedings of the International Conference Recent Advances in Natural Language Processing*, pages 379–387.

Joakim Nivre, Marie-Catherine De Marneffe, Filip Ginter, Yoav Goldberg, Jan Hajic, Christopher D Manning, Ryan T McDonald, Slav Petrov, Sampo Pyysalo, Natalia Silveira, et al. 2016. Universal Dependencies v1: A multilingual treebank collection. In *LREC*.

Antoni Oliver and Marko Tadić. 2004. Enlarging the Croatian morphological lexicon by automatic lexical acquisition from raw corpora. In *Fourth International Conference on Language Resources and Evaluation LREC2004*. ELRA.

Valentyna S. Perebyjnis, Nataliya P. Darchuk, and Tetiana O. Gryaznukhina. 1989. *Morphological analysis of scientific texts on computers / Morfologicheskiy analiz nauchnogo teksta na EVM*. Naukova Dumka, Kyiv, Ukraine.

Ian Press and Stefan Pugh. 2015. *Ukrainian: A comprehensive grammar*. Routledge.

Aarne Ranta. 2011. *Grammatical framework: Programming with multilingual grammars*, volume 173. CSLI Publications, Center for the Study of Language and Information Stanford.

Andriy Rysin and Vasyl Starko. 2019. Project to generate pos tag dictionary for Ukrainian language. *GitHub repository*. `https://github.com/brown-uk/dict_uk`.

Benoît Sagot. 2005. Automatic acquisition of a Slovak lexicon from a raw corpus. In *International Conference on Text, Speech and Dialogue*, pages 156–163. Springer.

Ilya Segalovich. 2003. A fast morphological algorithm with unknown word guessing induced by a dictionary for a web search engine. In *MLMTA*, pages 273–280. Citeseer.

Miikka Silfverberg, Ling Liu, and Mans Hulden. 2018. A computational model for the linguistic notion of morphological paradigm. In *Proceedings of the 27th International Conference on Computational Linguistics*, pages 1615–1626.

Jan Šnajder. 2013. Models for predicting the inflectional paradigm of Croatian words. *Slovenščina*, 20:1–34.

Andrew Spencer. 2001. The paradigm-based model of morphosyntax. *Transactions of the Philological Society*, 99(2):279–314.

Ludwig Wittgenstein. 2009. *Philosophical investigations*. Wiley-Blackwell.

Lawrence Wolf-Sonkin, Jason Naradowsky, Sebastian J Mielke, and Ryan Cotterell. 2018. A structured variational autoencoder for contextual morphological inflection. *arXiv preprint arXiv:1806.03746*.

Multiple Admissibility in Language Learning:
Judging Grammaticality Using Unlabeled Data

Anisia Katinskaia, **Sardana Ivanova**, **Roman Yangarber**
University of Helsinki, Department of Computer Science, Finland
`first.last@helsinki.fi`

Abstract

We present our work on the problem of detection Multiple Admissibility (MA) in language learning. Multiple Admissibility occurs when more than one grammatical form of a word fits syntactically and semantically in a given context. In second-language education—in particular, in intelligent tutoring systems/computer-aided language learning (ITS/CALL), systems generate exercises automatically. MA implies that multiple alternative answers are possible. We treat the problem as a grammaticality judgement task. We train a neural network with an objective to label sentences as grammatical or ungrammatical, using a "simulated learner corpus": a dataset with correct text and with artificial errors, generated automatically. While MA occurs commonly in many languages, this paper focuses on learning Russian. We present a detailed classification of the types of constructions in Russian, in which MA is possible, and evaluate the model using a test set built from answers provided by users of the Revita language learning system.

1 Introduction

The problem of *Multiple Admissibility* (MA) occurs in the context of language learning. In "cloze" exercises (fill-in-the-blank), the learner receives a text with some word removed, and a base form[1] of the removed word as a hint. The task is to produce the correct grammatical form of the missing word, given the context. The answer given by the user is checked automatically by the language learning system. Therefore, the system should be able to accept more than one answer, if there are grammatically and semantically valid alternatives in the given context. Otherwise, the language learning system returns negative (actually incorrect) feedback to the learner. This is a problem,

because negative feedback for an acceptable answer misleads and discourages the learner.

We examine MA in the context of our language learning system, Revita (Katinskaia et al., 2018). Revita is available online[2] for second language (L2) learning beyond the beginner level. It is in use in official university-level curricula at several major universities. It covers several languages, many of which are highly inflectional, with rich morphology. Revita creates a variety of exercises based on input text materials, which are selected by the users. It generates exercises and assesses the users' answers automatically.

For example, consider the sentence in Finnish: "Ilmoitus $\boxed{vaaleista}$ $\boxed{tulee}$ $\boxed{kotiin}$ $\boxed{postissa}$." ("Notice about elections comes to the house in the mail.")

In practice mode, Revita presents the text to the learner in small pieces—"snippets" (about 1 paragraph each)—with all generated exercises. This is important, because grammatical forms in exercises usually depend on a wider context.

For the given example, Revita can generate cloze exercises hiding several tokens (*surface forms*) and providing their lemmas as hints:
"Ilmoitus $\boxed{vaali}$ $\boxed{tulla}$ $\boxed{koti}$ $\boxed{posti}$."
("Notice $\boxed{\text{election}}$ $\boxed{\text{come}}$ $\boxed{\text{house}}$ $\boxed{\text{mail}}$.").

For the verb "*tulla*" ("come") and nouns "*vaali*" ("election"), "*koti*" ("home") and "*posti*" ("mail") the learner should insert the correct grammatical forms. Revita expects them to be the same as the forms in the original text, and will return negative feedback otherwise. However, in this example, *postitse* ("via email") is also acceptable, although it is not in the original text.

The MA problem is also relevant in the context of exercises that require a free-form answer, such as an answer to a question or an essay. The learner

---

[1] The base or "dictionary" form will be referred to as *lemma* in this paper.

[2] `https://revita.cs.helsinki.fi/`

Proceedings of the 7th Workshop on Balto-Slavic Natural Language Processing, pages 12–22,
Florence, Italy, 2 August 2019. ©2019 Association for Computational Linguistics

can produce "unexpected" but nevertheless valid grammatical forms.

In the current work, we restrict our focus to MA of multiple surface forms of the same lemma, given the context; we do not consider synonyms, which can also fit the same context. The latter topic is part of the future work.

The structure of the paper is as follows: In section 2 we formulate the problem and provide a detailed classification of the types of MA found in the learner data. In section 3 we describe our approach, in particular, the procedure for generating artificial grammatical errors and creating test sets. Section 4 presents previous work on artificial error generation. Section 5 describes our model and experimental setup. In section 6 we discuss the results and error analysis, and conclude in section 7.

2 Multiple Admissibility: Problem Overview

We use data from several hundred registered students learning Russian (and other languages), practicing with exercises based on texts, or answering questions in test sessions. Currently, Revita does not provide a mode for written essays, because it does not check free-form answers.

Except for cloze exercises, Revita also generates exercises where the users are asked to select among various surface forms based on a given lemma—a correct surface form and a set of automatically generated distractors; or to type the word they hear. This allows us to collect a wide range of errors, though not all kinds of possible errors; e.g., currently we do not track punctuation errors, word order errors, insertion errors, errors resulting from choosing an incorrect lemma, etc.

We annotated 2884 answers from the Revita database, which were automatically marked as "not matching the original text." This work was done by two annotators (90% agreement) both with native-level competency in Russian, and background in linguistics and teaching Russian. Among all annotated answers, 7.5% were actually correct, but differed from the original text. Also, we checked answers given by three students with C1 CEFR proficiency level in Russian (established independently by their teachers); 15.8% of these answers were grammatically and semantically valid in the context. Thus, for advanced users, the problem of MA is twice as relevant as on average; we plan to investigate these results with a larger base of Revita users.

2.1 Types of Multiple Admissibility

In analyzing the answers given by our users, we discovered several types of the most frequent contexts where MA appears.

Present/Past tense: The most clear case of MA in Russian (as in many other languages) is the case of interchangeable forms of present and past tense of verbs. Russian has three tenses (present, past, future), of which past and future tenses can have perfective or imperfective aspect.

In the next example, if both verbs are chosen for as exercises[3] and the learner sees two lemmas ("задержаться" and "вернуться"), she has a possibility to produce verb forms in any tense depending on the context *beyond the given sentence*. It may be narrative past tense or present tense, or the text may be a message where the communicative goal of the speaker is to inform the reader about future events, so future tense is expected.

"Мы задержались(PST)[4] у друзей и вернулись(PST) домой поздно."
"We were delayed with friends and returned home late."

The following option may be acceptable:

"Мы задержались(PST) у друзей и вернемся(FUT) домой поздно."
"We were delayed with friends and will return home late."

The future cannot precede the past in this sentence, so the next variant answer is grammatically incorrect:

* "Мы задержимся(FUT) у друзей и вернулись(PST) домой поздно."
"We will be delayed with friends and returned home late."[5]

Some cases are more difficult because the choice of tense can depend on knowledge beyond the text:

"Ученым удалось установить, что у минойцев существовало (PST) несколько видов письма."

---

[3]If one of the verbs is chosen as an exercise, the user may get a hint from the surface form of the other verb, that they should be coordinated.

[4]We use standard abbreviations from the Leipzig Glossing Rules.

[5]*Star is used to mark an incorrect sentence.

"Scientists were able to establish that the Minoans <u>had</u> several types of writing systems."

In a non-fictional narrative, only the past tense can be used, since the Minoans do not exist in the present. These examples show that deciding which tenses are acceptable in the context is difficult.

Singular/Plural: Singular and plural nouns can be grammatically valid in the same context, if there is no dependency on words beyond the sentence boundaries. For instance:

"Из последних разработок—скафандр для <u>работы</u> (SG.) в открытом космосе."
"Из последних разработок—скафандр для <u>работ</u> (Pl.) в открытом космосе."
"From the latest developments—the spacesuit for <u>work</u> in open space."

Short/Full adjective:[6] in many constructions, short and full forms of adjectives can be used as a part of a compound predicate (Vinogradov, 1972). The difference between these is that the short form typically expresses *temporal* meaning and that it is a phenomenon of *literary language*, whereas its full alternative form sounds more colloquial.

"Вы ужасно <u>болтливы</u> (short) и непоседливы " (short) (from I. Bunin)
"You are being terribly <u>talkative</u> (PRED) and <u>restless</u> (PRED)."
"Вы ужасно <u>болтливые</u> и непоседливые".
"You are terribly <u>talkative</u> (DESCR) and <u>restless</u> (DESCR)".

We treat these examples as MA, because even for native Russian speakers in many cases the choice can be unclear. So it would be too strict to treat one of the variants as incorrect.

Nominative/Instrumental case: nouns as part of compound named predicates can be in the nominative or instrumental case. The difference in meaning is similar to that of short/full adjectives (Rosenthal et al., 1994): nominative indicates a *constant* feature of a subject, whereas instrumental indicates a *temporary* feature of a subject. We consider the following examples as MA, because of a subtle difference in meaning:

"Она была <u>загадочная</u> (NOM) и <u>непонятная</u> (NOM) для меня". (from I. Bunin)

"Она была <u>загадочной</u> (INS) и <u>непонятной</u> (INS) для меня".
"She was <u>mysterious</u> and <u>incomprehensible</u> to me".

Genitive/Accusative case: usage of genitive vs. accusative is a complex topic, beyond the scope of this paper. We mention a few examples briefly, where MA can appear—denotation of *a part of the whole* and *negation*. Usually the genitive is used to denote a part of the whole. In the following example, usage of the accusative is incorrect:

"Пожалуйста, отрежь <u>хлеба</u>" (GEN)
* "Пожалуйста, отрежь <u>хлеб</u>" (ACC)
"Please, cut <u>some bread</u>."

In some contexts both meanings are possible—of a part and of the whole—resulting in MA:

"Нам оставили <u>хлеба</u> и <u>вина</u>" (GEN)
"We were left with <u>some bread</u> and <u>wine</u>."

"Нам оставили <u>хлеб</u> и <u>вино</u>" (ACC)
"We were left with <u>bread</u> and <u>wine</u>."

If both words appear in exercises, Revita should accept genitive or accusative (if the context specifies the expected meaning nowhere else).

The next case is negation constructions. The genitive is usually used where negation is stressed, whereas the accusative weakens the negation, (Rosenthal et al., 1994). However, it is worth noticing that the difference can be difficult to understand even for native Russian speakers.

"До вас никто еще <u>этого браслета</u> (GEN) не надевал." (from Kuprin.)
"**No one** has worn <u>this bracelet</u> before you."

Compare with a similar example in the accusative:

"Он не отвергнул тогда с презрением <u>эти сто</u> (ACC) рублей." (Dostoevsky)
"He **did not** reject <u>those one hundred</u> rubles with contempt."

It is not always possible for the learner to know which case expected in the sentence, because it implies that she should know which type of negation was mentioned. always possible, and both options fit semantically.

Perfective/Imperfective aspect: errors in aspect are very common (Rozovskaya and Roth,

---

[6]So-called full/short forms of adjectives correspond to descriptive/predicative adjectives in other languages: compare "the hungry(DESCR) dog" vs. "the dog is hungry(PRED)".

2019). Without going into detail, we show examples from (Rakhilina et al., 2014)—a heritage learner corpus.[7] Both sentences can be interpreted as correct, with a subtle difference in meaning:

"Он пишет ей, чтобы она не перестала (PFV) любить его."

"He writes to her that she should not stop loving him."

"Он пишет ей, чтобы она не переставала (IPFV) любить его."

"He writes to her that she continue to love him."

Gerund/Other verb forms: MA occurs in some contexts where gerunds are used. In the following example, both sentences can express the meaning of two actions happening at the same time. The only argument against using a past tense verb form is that it sounds somewhat unnatural without a conjunction "and" between verbs ("was saying and thinking"):

"... говорил я себе, думая (GERUND) об Охотном ряде" (from Bunin)

"... I was saying to myself, thinking about Okhotny Ryad"

"... говорил я себе, думал (PST) об Охотном ряде"

"... I was saying to myself, was thinking about Okhotny Ryad"

Prepositions with multiple cases: some prepositions can govern two different cases of the following noun, with no change in meaning:

"Она спряталась под одеялом." (INS)

"Она спряталась под одеяло." (ACC)

"She hid under a blanket."

Second Genitive (Partitive): and other forms common in spoken language can be valid alternatives, often unfamiliar to L2 learners.

"Я привозил ей коробки шоколаду (2GEN), новые книги..."

"Я привозил ей коробки шоколада (GEN), новые книги..."

"I was bringing her boxes of chocolate, new books..."

Other cases: some examples of MA contexts are exceptionally interesting and rare.

"На этой почве хорошо росла трава, что обеспечивало (Neu) пастбищами овец."

"На этой почве хорошо росла трава, что обеспечивала (Fem) пастбищами овец."

"The grass grew well on this soil, what provided sheep with pasture."

These sentences expresses similar meaning, although the verb "обеспечивать" ("*to provide*") appears in the neuter gender in the first and feminine in the second. This happens because in the first sentence the subordinative pronoun "что" ("*which*") refers to the entire preceding clause, whereas in the second it refers only to the word "трава" ("*grass*"), which is feminine.

We observe many other types of constructions with MA. This is not an exhaustive list, but covers only some of the types actually found among the answers given by the learners of Russian in Revita. The list should give us some intuitions about the problem of MA, and how difficult it is to identify automatically.

3 Overview of the Approach

How can we identify instances of Multiple Admissibility? One approach to this problem is to train a model with a language modeling objective—referred to as "LM-trained" in the literature. In such a scenario, the task of the model is to predict the next word at every point in the sentence, e.g., for the sentence "The keys to the cabinet [is/are] here"[8] the task of the model is to predict that $P(are|C) > P(is|C)$, where C is the context. Linzen (2016) experimented with this kind of language modeling in three setups: without any grammatically relevant supervision, with supervision on grammaticality (predicting which of two sentences[9] is grammatical/ungrammatical), and number prediction—predicting between two classes, "singular" or "plural". The last two setups are strongly supervised. The poorest results were obtained using a LM-trained model, despite using a large-scale language model (Jozefowicz et al., 2016).

Later, Gulordava (2018) reevaluated these results for the task of predicting long-distance agreement: for several languages, including Russian,

---

[7]Heritage learners are persons with a cultural connection to or proficiency in the language through family, community, or country of origin. (Definition from http://www.cal.org/heritage/research/)

[8]The example is from (Linzen et al., 2016).

[9]"The keys to the cabinet are here" vs. "The keys to the cabinet is here"

an LM-trained RNN approached the accuracy of the supervised models described in (Linzen et al., 2016). Marvin (2018) performed a targeted evaluation of several LMs—N-gram, LM-trained RNN, and Multitask RNN[10]—on the task of detecting errors in several grammatical constructions for English.[11] The results of even the strongest LM varied considerably depending on the syntactic complexity of the construction: 100% accuracy in the case of simple subject-verb agreement, and 0.52% accuracy for subject-verb agreement across an object relative clause (without "that").

In light of these results from prior research, we decided to approach the problem as a supervised grammaticality judgement task—a two-class classification task, (Linzen et al., 2016)).

Since MA answers are *correct* answers, sentences with alternative grammatical forms of the same lemma would be grammatically correct. One of the problems with this approach is the lack of annotated training data. The Revita database had only 7156 answers labeled "incorrect" for Russian, at the time when these experiments began. Therefore we generated a training dataset by *simulating* grammatical errors. We describe the simulation procedure in the following subsection, and briefly review prior approaches to generating artificial errors for grammatical error detection and correction tasks (GED/GEC). Every instance in the simulated dataset is labeled as correct or incorrect. The network reads the entire sequence in a bidirectional fashion and receives a supervised signal at the end. We describe the model and the experiments in the following sections.

3.1 Generating Artificial Errors

First, we describe the process of generating training data: the source of data, preprocessing steps and a brief analysis of what types of errors we obtain in the simulated data. In the following subsection, we proceed to describe the test sets which were build from real users' data containing "natural" errors.

Generating training datasets with artificial errors is a common approach, because obtaining large error-annotated learner corpora is extremely difficult and costly, (Granger, 2003): difficulties

relate to collecting data from language learners and very expensive annotation procedures.

Revita at present creates exercises only for words which do not exhibit *lemma ambiguity* (homography).[12] Lemma ambiguity occurs when a surface form has more than one lemma. An example of this type of ambiguity is the token "стекло", which has two morphological analyses:

стечь ("*to flow down*") Verb+Past+Sing+Neut, стекло ("*glass*") Noun+Sing+Nom/Acc.[13]

In this setting, we do not need to generate errors for surface forms with lemma ambiguity.

Training instances are generated by sliding a window of radius r over the list of input tokens, with the target token in the middle. The target is every n-th token (n is the stride). If the target token is unambiguous, is above a frequency threshold,[14] and has a morphological analysis, it is replaced by a *random* grammatical form from the paradigm to which the token belongs.[15]

We use $r = 10$, which results in a window wider than an average sentence in Russian, and we are interested in including wide context in training instances. All generated windows are labeled as negative/ungrammatical. The training dataset consists of a balanced number of grammatical and ungrammatical instances. Part of the generated data was removed from training dataset and used as a *validation set* for training the model.

Of the automatically generated errors that we checked, some appear very natural, while others may be less likely to be made by real students.

As Linzen (2016) notes, some of the generated instances will *not* in fact be ungrammatical. We analysed 500 randomly chosen generated windows; 3% of them happened to be grammatical (in Table 1 we refer to them as Multi-admissible). We provide the interpretation for all labels in Table 1 in the following subsection.

3.2 Test Data Analysis

To create test sets, we took 2884 answers from Revita's database, which were automatically marked as "incorrect," and manually annotated them using the labels below:

---

[10]Language modeling objective, combined with a supervised task of sequence tagging with CCG supertags.

[11]The authors expected that a LM would assign a higher probability to a grammatical sentence than to an ungrammatical one.

[12]Because it currently does not attempt to perform disambiguation, and only one lemma can be shown as the hint.

[13]This is an example not only of lemma ambiguity, but also of word sense and morphological ambiguity.

[14]We count frequencies from the entire corpus used for building the training set, to exclude words appearing once.

[15]We generate paradigms of inflected words using the pymorphy2 morphological analyzer (Korobov, 2015).

Label	(1) Training set	(2) Real student data	(3) Advanced students
Grammatical error	83.0%	21.4%	39.4%
Non-word error	—	20.8%	12.2%
Multiple-choice	—	12.0%	17.0%
Multi-admissible	**3.0%**	**7.5%**	**15.8%**
Pragmatic error	2%	1.6%	2.9%
Broken	12%	36.7%	12.7%
Total instances annotated	500	2884	170

Table 1: Data we annotated for verification and testing: (1) subset of the set of errors *automatically generated* for training (randomly sampled and manually annotated), (2) learners' answers (randomly sampled), marked by the System as *incorrect*, (3) subset of learner' incorrect answers—for *advanced* learners only (CEFR level C1/C2). "Broken": discarded instances (technical problems, too many unknown words, numbers, punctuation marks, etc.)

- **Grammatical error**: answer was a valid grammatical form of the word (exists in paradigm), but incorrect in the given context. This group includes only errors made in cloze exercises.
- **Non-word error**: spelling error—the word was rejected by the morphological analyzer.
- **Multiple-choice**: error in a choice of word from a list of options.
- **Multi-admissible**: as mentioned above, we consider these to be *correct* answers.
- **Pragmatic error**: a separate type of error where the given answer can fit grammatically, but is semantically/pragmatically unnatural in the context.

We provide one example of the last kind of error; it requires further investigation:

"У меня машина сломалась, и мне пришлось звонить в автосервис (ACC)".
"My car broke down and I had to call (to) the auto repair".

* "У меня машина сломалась, и мне пришлось звонить в автосервисе (LOC)".

* "My car broke down and I had to call (while being) in a car-service station".

Preposition "в" ("in") governs two cases—Nominative and Locative—but the second sentence does not make sense pragmatically. We have begun a more detailed annotation of all learner answers (i.e., the types of grammatical errors). This topic is beyond the scope of this paper.

- **Broken**: discarded instances (technical problems, words not in our training vocabulary, too many numbers, punctuation marks, answers given in languages different from expected, etc).

Table 1 represents the number of all mentioned data types in the real learners' answers (the second column) and in the subset of these real answers which were given only by advanced learners (the third column).

We separate the real, manually annotated data into four test sets (see Table 2).

A. The first test set contains only sentences exhibiting MA.

B. The second test set is randomly chosen correct sentences from a separate corpus (for a total of 500 instances) which was not used for generating training data.

C. The third test set is made to test the ability of our model to distinguish between grammatical and ungrammatical sentences (as it was trained to do)—thus it contains:

C1. sentences with grammatical errors made by Revita users;

C2. correct sentences from Revita's database.

D. The fourth test set contains sentences only with pragmatic errors.

In the next section, we shortly review prior work related to artificial error generation (AEG) for the grammaticality judgement task.

4 Related Work

Felice (2016) divides methods of AEG into deterministic vs. probabilistic. The **deterministic approach** consists of methods that generate errors in systematic ways, which do not make use of learner error distributions. Izumi et al. (2003) introduced a system for correction of article errors made by English learners, native in Japanese. The system was trained on artificial data where *a, an, the* or the zero article were replaced with a different option chosen randomly.

Sjöbergh and Knutsson (2005) created an artificial corpus consisting of two of the most frequent types of errors among non-native Swedish speakers: split compounds and word order errors.

Brockett et al. (2006) describe a statistical machine translation (SMT) system for correcting a set of 14 countable and uncountable nouns which are often confused by learners of English. They used rules to change quantifiers (e.g. *much–many*), to generate plural forms, and to insert unnecessary determiners. Lee and Seneff (2008) created an artificial corpus of verb form errors. They changed verbs in the original text to different forms, such as to-infinitive, 3rd person singular present, past, or -ing participle. Ehsan and Faili (2013) used SMT for AEG to correct grammatical errors and context-sensitive spelling mistakes in English and Farsi. Training corpora were obtained by injecting artificial errors into well-formed treebank sentences using predefined error templates.

Probabilistic approach: Rozovskaya and Roth describe several methods for AEG which include creation of article (Rozovskaya and Roth, 2010b) and preposition errors (Rozovskaya and Roth, 2010a, 2011) based on statistics from an English as a Second Language (ESL) corpora. They inject errors into Wikipedia sentences using different strategies (e.g., distribution before and after correction, L1-specific error distributions).

Rozovskaya et al. (2012) proposed an inflation method, which preserves the ability of the model to take into account learner error patterns. While also increasing the model's recall, this method reduced the confidence that the system has in the source word. Improvement in F-scores was achieved by this method when correcting determiners and prepositions. Further, this method was used by other researchers (Felice and Yuan, 2014; Putra and Szabó, 2013; Rozovskaya et al., 2013, 2014, 2017).

Dickinson (2010) introduce an approach to generate artificial syntactic errors and morphological errors for Russian. Imamura et al. (2012) adapt the method of Rozovskaya and Roth (2010b) for particle correction in Japanese. Cahill et al. (2013) examine automatically-compiled sentences from Wikipedia revisions for correcting errors in prepositions. Kasewa et al. (2018) use an off-the-shelf attentive sequence-to-sequence NN (Bahdanau et al., 2014) to learn to introduce errors.

5   Model and Experiment

Data: For generating the training/validation datasets, we use the open-source "Taiga" Russian corpus,[16] which is arranged by genre into several segments. We used all news segments, and part of the literary text segment, for a total of 809M words. We exclude social media, film subtitles, and poems, because their language has more deviations from the literary standard. All documents were lowercased, tokenized, and morphologically analyzed using Crosslator (Klyshinsky et al., 2011).[17] We replace all punctuation marks with a special token, to preserve information about sentence/clause boundaries. The size of the training vocabulary was around 1.2M words (after removing words with frequency less than 2). For validation, we randomly chose 5% of all generated data.

Model architecture: our baseline neural network (NN) is implemented in TensorFlow. Its architecture is a one-layer bidirectional LSTM with dropout (0.2), which has 512 hidden units. The hidden state of the BiLSTM is then fed to an Multi-layer Perceptron (MLP). The MLP uses one hidden layer with 1024 neurons, and Leaky ReLU activation function. The size of the output layer is 1, since we have only two classes to predict. The output of the MLP is then fed to a sigmoid activation function to obtain a prediction for the entire input sequence. To encode words, we use the FastText 300-dimensional pre-trained embeddings.[18]

The network and the word embeddings were trained in an end-to-end fashion. Optimization was done using Adam, dropout, and early stopping based on the loss on the validation set. We trained the network over only half of an epoch, since it was showing signs of overfitting—because we use a sliding window, the number of training instances was over 90M. The averaged accuracy on the validation set was 95 %. Table 2 reports the accuracy on the test sets, averaged across 5 runs.

6   Results

Table 2 shows the results of our experiments in terms of accuracy. 85.9% accuracy was achieved across all types of MA. However, we should stress that in the test set marked Multi-admissible (MA), the majority of the instances belong to the MA types of Present/Past tense and Singular/Plural.

Since the test set has a small number of instances of MA contexts with gerund/other verb

---

[16]https://tatianashavrina.github.io

[17]This analyzer was chosen because it is a part of Revita's text processing pipeline.

[18]https://fasttext.cc/docs/en/crawl-vectors.html

	Test set	#	Acc
A.	**Multi-admissible**	178	85.9
B.	Random correct	500	92.3
C.	Correct & incorrect	1290	81.0
C1.	Grammatically correct	650	73.3
C2.	Grammatically incorrect	640	88.6
D.	Pragmatic errors	46	54.3

Table 2: *Percent accuracy* of our NN model. Random correct: test set built from sentences which were not included in the training and validation sets and did not appear in Revita's database, randomly selected sentences from normal texts. Grammatically incorrect: test set with real grammatical errors from students' data. Pragmatic errors: test set with real pragmatic errors from students' data.

	MA types	#	Acc
1.	Perf/Imperf + Gerund/Other	14	92.8
2.	Case	24	91.7
3.	Present/Past	53	88.7
4.	Singular/Plural	78	82.0
5.	Short/Full adj	9	77.7

Table 3: *Percent accuracy* of our NN model for different MA contexts. Case combines all types of MA contexts listed in the Subsection 2.1 which differ by case (Nominative/Instrumental, Genitive/Accusative and others).

forms and MA contexts which differ by perfective/imperfective aspect, we grouped them together for testing the model. On these two types of MA the model achieved the highest accuracy, 92.8% (see Table 3). For the same reasons we grouped together MA contexts which differ by case (Nominative/Instrumental, Genitive/Accusative, Second Genitive and other). The overall accuracy for these contexts is 91.7%.

We plan to test all combined MA types separately as soon as we have more annotated data. The accuracy for Present/Past tense is 88.7%. The accuracy for Number agreement (including subject-verb agreement on number) is 81.0%. The lowest accuracy was achieved for Short/Full adjectives—77.7%. Some discussion of errors is in the following subsection.

We use additional test sets to assess other aspects of the trained NN model. The "Random correct" test set (B.) contains 500 randomly sampled sentences *without errors*, to compare with the MA test set. These sentences were sampled from a corpus which was not used for generating training/validation data, and are not present in the Revita database. On random correct sentences, the model achieved substantially better results than for MA instances (92.3%). It is interesting that the model has more difficulty with the syntactic structure of contexts with known MA than with some random correct contexts.

Another test set (C.) is made up of correct sentences from the Revita database, and sentences with grammatical errors made by the learners. We evaluate the model on this test set to gain insight into how well it can differentiate between various incorrect vs. correct sentences. The discussion of results for different grammatical error types is beyond the scope of this paper, and is left for the further work.

The pragmatic error test set (D.) was used to find out how difficult it is to predict labels for sentences which are correct grammatically but incorrect semantically/pragmatically. Clearly these instances pose the greatest challenge to the current model; (it was not explicitly trained to detect them).

Of the nearly 3000 manually annotated instances, the number of instances found to be pragmatic errors and MA was not large.

6.1 Error Analysis

We analysed some of the errors the model made on the MA test dataset. For all types of MA, we found some similar patterns: the model assigns very low scores to short sequences (which are padded), contexts with too many punctuation marks or names, and context with non-Russian words which are unknown to the model. For example, for constructions with Present/Past tense, the network made wrong predictions if the subject was a name or a number, which in most cases corresponds to the token "UNK" in our model's vocabulary. The same happens if the subject is outside the window. Sometimes the model confuses certain nouns or pronouns next to the verb with its subject, for example:

"Поезда (SUBJ) метро задерживаются (PRED).

"Trains of the metro are delayed."

In this case, the model might suppose that the (genitive) singular noun "метро" ("metro") is the subject of the plural verb "задерживаются" ("are delayed"), which is incorrect—the actual subject is the plural noun "поезда" ("trains")—but the genitive is closer to the predicate. As a result, the model will identify the sentence as grammatically incorrect, believing that the subject and predicate conflict in number.

We also should note that some instances marked by the model as incorrect are actually incorrect, but marked as MA by annotators, which means that MA instances need to be double-checked and that the model is able to identify ungrammatical contexts.

It is difficult to compare our results directly with prior work, because we have not yet found in the previous work a problem similar to Multiple Admissibility for Russian. A similar problem—grammatical acceptability judgment—is presented in (Warstadt et al., 2018), for English only. The best results they achieved in terms of percent accuracy is 77.2%. The average human accuracy is 85%.

For the task of grammatical error detection, the results obtained for Russian are much lower than for English. For example, the highest precision in (Rozovskaya and Roth, 2019) for errors in number agreement is 56.7.

Concerning the grammaticality judgement task, Marvin (2018) reported accuracies for subject-verb agreement from 50% to 99% depending on the syntactic complexity of the sentence (e.g., relations across relative clause). This is similar to Present/Past tense construction in our setup.

Linzen et al. (2016) also concludes that the grammaticality judgment objective is more difficult than, for example, the number prediction objective. The LSTM model can have up to 23% error on this task, as sentence complexity grows. This work studied only number agreement and subject-verb dependencies in English.

7 Conclusions and Future Work

We address the problem of *Multiple admissibility* in automatically generated exercises, by approaching it as a grammaticality judgment task. We offer a detailed study of examples, where our language learning system mistakenly assesses admissible answers as incorrect. We classify these contexts into 10 types, where only some of these types have been in the focus of prior research, especially for Russian. We train a NN model with the grammaticality objective, independent of the type of test set we use for evaluation. The problem of

lacking labeled training data was approached by generating a dataset with artificial errors. We also observed that the MA problem is more relevant for advanced language learners. Another observation is that for a trained model it is more difficult to make prediction about MA contexts than about random correct sentences.

We plan to extend and improve our training data by marking numbers with special tokens, or by mapping them into words. We also plan to mark names with a name tag by using some of the existing NER models, and mark rare words with their part of speech. We also believe that providing the model with syntactic information (parsing) can help, so that we can train a model in a multitask fashion: predict tags of words, as well as their correctness. Also, it is worth trying to use new large-scale language models, which proved to be more effective on a variety of tasks.

Additional annotation of student data collected in Revita's database is needed; in the current work, the annotation was done by two experts, and all disagreements were resolved. We plan to extend our experiments to other languages available in Revita. Each has its own language-specific types of MA. Generating all paradigms of a word could be problematic for some highly inflected languages (e.g., Finnish, etc.).

The goal of this paper is to introduce the problem of Multiple Admissibility and to attract more attention to experimenting with morphologically rich languages and languages other than English in this context.

References

Dzmitry Bahdanau, Kyunghyun Cho, and Yoshua Bengio. 2014. Neural machine translation by jointly learning to align and translate. *arXiv preprint arXiv:1409.0473*.

Chris Brockett, William B Dolan, and Michael Gamon. 2006. Correcting ESL errors using phrasal SMT techniques. In *Proceedings of the 21st International Conference on Computational Linguistics and the 44th annual meeting of the Association for Computational Linguistics*, pages 249–256. Association for Computational Linguistics.

Aoife Cahill, Nitin Madnani, Joel Tetreault, and Diane Napolitano. 2013. Robust systems for preposition error correction using Wikipedia revisions. In *Proceedings of the 2013 Conference of the North American Chapter of the Association for Computational Linguistics: Human Language Technologies*, pages 507–517.

Markus Dickinson. 2010. Generating learner-like morphological errors in russian. In *Proceedings of the 23rd International Conference on Computational Linguistics (Coling 2010)*, pages 259–267.

Nava Ehsan and Heshaam Faili. 2013. Grammatical and context-sensitive error correction using a statistical machine translation framework. *Software: Practice and Experience*, 43(2):187–206.

Mariano Felice. 2016. Artificial error generation for translation-based grammatical error correction. Technical report, University of Cambridge, Computer Laboratory.

Mariano Felice and Zheng Yuan. 2014. Generating artificial errors for grammatical error correction. In *Proceedings of the Student Research Workshop at the 14th Conference of the European Chapter of the Association for Computational Linguistics*, pages 116–126.

Sylviane Granger. 2003. Error-tagged learner corpora and CALL: A promising synergy. *CALICO journal*, 20(3):465–480.

Kristina Gulordava, Piotr Bojanowski, Edouard Grave, Tal Linzen, and Marco Baroni. 2018. Colorless green recurrent networks dream hierarchically. *arXiv preprint arXiv:1803.11138*.

Kenji Imamura, Kuniko Saito, Kugatsu Sadamitsu, and Hitoshi Nishikawa. 2012. Grammar error correction using pseudo-error sentences and domain adaptation. In *Proceedings of the 50th Annual Meeting of the Association for Computational Linguistics: Short Papers-Volume 2*, pages 388–392. Association for Computational Linguistics.

Emi Izumi, Kiyotaka Uchimoto, Toyomi Saiga, Thepchai Supnithi, and Hitoshi Isahara. 2003. Automatic error detection in the Japanese learners' English spoken data. In *The Companion Volume to the Proceedings of 41st Annual Meeting of the Association for Computational Linguistics*.

Rafal Jozefowicz, Oriol Vinyals, Mike Schuster, Noam Shazeer, and Yonghui Wu. 2016. Exploring the limits of language modeling. *arXiv preprint arXiv:1602.02410*.

Sudhanshu Kasewa, Pontus Stenetorp, and Sebastian Riedel. 2018. Wronging a right: Generating better errors to improve grammatical error detection. *arXiv preprint arXiv:1810.00668*.

Anisia Katinskaia, Javad Nouri, and Roman Yangarber. 2018. Revita: a language-learning platform at the intersection of ITS and CALL. In *Proceedings of LREC: 11th International Conference on Language Resources and Evaluation*, Miyazaki, Japan.

E.S. Klyshinsky, N.A. Kochetkova, M.I. Litvinov, and V.Yu. Maximov. 2011. Method of POS-disambiguation using information about words cooccurrence (for Russian). *Proceedings of GSCL*, pages 191–195.

Mikhail Korobov. 2015. Morphological analyzer and generator for Russian and Ukrainian languages. In *International Conference on Analysis of Images, Social Networks and Texts*, pages 320–332. Springer.

John Lee and Stephanie Seneff. 2008. Correcting misuse of verb forms. *Proceedings of ACL-08: HLT*, pages 174–182.

Tal Linzen, Emmanuel Dupoux, and Yoav Goldberg. 2016. Assessing the ability of lstms to learn syntax-sensitive dependencies. *Transactions of the Association for Computational Linguistics*, 4:521–535.

Rebecca Marvin and Tal Linzen. 2018. Targeted syntactic evaluation of language models. *arXiv preprint arXiv:1808.09031*.

Desmond Darma Putra and Lili Szabó. 2013. UdS at CoNLL 2013 Shared Task. In *Proceedings of the Seventeenth Conference on Computational Natural Language Learning: Shared Task*, pages 88–95.

E.V. Rakhilina, A.S. Vyrenkova, and M.S. Polinskaya. 2014. Grammar of errors and grammar of constructions: "Heritage" ("inherited") Russian language. *Questions of linguistics*, 3(2014):3–19.

Ditmar Elyashevich Rosenthal, E.V. Dzhandzhakova, and N.P. Kabanova. 1994. *Reference on Spelling, Pronunciation, and Literary Editing*. Moscow International School of Translators.

Alla Rozovskaya, Kai-Wei Chang, Mark Sammons, and Dan Roth. 2013. The University of Illinois system in the CoNLL-2013 shared task. In *Proceedings of the Seventeenth Conference on Computational Natural Language Learning: Shared Task*, pages 13–19.

Alla Rozovskaya, Kai-Wei Chang, Mark Sammons, Dan Roth, and Nizar Habash. 2014. The Illinois-Columbia system in the CoNLL-2014 shared task. In *Proceedings of the Eighteenth Conference on Computational Natural Language Learning: Shared Task*, pages 34–42.

Alla Rozovskaya and Dan Roth. 2010a. Generating confusion sets for context-sensitive error correction. In *Proceedings of the 2010 Conference on Empirical Methods in Natural Language Processing*, pages 961–970. Association for Computational Linguistics.

Alla Rozovskaya and Dan Roth. 2010b. Training paradigms for correcting errors in grammar and usage. In *Human language technologies: The 2010 annual conference of the north american chapter of the association for computational linguistics*, pages 154–162. Association for Computational Linguistics.

Alla Rozovskaya and Dan Roth. 2011. Algorithm selection and model adaptation for ESL correction tasks. In *Proceedings of the 49th Annual Meeting of the Association for Computational Linguistics: Human Language Technologies-Volume 1*, pages 924–933. Association for Computational Linguistics.

Alla Rozovskaya and Dan Roth. 2019. Grammar error correction in morphologically rich languages: The case of Russian. *Transactions of the Association for Computational Linguistics*, 7:1–17.

Alla Rozovskaya, Dan Roth, and Mark Sammons. 2017. Adapting to learner errors with minimal supervision. *Computational Linguistics*, 43(4):723–760.

Alla Rozovskaya, Mark Sammons, and Dan Roth. 2012. The UI system in the HOO 2012 shared task on error correction. In *Proceedings of the Seventh Workshop on Building Educational Applications Using NLP*, pages 272–280. Association for Computational Linguistics.

Jonas Sjöbergh and Ola Knutsson. 2005. Faking errors to avoid making errors: Very weakly supervised learning for error detection in writing. In *Proc. RANLP*, volume 2005.

Viktor Vladimirovich Vinogradov. 1972. *Russian language: The grammatical doctrine of the word*, volume 21. High School.

Alex Warstadt, Amanpreet Singh, and Samuel R Bowman. 2018. Neural network acceptability judgments. *arXiv preprint arXiv:1805.12471*.

Numbers Normalisation in the Inflected Languages: a Case Study of Polish

Rafał Poświata and Michał Perełkiewicz
National Information Processing Institute
al. Niepodległości 188b, 00-608 Warsaw, Poland
`{rposwiata, mperelkiewicz}@opi.org.pl`

Abstract

Text normalisation in Text-to-Speech systems is a process of converting written expressions to their spoken forms. This task is complicated because in many cases the normalised form depends on the context. Furthermore, when we analysed languages like Croatian, Lithuanian, Polish, Russian or Slovak there is additional difficulty related to their inflected nature. In this paper we want to show how to deal with this problem for one of these languages: Polish, without having a large dedicated data set and using solutions prepared for other NLP tasks. We limited our study to only numbers expressions, which are the most common non-standard words to normalise. The proposed solution is a combination of morphological tagger and transducer supported by a dictionary of numbers in their spoken forms. The data set used for evaluation is based on the part of 1-million word subset of the National Corpus of Polish. The accuracy of the described approach is presented with a comparison to a simple baseline and two commercial systems: Google Cloud Text-to-Speech and Amazon Polly.

1 Introduction

In Text-to-Speech (TTS) or automatic speech recognition (ASR) text normalisation is a task of converting written expressions to their spoken equivalents. For example in English, sentence "I have 3 dogs" will be normalised to "I have three dogs". In inflected languages, like Polish, this task is much harder as presented in Table 1. We can see that for English sentences number "2" is always normalised to "two", but for Polish, this is more complicated. Each of the Polish sentences has a different normalised form of number "2" (dwóch, dwie, dwaj). These forms are only a small part of all possible forms of this number which is one of the reasons why text normalisation for the Polish language is more complicated than for English.

This paper presents the solution for this specific problem – normalising number expressions in the Polish language.

The rest of the paper is organised as follows. Section 2 briefly shows the related work and our motivation. Next, we describe the architecture of our system. Section 4 elaborates on experiments and evaluation. It presents the prepared data set and the results of two experiments. Finally, Section 5 concludes our work.

2 Related Work

Text normalisation has been known since the appearance of the first TTS systems. Initial approaches were based on hand-made rules (Allen et al., 1987; Sproat, 1997). These methods were quite effective even for non-standard words, but also challenging to maintain and develop, due to the richness of the language. Next generation of text normalisation systems used the combination of rules and language model (Sproat et al., 2001; Graliński et al., 2006; Brocki et al., 2012). Latest research focused on neural networks (Sproat and Jaitly, 2016, 2017; Zare and Rohatgi, 2017; Pramanik and Hussain, 2018; Zhang et al., 2019). Especially recurrent neural networks (RNN) have promising results, but also tend to fail in some unexpected and unacceptable cases, such as translating large numbers with one digit mistake or treating cm as kilometres (Zhang et al., 2019). RNN approaches known for English are difficult to transfer to Polish because there are no publicly available resources of Polish texts in spoken forms which are necessary. The proposed solution does not require a large data set and, at the same time, it takes advantages of neural networks by using them for morphological tagging (one of the modules of the system). Furthermore, in contrast to the mentioned articles, this paper focuses only on number expressions. Normalising

Proceedings of the 7th Workshop on Balto-Slavic Natural Language Processing, pages 23–28,
Florence, Italy, 2 August 2019. ©2019 Association for Computational Linguistics

Sentence in Polish	Normalized sentence	English translation	Normalized translation
Rozmawia 2 mężczyzn.	Rozmawia **dwóch** mężczyzn.	2 men are talking.	**Two** men are talking.
Rozmawiają 2 kobiety.	Rozmawiają **dwie** kobiety.	2 women are talking.	**Two** women are talking.
Rozmawiają 2 przyjaciele.	Rozmawiają **dwaj** przyjaciele.	2 friends are talking.	**Two** friends are talking.

Table 1: The difference between text normalization for Polish and English language.

numbers is very demanding so deeper exploration of this topic is understandable, which confirms the existence of publications describing only this issue (Kanis et al., 2005; Sproat, 2010; Mya Hlaing et al., 2018).

3 System Architecture

To manage all aspects of normalising Polish sentences, especially inflected forms and different types of numbers (cardinal, ordinal, decimal, etc.), we created the system presented in Figure 1. This system contains five components: a tokeniser, morphological tagger, classifier, transducer and post-processor. The tokeniser is used to transform a sentence into a list of tokens (words). The morphological tagger gets the list of tokens and adds to them morphological tags (morphosyntactic tag is a sequence of colon-separated values which determines the grammatical class and categories used in the National Corpus of Polish[1]). To create these two components we integrated our system with KRNNT, a morphological tagger for Polish based on recurrent neural networks (Wróbel, 2017). The main advantage of this tagger is the correct interpretation of words in the context which results from the use of RNNs. Next component, the classifier, assigns to each token one of the eleven classes, shown in Table 2. This classifier works on two levels. On the first level, it uses a decision tree created from token characteristics and morphological tags to assign to each token non-complex class (PLAIN, PUNCT, CARDINAL, ORDINAL, NUMBER_WITH_SUFFIX, DECIMAL, FRACTION, TELEPHONE or IDENTIFIER). To train this classifier, we divided the data set into 5 folds and used k-fold Cross-Validation method. The average accuracy of our model was 97.92%. On the second level, it uses hand-made rules to group some of these tokens to one of the complex tokens (DATE or TIME). When we have tokens with tags and classes, we can go to the core component: transducer. The transducer has two main tasks: it decides whether a given token requires normalisa-

tion and it prepares tokens for transfer to a function that converts numbers into Polish words. This function utilises rules and a dictionary of numbers in their spoken forms. These rules implement the pronunciation principles of individual numbers in Polish. Some of these principles required linguistic knowledge, especially in the case of large ordinal numbers. The dictionary contains all cardinal and ordinal forms of base numbers (0-19, 20-90, 100-900, 10^3, 10^6, 10^9, 10^{12} and 10^{15}) which can be used to create complex ones. To prepare this dictionary, we filtered and processed Polimorf morphological dictionary (Wolinski et al., 2012). Polimorf is an open-source Polish morphological dictionary containing over 7 million word forms with assigned category, word lemma and part-of-speech tag. The last step is post-processing when normalised tokens are transformed to lower case, punctuation is removed, and finally, they are combined to create a normalised sentence. This component is configurable, which means that you can, for example, keep the punctuation.

Class name	Example token
PLAIN	Dom
PUNCT	.
CARDINAL	2
ORDINAL	3.
NUMBER_WITH_SUFFIX	5-letni
DECIMAL	2,3
FRACTION	1/3
DATE	31 lipca 1989
TIME	godzina 8.00
TELEPHONE	789-123-456
IDENTIFIER	B-52

Table 2: Classes of tokens with examples.

4 Experiments and Evaluation

We prepared two experiments to evaluate the correctness of our system. The first experiment was only for the transducer, second for the whole system with the comparison to baseline and two commercial systems: Google Cloud Text-to-Speech

---

[1]http://nkjp.pl/poliqarp/help/ense2.html

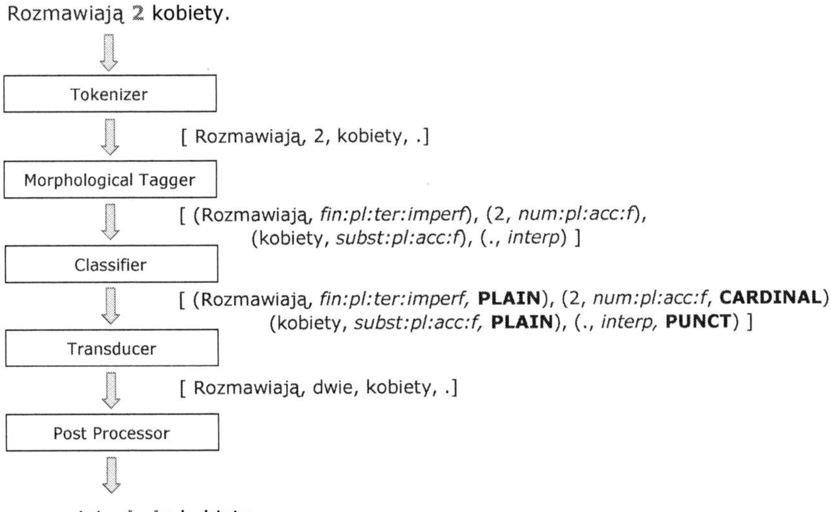

Figure 1: High level architecture of our system with example of usage and intermediate states between components.

and Amazon Polly. The above experiments used the data set of sentences with their spoken forms and additional information like morphological tags and classes. Details about the data set and experiments are shown in the next subsections.

4.1 Data

There are no publicly available data sets for the Polish language designed for text normalisation. However, there are some resources, created for other NLP tasks, which can be used as a base to prepare one. We chose the largest publicly available manually annotated data set for Polish - 1-million subcorpus of the National Corpus of Polish (Przepiórkowski et al., 2012). The corpus includes books, articles, transcriptions of spoken conversations and content from the web. What is more, it assigns some of the tokens to categories like person name, organisation name, place name, time or date. For our data set, we selected only sentences with numerical tokens and without abbreviations. Next, we processed them to create hints of probable classes and normalised forms, which we used during manual annotation. For more efficient annotation process we created a simple web application with a customised user interface. As a result, we got the data set of 5,444 sentences, which contained 7,170 numerical tokens. The distribution of numerical token classes is presented in Table 3.

Class name	Number of tokens	Frequency [%]
CARDINAL	3735	52.09
DATE	1899	26.49
ORDINAL	661	9.22
NUMBER_WITH_SUFFIX	389	5.43
IDENTIFIER	197	2.75
TIME	156	2.18
DECIMAL	106	1.48
FRACTION	16	0.22
TELEPHONE	11	0.15

Table 3: The distribution of numerical token classes in the data set.

4.2 Transducer Evaluation

In the first experiment, we tested the hypothesis that having a class and morphological tags is sufficient to normalise a token properly. For this pur-

Class name	Accuracy [%]
ALL	95.75
CARDINAL	95.26
DATE	96.95
ORDINAL	97.43
NUMBER_WITH_SUFFIX	93.06
IDENTIFIER	97.46
TIME	95.51
DECIMAL	90.57
FRACTION	75.0
TELEPHONE	100.0

Table 4: The accuracy of the transducer component.

Class name	Number of tokens	Accuracy [%]			
		Baseline	Amazon Polly	Google Cloud TTS	Our system
ALL	407	30.47	34.15	57.99	**90.91**
CARDINAL	173	24.86	24.28	78.61	**94.8**
ORDINAL	73	9.59	10.96	32.88	**93.15**
DATE	60	18.33	35.0	48.33	**80.0**
NUMBER_WITH_SUFFIX	34	82.35	**97.06**	26.47	94.12
TIME	24	0.0	16.67	4.17	**87.5**
DECIMAL	18	83.33	**100.0**	94.44	83.33
IDENTIFIER	13	84.62	**100.0**	92.31	92.31
FRACTION	8	**87.5**	0.0	75.0	**87.5**
TELEPHONE	4	**50.0**	0.0	**50.0**	**50.0**

Table 5: Our system evaluation with comparison to baseline, Google Cloud Text-to-Speech and Amazon Polly. Bold values indicate the highest scores in the category.

pose, we examined the transducer component. Results of this experiment are presented in Table 4. The transducer achieved 95.75% accuracy. We observed several types of problems. Firstly, there were situations where the cardinal number had two possible forms for a given case and gender (e.g. "trzej", "trzech") and the transducer did not know which of these forms to chose (in the presented example it chose "trzech"). The second problem was related with messy data which were unexpected by the transducer (e.g. "5- -letni"). The Accuracy on the FRACTION class was caused by cases when the fraction did not have an inflected form (e.g. 1/3 sometimes should be normalised to "jedną trzecią" not to "jedna trzecia"). For the DECIMAL class individual tokens should be replaced not directly but in a context-sensitive manner (e.g. 0.5 should be normalised to "pół"). However, we assumed that the results of this component are acceptable and it can be used in the designed system.

4.3 System Evaluation

To estimate how well our system works we compared it with three solutions: baseline that does not rely on morphological tags and two commercial systems: Google Cloud Text-to-Speech[2] and Amazon Polly[3]. For this experiment, we selected 250 sentences with 407 tokens for normalisation. We reduced the number of sentences for this experiment because of two reasons. First of all most of the sentences in the data set represent the same context and difference is only in the number value which does not bring anything interesting to the

analysis. A better solution is to choose those who represent different contexts. The second reason is that analysed commercial systems are full Text-to-Speech systems so to evaluate them we had to listen and write the answers, which is very time-consuming. Summary of this evaluation is shown in Table 5.

Baseline   The baseline is our main system but with disabled morphological tags interpretation. We saw that for almost all classes morphological tags were crucial and the baseline system had a very weak accuracy. For classes where tags are not required baseline achieves results close or equal to our main system.

Amazon Polly   The main problem with the Amazon Polly is that the word form is not taken into account, which for tag-dependent classes leads to results similar to those of the baseline system. At the same time, this system has the best results for NUMBER_WITH_SUFFIX, DECIMAL and IDENTIFIER classes.

Google Cloud Text-to-Speech   When we analysed the results of Google Cloud Text-to-Speech, we observed that the wrong interpretation of tokens causes most of the mistakes. For example, time expressions were interpreted as decimals, or ordinal numbers and dates as cardinals. For the NUMBER_WITH_SUFFIX class, Google Cloud TTS did not include suffix (e.g. "5-letni" was normalised to "pięć letni", not to "pięcioletni").

Our system   The incorrect predictions of our system were, in most cases, results of incorrect morphological tagging or classification. For the

[2]https://cloud.google.com/text-to-speech/
[3]https://aws.amazon.com/polly/

DECIMAL class, our system had the worst accuracy which was the consequence of the transducer behaviour. For almost all classes our system achieves the best results; for the others, it does not stand out significantly. Accuracy for the TELEPHONE class results from the specific reading of the telephone numbers (e.g. four digits numbers like 7128 are read in pairs so correct normalised form will be "siedemdziesiąt jeden dwadzieścia osiem").

5 Conclusion

The article described the problem of numbers normalisation in the Polish language. We presented difficulties, previous work and architecture of our system. Then we showed the performance of our core component (the transducer). The last subsection described the evaluation of our system with comparison to the baseline and two commercial TTS systems. Our system for tokens with the most common class in texts (CARDINAL, ORDINAL, DATE) achieves the best results. For other classes, the results are close to or exceed those of the other systems. Our future work will focus on correcting the errors mentioned in the previous sections. We believe that the architecture we use can also be adopted for other inflected languages. In addition, our solution can be used to create a data set that will then be used to train neural networks. We are aware that this work does not cover all possible cases of numerical tokens to normalised because there are also classes related to abbreviations like measure or money expressions. Next aspect of our future work will be focused on these classes. The first step will be recovering morphological information lost in abbreviated forms in National Corpus of Polish (Żelasko, 2018).

Resources Our data set used during evaluation and written answers of Google Cloud Text-to-Speech and Amazon Polly in json format are available at `https://github.com/rafalposwiata/text-normalization`. Data acquisition from TTS systems took place in March 2019.

References

Jonathan Allen, M. Sharon Hunnicutt, and Dennis Klatt. 1987. From Text to Speech: the MITalk System. In *Cambridge University Press, Cambridge*.

Łukasz Brocki, Krzysztof Marasek, and Danijel Koržinek. 2012. Multiple Model Text Normalization for the Polish Language. In *Foundations of Intelligent Systems: 20th International Symposium, ISMIS 2012, Macau, China, December 4-7, 2012. Proceedings*, pages 143–148.

Filip Graliński, Krzysztof Jassem, Agnieszka Wagner, and Mikołau Wypych. 2006. Linguistic Aspects of Text Normalization in a Polish Text-to-Speech System. *Systems Science*, 32.

Jakub Kanis, Jan Zelinka, and Ludek Müller. 2005. Automatic Numbers Normalization in Inflectional Languages. pages 663–666. Moscow State Linguistic University.

Aye Mya Hlaing, Win Pa Pa, and Ye Kyaw Thu. 2018. Myanmar Number Normalization for Text-to-Speech. In *Computational Linguistics*, pages 263–274.

Subhojeet Pramanik and Aman Hussain. 2018. Text Normalization using Memory Augmented Neural Networks.

Adam Przepiórkowski, Mirosław Banko, Rafał L Górski, and Barbara Lewandowska-Tomaszczyk. 2012. Narodowy Korpus Jezyka Polskiego [Eng.: National Corpus of Polish]. *Wydawnictwo Naukowe PWN, Warsaw*.

Richard Sproat. 1997. In Multilingual Text to Speech Synthesis: the Bell Labs Approach. In *Kluwer Academic Publishers, Boston, MA*.

Richard Sproat. 2010. Lightly supervised learning of text normalization: Russian number names. In *2010 IEEE Spoken Language Technology Workshop*, pages 436–441.

Richard Sproat, Alan W. Black, Stanley Chen, Shankar Kumar, Mari Ostendorfk, and Christopher Richards. 2001. Normalization of non-standard words. *Computer Speech and Language*, 15(3):287–333.

Richard Sproat and Navdeep Jaitly. 2016. RNN Approaches to Text Normalization: A Challenge. *arXiv preprint arXiv:1611.00068*.

Richard Sproat and Navdeep Jaitly. 2017. An RNN Model of Text Normalization. pages 754–758.

Marcin Wolinski, Marcin Milkowski, Maciej Ogrodniczuk, and Adam Przepiórkowski. 2012. PoliMorf: a (not so) new open morphological dictionary for Polish. In *LREC*, pages 860–864.

Krzysztof Wróbel. 2017. KRNNT: Polish Recurrent Neural Network Tagger. In *Proceedings of the 8th Language & Technology Conference: Human Language Technologies as a Challenge for Computer Science and Linguistics*, pages 386–391. Fundacja Uniwersytetu im. Adama Mickiewicza w Poznaniu.

Maryam Zare and Shaurya Rohatgi. 2017. DeepNorm-A Deep Learning Approach to Text Normalization. *arXiv preprint arXiv:1712.06994*.

Piotr Żelasko. 2018. Expanding Abbreviations in a Strongly Inflected Language: Are Morphosyntactic Tags Sufficient? In *Proceedings of the Eleventh International Conference on Language Resources and Evaluation (LREC-2018)*. European Language Resource Association.

Hao Zhang, Richard Sproat, Axel H. Ng, Felix Stahlberg, Xiaochang Peng, Kyle Gorman, and Brian Roark. 2019. Neural Models of Text Normalization for Speech Applications. *Computational Linguistics*, pages 1–49.

What does Neural Bring? Analysing Improvements in Morphosyntactic Annotation and Lemmatisation of Slovenian, Croatian and Serbian

Nikola Ljubešić
Jožef Stefan Instute
Jamova cesta 39
1000 Ljubljana, Slovenia
nikola.ljubesic@ijs.si

Kaja Dobrovoljc
Jožef Stefan Institute
Jamova cesta 39
1000 Ljubljana, Slovenia
kaja.dobrovoljc@ijs.si

Abstract

We present experiments on Slovenian, Croatian and Serbian morphosyntactic annotation and lemmatisation between the former state-of-the-art for these three languages and one of the best performing systems at the CoNLL 2018 shared task, the Stanford NLP neural pipeline. Our experiments show significant improvements in morphosyntactic annotation, especially on categories where either semantic knowledge is needed, available through word embeddings, or where long-range dependencies have to be modelled. On the other hand, on the task of lemmatisation no improvements are obtained with the neural solution, mostly due to the heavy dependence of the task on the lookup in an external lexicon, but also due to obvious room for improvements in the Stanford NLP pipeline's lemmatisation.

1 Introduction

Morphosyntactic annotation and lemmatisation are crucial tasks for languages that are rich in inflectional morphology, such as Slavic languages. These tasks are far from solved, and the recent CoNLL 2017 (Zeman et al., 2017) and CoNLL 2018 (Zeman et al., 2018) shared tasks on multilingual parsing from raw text to Universal Dependencies (Nivre et al., 2016) have given the necessary spotlight to these problems. In addition to the advances due to multi- and cross-lingual settings, the participating systems have also confirmed the predominance of neural network approaches in the field of natural language processing.

In this paper we compare the improvements obtained on these two tasks in three South Slavic languages (Slovenian, Croatian and Serbian) by moving from traditional approaches to the neural ones. The tool that we use as the representative of the traditional approaches is reldi-tagger (Ljubešić and Erjavec, 2016;

Ljubešić et al., 2016), the previous state-of-the-art for morphosyntactic tagging and lemmatisation of the three focus languages due to (1) carefully engineered features for the CRF-based tagger, (2) integration of an inflectional lexicon both for the morphosyntactic tagging and the lemmatisation task and (3) lemma guessing for unknown word forms via morphosyntactic-tag-specific Naive Bayes classifiers, predicting the transformation of the surface form. The tool that we use as the representative for the neural approaches is stanfordnlp, the Stanford NLP pipeline (Qi et al., 2018), a state-of-the-art in neural morphosyntactic and dependency syntax text annotation. The system took part in the CoNLL 2018 shared task (Zeman et al., 2018) as one of the best-performing systems, which would have, with "an unfortunate bug fixed", placed among the top-three for all evaluation metrics, including lemmatisation and morphology prediction. The tool is, additionally, released as open source and has a vivid development community,[1] with a named entity recognition module being in development.

2 Experiment Setup

We perform our comparison of the traditional and the neural tool of choice on the two tasks on data splits defined in the babushka-bench benchmarking platform[2] which currently hosts data and results for the three South Slavic languages we use in these experiments, namely Slovenian, Croatian and Serbian. It is organised as a git repository, with scripts for transferring datasets from the CLARIN.SI repository,[3] and splitting them into

---

[1] https://github.com/stanfordnlp/
stanfordnlp
[2] https://github.com/clarinsi/
babushka-bench
[3] https://www.clarin.si/repository/
xmlui

Proceedings of the 7th Workshop on Balto-Slavic Natural Language Processing, pages 29–34,
Florence, Italy, 2 August 2019. ©2019 Association for Computational Linguistics

training, development, and testing portions. While the primary usage of this platform are in-house experiments on the available and emerging technologies, other researchers are more than welcome to further enrich the repository.

The name of the repository has its roots in the erroneous, but popular naming of the Matryoshka doll in South Slavic languages, as the datasets are split into train, dev and test portions in a random fashion, but with a fixed random seed. This enables splitting the same datasets on the annotation layers that were not applied over the whole dataset (as is often the case with costly annotations of syntax, semantic etc.), and simultaneously ensuring that no spillage between train, dev and test between the various layers would occur. There are many cases where such a split comes handy for benchmarking, one example being using the whole datasets for training taggers and just portions of the datasets (i.e. the manually parsed subsets) to train parsers that require tagging as upstream processing.

For evaluating morphosyntactic tagging and lemmatisation in `babushka-bench`, we use a modified CoNLL 2018 shared task evaluation script to enable evaluation without parsing present. This script calculates the F1 metric between the gold and the real annotations, taking into account the possibility of different segmentation, which is not the case in these experiments as we use gold segmentation from the datasets to focus on the tasks of morphosyntactic tagging and lemmatisation. When modelling morphosyntax, we predict morphosyntactic descriptions (MSDs), position-based encodings of part-of-speech and feature-value pairs, as defined in the MULTEXT-East tagset (Erjavec, 2012). The training-data-defined size of the tagset for each of the three languages lies between 600 and 1300 MSDs, depending on the language and the size of the training data. This is the default tagset for the `reldi-tagger` and is also supported by the `stanfordnlp` tool, where language-specific tags (XPOS) are predicted as one of the three outputs by the tagging module (the other two being UD parts-of-speech (UPOS) and features (FEATS)). The datasets we use for our experiments are the three official datasets for training standard language technologies for these languages. These are the ssj500k dataset for Slovenian (Krek et al., 2019), the hr500k dataset for

Croatian (Ljubešić et al., 2018) and the SE-Times.SR dataset for Serbian (Batanović et al., 2018). While the Slovenian and Croatian datasets are both around 500 thousand tokens in size, the Serbian dataset is significantly smaller with only 87 thousand tokens in size. We additionally make use of the inflectional lexicons of these three languages, Sloleks for Slovenian (Dobrovoljc et al., 2019), hrLex for Croatian (Ljubešić, 2019a) and srLex for Serbian (Ljubešić, 2019b), all containing more than 100 thousand lemmas with around 3 million inflected forms.

While learning neural morphosyntactic taggers, we also experiment with various embeddings, mostly (1) the original CoNLL 2017 word2vec (w2v) embeddings for Slovenian and Croatian (Ginter et al., 2017) (there are none available for Serbian), based on the Common-Crawl data, and (2) the CLARIN.SI embeddings for Slovenian (Ljubešić and Erjavec, 2018), Croatian (Ljubešić, 2018a) and Serbian (Ljubešić, 2018b), either trained with fastText (fT) or with word2vec (w2v)[4] on large, just partially publicly available texts due to copyright restrictions.

Our experiments are split into two main parts: experiments on morphosyntactic tagging in Section 3.1, backed with the comparison of the difference of the most frequent errors in the traditional and neural approaches, and the experiments on lemmatisation in Section 3.2.

3 Results

3.1 Morphosyntax

We first compare the results of the two tools on morphosyntactic annotation, trained on the training portion of the datasets of the three languages, with development data used if necessary.[5] The results of the two taggers on the two languages are presented in Table 1.

The results show significant differences between `reldi-tagger` and `stanfordnlp`, with relative error reduction of 43% for Slovenian, 27% for Croatian and 40% for Serbian. Regarding

---

[4]Currently only the fastText versions are available for download in the repository.

[5]While `stanfordnlp` uses the development data for updating the learning rate and optimization algorithm, `reldi-tagger` did not make any use of the development data during this training phase. However, during the development of `reldi-tagger`, a series of feature selections and hyperparameter values were investigated on held-out data, so we can consider for that tool to have used development data indirectly, as well.

tool	distributional information	Slovenian	Croatian	Serbian
reldi-tagger	Brown clusters	94.21	91.91	92.03
stanfordnlp	CoNLL w2v embeddings	96.45	93.85	94.78
stanfordnlp	CLARIN.SI w2v embeddings	**96.79**	**94.18**	94.91
stanfordnlp	CLARIN.SI fT embeddings	96.72	94.13	**95.23**

Table 1: F1 results in morphosyntactic annotation with the traditional and neural tool and different distributional information.

		Slovenian		Croatian			Serbian		
	true	pred	freq	true	pred	freq	true	pred	freq
reldi-tagger	Ncmsan	Ncmsn	109	Xf	Npmsn	162	Xf	Npmsn	28
	Ncmsn	Ncmsan	71	Qo	Cc	118	Ncmsan	Ncmsn	22
	Ncnsa	Ncnsn	61	Ncmsan	Ncmsn	117	Npmsan	Npmsn	13
	Ncfpa	Ncfsg	47	Ncmsn	Ncmsan	98	Ncmsn	Ncmsan	12
	Agpnsn	Rgp	41	Ncfpa	Ncfsg	56	Ncmsg	Ncmpg	12
	Ncfpn	Ncfsg	36	Cs	Rgp	55	Ncfpn	Ncfsg	12
	Ncnsn	Ncnsa	35	Ncmpg	Ncmsg	53	Ncmpg	Ncmsg	11
	Agpnsa	Agpnsn	31	Ncmsg	Ncmpg	50	Npmsay	Npmsg	9
	Sa	Sl	27	Agpnsny	Rgp	48	Ncnsn	Ncnsa	8
	Npmsay	Npmsg	27	Ncnsa	Ncnsn	43	Ncfpa	Ncfsg	8
stanfordnlp	Ncmsn	Npmsn	54	Xf	Npmsn	111	Xf	Npmsn	20
	Pp3fpa–y	Pp3mpa–y	31	Qo	Cc	96	Ncmsan	Ncmsn	10
	Ncmsan	Ncmsn	28	Cs	Rgp	75	Ncmpg	Ncmsg	10
	Cc	Rgp	28	Npmsn	Xf	74	Npfsn	Npmsn	8
	Ncmsn	Ncmsan	27	Mro	Mdo	57	Ncmsn	Ncmsan	8
	Xf	Npmsn	20	Ncmsg	Ncmpg	50	Npmsan	Npmsn	7
	Ncnsn	Ncnsa	18	Ncmsan	Ncmsn	42	Ncnsn	Ncnsa	5
	Pp3nsa–y	Pp3msa–y	17	Ncmpg	Ncmsg	38	Ncmsg	Ncmpg	5
	Npfsn	Npmsn	17	Rgp	Cs	37	Npmsn	Npmsan	4
	Mlc-pn	Mlc-pa	17	Cc	Qo	36	Ncnsa	Ncnsn	4

Table 2: Most frequent errors by the traditional and neural tagger on Slovenian, Croatian and Serbian.

the usage of different embedding collections with stanfordnlp, there are no drastic differences, but the CLARIN.SI embeddings show to be better suited than the CoNLL embeddings, which does not come as a surprise as the former are based on more text, which is frequently also of higher quality. The distinction between word2vec (w2v) and fastText (fT) embeddings shows to be minimal, but fastText seems to be more beneficial when smaller amounts of training data are available, as is the case with Serbian.

For the error analysis, as well as downstream experiments on lemmatisation, for which morphosyntactic annotation is a prerequisite, we take the stanfordnlp tool with CLARIN.SI fastText embeddings, as these settings achieve the best results on average.

To identify the differences in morphosyntactic tagging errors between the traditional and neural tagger, we analyse the 10 most frequent confusions per tagger for each of the three languages. Our results presented in Table 2 show that some of the most frequent errors in reldi-tagger are substantially reduced by stanfordnlp, such as the confusion between masculine nouns in singular accusative (Ncmsan) and nominative (Ncmsn), which shows the neural tagger to be more capable in modelling long-range dependencies. Namely, whether a male noun is in the nominative or accusative case depends mostly on whether one of these two cases already occurred somewhere in the clause.

Another regular confusion in morphosyntactic tagging in general, which is also heavily resolved

tool	morphosyntax	Slovenian	Croatian	Serbian
`reldi-tagger`	gold	99.46	98.17	97.89
`reldi-tagger`	`reldi-tagger`	98.35	96.82	96.44
`reldi-tagger`	`stanfordnlp`	98.77	97.22	97.26
`stanfordnlp`	gold	97.75	96.22	95.29
`stanfordnlp`	`stanfordnlp`	97.51	95.85	95.18
`stanfordnlp+lex`	gold	99.30	98.11	97.78
`stanfordnlp+lex`	`stanfordnlp`	98.74	97.22	97.13

Table 3: F1 results in lemmatisation with the traditional and neural tool and different upstream processing.

by the neural tagger, is that between adjectives in the neutrum nominative (Agpnsn) and adverbs (Rgp), which, again, requires information from a wider context, i.e., whether there is a noun to which the potential adjective can be attached to.

An error type which requires more of a semantic understanding is the distinction between proper nouns (Npmsn) and foreign residuals (Xf) in Croatian and Serbian. In these two languages, the rule is that proper nouns of foreign origin (*Easy Jet, Feng Shui*) are annotated as foreign residuals. This type of error is in good part resolved via word embedding information where this distinction is obviously encoded, while in the 1000 hierarchical Brown clusters this is obviously not the case.

Interestingly, some shared errors are even more frequent in the neural `stanfordnlp` predictions, such as the disambiguation between homonymous conjunctions (Cc, Cs) and adverbs (Rgp) for Croatian and Slovenian (e.g. *već, tako, zato*), which does come as a surprise as this distinction requires long-range information which should be more available in the neural approach.

3.2 Lemmatisation

Given that morphosyntactic information is usually expected as the input to lemmatisation, we compare the lemmatisation performance of the two tools if (1) gold morphosyntax is given, (2) the morphosyntax predicted by the tool itself is used and (3) the best predicted morphosyntax by `stanfordparser` is used. In addition to that, we also expand `stanfordnlp` with a simple intervention in the lemmatisation procedure, in which the lexicon lookup is not performed over the training data only, but the external inflectional lexicons as well, naming this modified tool `stanfordnlp+lex`.

The results of the lemmatisation experiments are given in Table 3. The results show that `reldi-tagger` outperforms the original `stanfordnlp` by a substantial margin, which does not come as a surprise as `reldi-tagger` uses a large inflectional lexicon. A simple lexicon intervention with `stanfordnlp+lex` closes the gap between the two, with almost no difference in lemmatisation quality for any of the languages.

Regarding different upstream processing, as expected, preprocessing with `stanfordnlp` closes one third of the gap between preprocessing with `reldi-tagger` and having perfect, gold morphosyntactic annotation.

Investigating the differences between the decisions of `reldi-tagger` and `stanfordnlp+lex` shows that these mostly differ in handling named entities, with both tools missing the correct lemma with similar frequency. For `stanfordnlp+lex` in particular, some errors can be attributed to the fact it does not rely on the morphological feature (FEATS) information when looking up the lexicon and producing lemma predictions, causing errors such as generating a feminine proper noun lemma for a correctly tagged masculine proper noun.

4 Conclusion

In this paper we have presented the set up of the long-term evaluation platform for benchmarking current and future NLP tools for the three South Slavic languages, a practice which is still far too rare. We did a comparative evaluation of two state-of-the art tools with different architectures (traditional vs. neural) and confirmed that the neural approach yields significant improvements in tagging, especially because of better long-range dependency modelling and more distributional semantic information available.

For lemmatisation, the results of both approaches are very close, especially because of a heavy dependence on the lookup in a large inflectional lexicon, but with obvious room for improvement in the neural lemmatisation process.

The presented results give important pointers for the development of future state-of-the-art tools for the three languages, but also Slavic languages in general.

Acknowledgments

The work described in this paper was funded by the Slovenian Research Agency within the national basic research projects "Resources, methods and tools for the understanding, identification and classification of various forms of socially unacceptable discourse in the information society" (J7-8280, 2017–2020) and "New grammar of contemporary standard Slovene: sources and methods" (J6-8256, 2017–2020), the national research programme "Language Resources and Technologies for Slovene" (P6-0411), the Slovenian-Flemish bilateral basic research project "Linguistic landscape of hate speech on social media" (N06-0099, 2019–2023), and the Slovenian research infrastructure CLARIN.SI.

References

Vuk Batanović, Nikola Ljubešić, Tanja Samardžić, and Tomaž Erjavec. 2018. *Training corpus SE-Times.SR 1.0.* Slovenian language resource repository CLARIN.SI.

Kaja Dobrovoljc, Simon Krek, Peter Holozan, Tomaž Erjavec, Miro Romih, špela Arhar Holdt, Jaka Čibej, Luka Krsnik, and Marko Robnik-šikonja. 2019. *Morphological lexicon Sloleks 2.0.* Slovenian language resource repository CLARIN.SI. http://hdl.handle.net/11356/1230.

Tomaž Erjavec. 2012. Multext-east: morphosyntactic resources for central and eastern european languages. *Language Resources and Evaluation*, 46(1):131–142. https://doi.org/10.1007/s10579-011-9174-8.

Filip Ginter, Jan Hajič, Juhani Luotolahti, Milan Straka, and Daniel Zeman. 2017. *CoNLL 2017 Shared Task - Automatically Annotated Raw Texts and Word Embeddings.* LINDAT/CLARIN digital library at the Institute of Formal and Applied Linguistics (ÚFAL), Faculty of Mathematics and Physics, Charles University.

Simon Krek, Kaja Dobrovoljc, Tomaž Erjavec, Sara Može, Nina Ledinek, Nanika Holz, Katja Zupan, Polona Gantar, Taja Kuzman, Jaka Čibej, Špela Arhar Holdt, Teja Kavčič, Iza Škrjanec, Dafne Marko, Lucija Jezeršek, and Anja Zajc. 2019. *Training corpus ssj500k 2.2.* Slovenian language resource

repository CLARIN.SI. http://hdl.handle.net/11356/1210.

Nikola Ljubešić. 2018a. *Word embeddings CLARIN.SI-embed.hr 1.0.* Slovenian language resource repository CLARIN.SI.

Nikola Ljubešić. 2018b. *Word embeddings CLARIN.SI-embed.sr 1.0.* Slovenian language resource repository CLARIN.SI.

Nikola Ljubešić and Tomaž Erjavec. 2018. *Word embeddings CLARIN.SI-embed.sl 1.0.* Slovenian language resource repository CLARIN.SI.

Nikola Ljubešić. 2019a. *Inflectional lexicon hrLex 1.3.* Slovenian language resource repository CLARIN.SI. http://hdl.handle.net/11356/1232.

Nikola Ljubešić. 2019b. *Inflectional lexicon sr-Lex 1.3.* Slovenian language resource repository CLARIN.SI. http://hdl.handle.net/11356/1233.

Nikola Ljubešić, Željko Agić, Filip Klubička, Vuk Batanović, and Tomaž Erjavec. 2018. *Training corpus hr500k 1.0.* Slovenian language resource repository CLARIN.SI. http://hdl.handle.net/11356/1183.

Nikola Ljubešić and Tomaž Erjavec. 2016. Corpus vs. Lexicon Supervision in Morphosyntactic Tagging: the Case of Slovene. In *Proceedings of the Tenth International Conference on Language Resources and Evaluation (LREC 2016)*, Paris, France. European Language Resources Association (ELRA).

Nikola Ljubešić, Filip Klubička, Željko Agić, and Ivo-Pavao Jazbec. 2016. New Inflectional Lexicons and Training Corpora for Improved Morphosyntactic Annotation of Croatian and Serbian. In *Proceedings of the Tenth International Conference on Language Resources and Evaluation (LREC 2016)*, Paris, France. European Language Resources Association (ELRA).

Joakim Nivre, Marie-Catherine de Marneffe, Filip Ginter, Yoav Goldberg, Jan Hajic, Christopher D. Manning, Ryan McDonald, Slav Petrov, Sampo Pyysalo, Natalia Silveira, Reut Tsarfaty, and Daniel Zeman. 2016. Universal Dependencies v1: A Multilingual Treebank Collection. In *Proceedings of the Tenth International Conference on Language Resources and Evaluation (LREC 2016)*, Paris, France. European Language Resources Association (ELRA).

Peng Qi, Timothy Dozat, Yuhao Zhang, and Christopher D. Manning. 2018. Universal dependency parsing from scratch. In *Proceedings of the CoNLL 2018 Shared Task: Multilingual Parsing from Raw Text to Universal Dependencies*, pages 160–170, Brussels, Belgium. Association for Computational Linguistics. https://nlp.stanford.edu/pubs/qi2018universal.pdf.

Daniel Zeman, Jan Hajič, Martin Popel, Martin Pot-
thast, Milan Straka, Filip Ginter, Joakim Nivre,
and Slav Petrov. 2018. CoNLL 2018 shared
task: Multilingual parsing from raw text to universal dependencies. In *Proceedings of the CoNLL
2018 Shared Task: Multilingual Parsing from
Raw Text to Universal Dependencies*, pages 1–
21, Brussels, Belgium. Association for Computational Linguistics. http://www.aclweb.org/
anthology/K18-2001.

Daniel Zeman et al. 2017. CoNLL 2017 Shared Task:
Multilingual parsing from raw text to Universal De-
pendencies. In *Proceedings of the CoNLL 2017
Shared Task: Multilingual Parsing from Raw Text
to Universal Dependencies*, pages 1–19, Vancouver,
Canada. Association for Computational Linguistics.

AGRR-2019: A Corpus for Gapping Resolution in Russian

Maria Ponomareva[♠] **Kira Droganova**[†] **Ivan Smurov**[♠,♣] **Tatiana Shavrina**[◇,♡]
[♠]ABBYY, Moscow, Russia
[†]Charles University, Faculty of Mathematics and Physics
[♣]Moscow Institute of Physics and Technology, Moscow
[◇]Sberbank, Moscow, Russia
[♡]National Research University Higher School of Economics, Moscow
{maria.ponomareva,ivan.smurov}@abbyy.com
droganova@ufal.mff.cuni.cz
Shavrina.T.O@sberbank.ru

Abstract

This paper provides a comprehensive overview of the gapping dataset for Russian that consists of 7.5k sentences with gapping (as well as 15k relevant negative sentences) and comprises data from various genres: news, fiction, social media and technical texts. The dataset was prepared for the Automatic Gapping Resolution Shared Task for Russian (AGRR-2019) - a competition aimed at stimulating the development of NLP tools and methods for processing of ellipsis.

In this paper, we pay special attention to the gapping resolution methods that were introduced within the shared task as well as an alternative test set that illustrates that our corpus is a diverse and representative subset of Russian language gapping sufficient for effective utilization of machine learning techniques.

1 Introduction

During the last two years gapping (i.e., the omission of a repeated predicate which can be understood from context (Ross, 1970)) has received considerable attention in NLP works, both dedicated to parsing (Schuster et al., 2018; Kummerfeld and Klein, 2017) and to corpora enhancement and enrichment (Nivre et al., 2018; Droganova et al., 2018). At the same time, just a few works dealt with compiling a corpus that would represent different types of ellipsis, and almost exclusively for English. Most of these works address VP-ellipsis, which refers to the omission of a verb phrase whose meaning can be reconstructed from the context (Johnson, 2001), for instance, in "Mary loves flowers. John does too" (Hardt,

1997; Nielsen, 2005; Bos and Spenader, 2011). The research has mainly been conducted so far on rather small amounts of data, not exceeding several hundreds of sentences. In this work we aim to create a resource with a decent amount of data that would include a broad variety of genres and would rely minimally on any specific NLP frameworks and parsing systems.

This work consists of four parts. First, we describe the dataset, its features, and provide examples of Russian-specific constructions with gapping. Second, we describe an alternative test set that we have prepared to demonstrate that our corpus is representative enough. Then we briefly describe the key metrics that have been proposed to evaluate the quality of gapping resolution methods within the shared task. Finally, we provide a detailed analysis of the methods that have successfully solved the gapping resolution task as well as the results that were achieved on the alternative test.

2 Gapping

We confine ourselves to the types of elliptical constructions for Russian that involve omission of a verb, a verb phrase or a full clause.

In this work we use the following terminology for gapping elements. We call the pronounced elements of the gapped clause remnants. Parallel elements found in a full clause that are similar to remnants both semantically and syntactically are called remnant correlates. The missing material is called the gap (Coppock, 2001).

Traditionally, gapping is defined as the omission of a repeating predicate in non-initial composed and subordinate clauses where both remnants to the left and to the right remain expressed.

Proceedings of the 7th Workshop on Balto-Slavic Natural Language Processing, pages 35–43,
Florence, Italy, 2 August 2019. ©2019 Association for Computational Linguistics

(1) Я принял её за итальянку, а его за
     I mistook her for Italian   and him for
     шведа.
     Swede

     'I mistook her for Italian and I̶ ̶m̶i̶s̶t̶o̶o̶k̶ him for
     Swede'

However, a broader interpretation is possible
(Testelets, 2011). Some features of gapping worth
mentioning are listed below.

Elements remaining after predicate omission
can be of different types. Consider the following
examples where remnants are predicates (2),
preposition phrases (3), adverbs (4), adjectives (5)
potentially with their dependents.

(2) Одно может вдохновлять, а   другое
     one can inspire   and other
     вгонять в тоску.
     put   in melancholy
     'One thing can inspire and the other c̶a̶n̶ put you in
     a melancholic mood.'

(3) Советую   вам поменьше думать о
     recommend you less   think   about
     проблемах, и   побольше — об   их
     problems   and more   - about their
     решении.
     solution
     'I recommend you to think less about problems, and
     t̶h̶i̶n̶k̶ more about their solutions.'

(4) Вначале они играли интересно,   потом
     at.first they played interesting.ADV after
     — прескучно.
     - boring.ADV.INT
     'At first they played interestingly, then t̶h̶e̶y̶ ̶p̶l̶a̶y̶e̶d̶
     extremely dully.'

(5) Сердце ее было слишком чистым, чувства
     heart   her was too   pure   feelings
     слишком искренними.
     too   sincere
     'Her heart was too pure and her feelings w̶e̶r̶e̶ too
     sincere.'

The set of constructions for Russian that
implement stripping (Merchant, 2016) seems to be
broader than for English and the difference between
gapping and stripping in Russian is less clear. We
encountered a wide variety of examples that go
beyond the canonical examples. Examples (6) and
(7) illustrate the cases when arguments/adjuncts
of the elided verb do not fully correspond to the
arguments/adjuncts of the pronounced verb, thus
some of them (*в конце* 'in the end' in (6), *за 2009
год* 'during year 2009') do not have correlates. We
consider such examples gapping with one remnant
and include them in the corpus.

(6) Добавляем муку, крахмал и
     add   flour starch and
     разрыхлитель, а   **в конце** сметану.
     baking.powder and in end   sour.cream
     'We add flour, starch and baking powder, and at the
     end w̶e̶ ̶a̶d̶d̶ sour cream.'

(7) Рост цен   составил   11,9 процента
     growth prices amounted.to 11.9 percent
     (**за 2009 год** - 4,4 процента)
     in 2009 year - 4.4 percent
     'Price growth amounted to 11.9 percent (in 2009 i̶t̶
     a̶m̶o̶u̶n̶t̶e̶d̶ ̶t̶o̶ 4.4 percent)'

3   Corpus Description

Since the publicly available markup with gapping
is sparse, one of our key motivations was to create a
corpus that contains as many examples of gapping
as possible. To the best of our knowledge, no other
publicly available dataset contains a comparable
amount of gapping examples.

With that in mind, we decided to base
our corpus on the markup obtained with
Compreno (Anisimovich et al., 2012). Compreno
is a syntactic and semantic parser that contains a
module for predicting null elements in the syntactic
structure of a sentence. An overview of the module
can be found in (Bogdanov, 2012).

While cleaning up the output of a specific
system allows us to obtain markup much faster
than annotating from scratch, training on the
resulting corpus may yield systems that would
reproduce the original system's output instead of
properly modeling the real-world natural language
phenomenon. We took this risk because even if the
corpus we have created contains Compreno bias,
the selection is representative enough. Moreover,
in order to further test for the presence of such
bias, we evaluated the top systems of the shared
task on an alternative test set that was created from
SynTagRus (see Section 4).

The corpus is available on the shared task's
GitHub [1].

3.1   Annotation Scheme

We utilize the following labels for fully annotated
sentences with gapping:

- The gap is labeled V.
- The head of the pronounced predicate
  corresponding to the elided predicate is
  labeled cV.

---

[1] https://github.com/dialogue-evaluation/AGRR-2019

- Remnants and their correlates are labeled Rn and cRn respectively, where n is the pair's index

For gapping annotation we use square brackets to mark all gapping elements (whole NP, VP, PP etc. for remnants and their correlates and the predicate controlling the gap), the gap is marked with $[v]$. Example (8) shows an example of bracket annotation of (1).

(8) Я [cV принял] [cR1 её] [cR2 за итальянку],
    I   mistook   her   for Italian
    а [R1 его] [R2 за шведа].
    and him   for Swede
    'I mistook her for Italian and I mistook him for Swede'

Therefore, the full list of annotation labels is as follows: cV, $cR1$, $cR2$, V, $R1$, $R2$.

3.2 Obtaining the Data

In this section we provide a detailed description of the process of compiling the corpus. The bulk of the collection comprises Russian texts of various genres: news, fiction, technical texts. To our understanding, many NLP tasks that could benefit from gapping resolution are often applied to social network data. Therefore, we balanced the corpus by adding texts from the popular Russian social network VKontakte. They make up a quater of the collection.

First, all texts in the text collection were parsed with Compreno. We identified the sentences in which gapping was predicted. Using the Compreno parser, we generated bracketed annotation for each sentence (in which every gapping element X has an opening bracket $[X$ and closing bracket $]$).

Mindful of our main goal (i.e., to maximize the amount of data in the corpus), we decided to avoid fixing the annotation errors manually. Instead 11 assessors were asked to evaluate the annotation, assigning one of four classes:

0 no gapping, no markup is needed;

1 all gapping elements are annotated correctly;

2 some gapping elements are annotated incorrectly;

3 problematic example.

Each sentence was evaluated by two assessors. Table 1 shows that 41% out of 17411 sentences have correct annotation and 19% were erroneously attributed to the examples with gapping, according to both annotators.

	0	1	2	3
0	**3350 (19%)**	370 (2.1%)	303 (1.7%)	254 (1.5%)
1	394(2.3%)	**7201(41%)**	1163 (6.7%)	283 (1.6%)
2	288 (1.7%)	581 (3.3%)	1960 (11%)	302 (1.7 %)
3	446 (2.5 %)	230 (1.3%)	153 (0.9%)	133 (0.8 %)

Table 1: Assessment analysis for the AGRR corpus; 0, 1, 2, 3 - annotation classes.

The main application of our corpus is in machine learning, therefore the corpus has to include negative examples (i.e., sentences without gapping). We considered two types of negative examples to select more relevant sentences. The first type comprises problematic negative sentences on which the Compreno parser false positively predicted gapping (labeled 0 by both assessors). Introducing negative examples of this type (i.e. hard negatives) supposedly would allow a system to improve upon the results of the source parser. The second type comprises sentences of at least 6 words that contain a dash or a comma, and a verb. We made the negative class twice as large as the positive one.

It is worth mentioning that cases marked 2 and 3 noticeably overlap with cases of gapping from the SynTagRus gapping test set, which we use to validate our AGRR corpus (see section 4; for cases 2 and 3 examples see the official shared task report (Smurov et al., 2019)).

The test set contains ten times fewer examples than the combined training and development sets with the same distribution of genres - 75% from fiction and technical literature, 25% from social media - and the same 1:2 ratio of positive to negative classes.

		0		1		sum
dev	vk	670	2760	326	1382	20548
	other	2090		1056		
train	vk	2860	10864	1366	5542	
	other	8004		4176		
test	vk	343	1365	185	680	2045
	other	1022		495		
sum			14989		7604	**22593**

Table 2: # examples by class; vk stands for social media texts

3.3 Dataset Format

When choosing the annotation format, we aimed to minimize reliance on any specific NLP frameworks and parsers. Since tokenization is often an integral part of NLP pipelines, we decided not to provide any gold standard tokenization and thus did not choose the commonly used CoNLL-U format.

Instead, markup of each sentence contains a class label (1 if gapping is present in the sentence, 0 otherwise) and character offsets for each gapping element (no offsets if sentence does not contain the corresponding gapping element).

4 SynTagRus Gapping Test Set

In order to test how well our corpus represents the phenomenon in question, we employ an alternative test set[2] obtained from SynTagRus - the dependency treebank for Russian that provides comprehensive manually-corrected morphological and syntactic annotation (Boguslavsky et al., 2009; Dyachenko et al., 2015).

To detect and extract relevant sentences, we rely on the original SynTagRus annotation (Iomdin and Sizov, 2009), i.e., the Nodetype attribute, which, if present with the value "FANTOM", indicates an omission in surface representation.

All the sentences were manually verified and divided into three categories:

1 cases similar to the ones encountered in the AGRR corpus;

2 cases of gapping not included in the AGRR corpus;

3 cases considered other types of ellipsis rather than gapping.

Sentences from all three categories as well as the number of aooripriate negative examples (obtained from SynTagRus with simple heuristics) will be further jointly referred to as the SynTagRus gapping test set.

We expect the systems trained on the AGRR corpus to show better results for category 1, because the examples may differ stylistically and thematically but not on a structural level. High scores obtained for category 2 would demonstrate that the corpus and the top systems were transferable to a broader range of gapping cases. Additionally, we provide the results obtained by the top systems for category 3.

We further illustrate the diversity of ellipsis cases in categories 2 and 3 using examples adapted from the SynTagRus gapping test corpus.

[2]https://lindat.mff.cuni.cz/repository/xmlui/handle/11234/1-3001

4.1 Gapping not Included in the AGRR Corpus

In Russian, the number of remnants is limited only by the valency of the predicate and can exceed two. Consider an example (9) with three remnants.

(9) [cR1 В Испании] [cR2 в 1923 году] [cV
. In Spain in 1923 year
установил] диктатуру [cR3
established dictatorship
генерал Педро де Ривера], [R1 в
general Pedro de Rivera, in
Польше] [R2 в 1926-м] - [R3 Пилсудски].
Poland in 1926 - Pilsudski
'In Spain, the dictatorship of General Pedro de Rivera was established in 1923, while in Poland the dictatorship ~~was established~~ by Pilsudski in 1926.'

The AGRR corpus does not contain examples where the order of remnants differs from the order of correlates, though the structure is possible under certain conditions (Paducheva, 1974).

(10) [cR1 Школа и уроки] [cV
. school and lessons
принадлежали] [cR2 кругу мучительных
belonged.to circle painful
обязанностей], а [R2 душевному выбору]
duties and soul.ADJ choice
- [R1 зеленая птица с красной головой].
- green bird with red head
'School and lessons belonged to the circle of painful duties, while a green bird with a red head ~~belonged~~ to the choice of the soul.'

The cases with two independent instances of gapping are not seen by the systems trained on the AGRR corpus. In (11) the bracketed sentence has its own gapping with overt predicate имеет 'has' not connected to the first occurrence of gapping, where predicate достигает 'reaches' is elided.

(11) [cR1 Ширина долины] [cV **достигает**] [cR2
. width valley reaches
600 км], [R1 глубина] - [R2 8 км] (для
600 km, depth - 8 km for
сравнения: Большой каньон [cV **имеет**] [R1
comparison Grand Canyon has
ширину] [R2 до 25 км] [R1 и глубину] [R2
width to 25 km and depth
1,8 км]).
1.8 km
'The width of the valley reaches 600 kilometers, the depth ~~reaches~~ 8 kilometers (for comparison: the width of the Grand Canyon is about 25 kilometers and the depth ~~is~~ 1.8 kilometers).'

In Russian, gapping is not necessarily formed by omission of a verb. See (12), where the elided predicate is a noun (отчуждение 'isolation').

(12) Бюрократизм привел к [cV
red.tape   led   to
отчуждению] [cR1 трудящихся] [cR2 от
alienation   working.people   from
власти], [R1 крестьян] [R2 от   земли].
power   peasants   from land

> 'Red tape led to the alienation of working people
> from power, and ~~alienation~~ of peasants from the
> land'

The SynTagRus gapping test set contains several examples illustrating a particular type of gapping that we refer to as gapping with generalization. In this type of gapping, the correlate clause semantically generalizes over instances described in subsequent gapped clauses. Furthermore, the main clause may lack the correlates of some remnants, e.g. промышленностью 'industry', наукой 'science' in (13).

(13) [cR1 Средства и   способы] создаются
     .   means   and methods are.created
    талантливыми учеными, а [cV
    talented   scientists and
    реализуются]: [R1 средства] - [R2 **военной**
    are.realized   means   -   military
    промышленностью], а [R1 способы] - [R2
    industry   and methods -
    военной наукой и   опытом]
    military science and experience.

> 'Means and methods are created by talented
> scientists, and are realized: the means ~~are realized~~ by
> the military industry, and the methods ~~are realized~~
> by military science and experience.'

According to (Kazenin, 2007), gapping in Russian cannot elide an intermediate node in the tree structure. However, our data shows that such elision is possible. Consider (14), where the left correlate is higher syntactically than the elided predicate.

(14) Если [cR1 можно] [cV передать] [cR2 один
     if   is.possible transfer.INF   one
    университет], то   почему [R1 нельзя] [R2
    university,   then why   not.possible
    другие]?!
    others

> 'If it is possible to transfer one university, then why
> can't others ~~be transferred~~?!'

4.2 Other Types of Ellipsis

Along with cases of gapping not included in the AGRR corpus, we categorized sentences from the SynTagRus gapping test set that contain types of ellipsis other than gapping. Below we provide frequent categories of ellipsis with illustrations.

Ellipsis in comparative constructions (Bacskai-Atkari, 2018; Kennedy and Merchant, 2000) has restrictions that differ from gapping.

(15) От сна   за   рулем погибает
     from sleeping behind wheel die
    столько же водителей, сколько   от
    as.many   drivers   how.many/as from
    алкоголя
    alcohol

> 'As many drivers die from sleeping behind the
> wheel, as ~~many drivers die~~ from alcohol'

Cases where the second remnant is missing and the second clause contains just one remnant are called stripping (Merchant, 2016). Canonical examples of stripping are limited to a small number of constructions (16) - (17). According to (Hankamer and Sag, 1976), who introduced the term: "Stripping is a rule that deletes everything in a clause under identity with corresponding parts of a preceding clause except for one constituent (and sometimes a clause-initial adverb or negative)."

(16) The man stole the car after midnight, **but not** the diamonds. (Merchant, 2016)

(17) Abby can speak passable Dutch, and Ben, **too**. (Wurmbrand, 2013)

Our SynTagRus gapping test corpus contains examples with more (нет in (18)) and less canonical (причем in (19)) markers, but all of them can be distinguished from gapping with one remnant by the presence of closed set markers (see Section 2).

(18) Тогда деньги стали   общими, а
     Then money became shared   and
    экономики – **нет**.
    economy   - not.

> 'Then the money became shared, but the economy
> did not ~~become shared~~.'

(19) В Сталинграде каждый   сражается,
     in Stalingrad, everyone fights
    причем как мужчины, так и женщины
    and   both men   and women.'

> 'In Stalingrad, everyone continuously fights, both
> men and women ~~fight~~.'

Another type of   ellipsis   encountered in the SynTagRus gapping test corpus is sluicing (Merchant, 2001). Sluicing deletes the predicate from an embedded interrogative clause with no arguments remaining.

(20) Медикам дается указание как-то
doctors   are.given instructions somehow
бороться с   этим явлением,   а   как —
cope   with this phenomenon and how -
никому не   известно.
no.one NEG knows

'Doctors are instructed to somehow cope with this
phenomenon, but no one knows how ~~to cope with
it~~.'

Finally, in the SynTagRus gapping test set there are numerous sentences with the following type of ellipsis: the repeating predicate is elided leaving only its arguments, and there are no correlates for arguments in the full clause. In sentences of this category, the second clause adds further details to the situation mentioned in the full clause.

Consider (20), where the predicate меняются ('they change') has no subject in the full clause, while it is added in the elided clause with одним игроком ('by one player').

(21) Правила меняются по ходу   игры
rules   are.changed with progress game
и   всегда почему-то   одним
and always for.some.reason one
игроком
player.INST

'The rules are changed as the game progresses and for some reason ~~the rules are changed~~ always by one player'

In (22) the elided clause adds the manner справкой('by certificate') to the action подтвердить ('to verify')

(22) Студент должен подтвердить свои доходы,
student must   confirm   his   income
причем желательно справкой.
and   preferably   certificate.INST

'The student must confirm their income, and preferably ~~confirm~~ with a certificate.'

5 Shared Task

In this paper, we revisit the information about the shared task that is essential for understanding the results of this paper (for details see the shared task report (Smurov et al., 2019))

We have formulated 3 different tasks concerning gapping with increasing complexity:

1. Binary presence-absence classification - for every sentence, decide if there is a gapping construction present.

2. Gap resolution - for every sentence with gapping, predict the position of the elided predicate and the head of the pronounced predicate in the antecedent clause.

3. Full annotation - for every sentence with gapping, predict the linear position of the elided predicate and positions of its remnants in the clause with the gap, as well as the positions of remnant correlates and the head of the pronounced predicate in the antecedent clause.

Solutions of all three tasks can be utilized by researchers studying gapping. Since sentences with gapping are naturally rare, the solution of the binary classification task will help researchers to find sentences with gapping for further analysis and data enrichment. Solutions of the other two tasks can be used to facilitate gapping resolution for parsing systems as well as to verify the quality of gapping annotation in syntactic corpora.

5.1 Metrics

The main metric for the binary classification task is standard f-measure. Two other tasks were scored based on symbolwise f-measure on gapping elements relevant to the particular task (all 6 for full annotation, V and cV for gap resolution).

The following is a description of symbolwise f-measure:

- true negative samples for binary classification task do not affect total f-measure;

- for true positive samples, symbolwise f-measure is obtained for each relevant gapping element separately, thus generating 6 scores for the full annotation task and 2 scores for the gap resolution task (if the evaluated sentence is either false positive or false negative, all the generated scores are equal to 0);

- the obtained f-measures are macro-averaged over the whole corpus.

One particular feature of the described metrics is that the second and the third task scores cannot exceed the first task score and thus binary classification errors are relatively harshly penalized in all three tasks. We have deliberately chosen such metrics since ellipsis is a rare language phenomenon and thus misclassification (false positive in particular) should be treated with caution.

6 Results and Analysis

6.1 Evaluation Results

Results of the top two participants on both the AGRR-2019 and the SynTagRus gapping test set are presented in Table 3. The implemented solutions are described in detail in the next section. The full table with shared task results as well as brief description of each participating system is available in the official report.

Corpus	Team	Binary	Gap	Full
AGRR	Winner	0.96	0.90	0.89
AGRR	2nd best	0.95	0.86	0.84
SynTagRus	Winner	0.91	0.76	0.77
SynTagRus	2nd best	0.88	0.67	0.64

Table 3: Top systems F1 scores on AGRR-2019 and SynTagRus test set. Binary: binary classification; Gap: gap resolution; Full: full annotation.

F1 scores on the SynTagRus gapping test set are measured for the subset consisting of categories 0 and 1. While examples of categories 2 and 3 cannot be reliably measured with the shared task metrics, we have calculated the number of examples of each category classified by the top systems as gapping. These results are shown in Table 4.

Cat	Total	Team	positives	positives, %
0	1166	Winner	8	0.7%
0	1166	2nd best	30	2.6%
1	507	Winner	433	85.4%
1	507	2nd best	420	82.8%
2	75	Winner	26	35%
2	75	2nd best	37	49%
3	100	Winner	6	6%
3	100	2nd best	13	13%

Table 4: Number of sentences classified as gapping for each category of SynTagRus gapping test set.

Table 3 demonstrates that the AGRR-2019 corpus contains enough data for effective utilization of machine learning techniques. The results on the SynTagRus gapping test set in particular show that systems trained on the AGRR-2019 corpus are able to yield reasonably good results on a dataset obtained without any usage of the Compreno parser. While both systems experience a performance drop relative to scores on the AGRR-2019 test set, this can be attributed to domain shift (as two corpora have different genre composition etc.). In our opinion these results provide enough evidence to state that while the AGRR-2019 corpus has some inherent restrictions (see Section 4), it reflects a real-world linguistic phenomenon rather than the output of the Compreno system.

Performance on category 0 examples, as is shown in Table 4, demonstrates that high-precision systems can be trained on the AGRR-2019 corpus[3].

Performance on category 2 examples demonstrates that such systems can potentially recognize gapping examples of types completely unrepresented in the training set (obviously, performance on such sentences could be improved if similar examples were be added to the training set).

Performance on category 3 examples, by contrast, demonstrates that such systems can differentiate gapping from other types of ellipsis (including rather similar ones such as stripping and sluicing).

6.2 General Analysis

Most participants, including all top systems, treated gap resolution and full annotation tasks as sequence labeling tasks. The most popular approaches were to enhance the standard BLSTM-CRF architecture (Lample et al., 2016; Ma and Hovy, 2016), to pretrain an LSTM-based language model or to use transformer-based solutions (Vaswani et al., 2017; Devlin et al., 2018).

Most participating systems did not use any token-level features other than word embeddings, character-level embeddings, or language model embeddings (Peters et al., 2018; Devlin et al., 2018; Howard and Ruder, 2018). Of particular note is that neither of the 2 top-scoring systems used morphological or syntactic features. While it may be theorized that using such features could yield some improvements, we presume that language model embeddings (especially when coupled with self-attention as in the top two systems) contain most syntactic information relevant to ellipsis resolution.

6.3 Top Systems Analysis

The top two systems share several important elements: language model embeddings, self-attention (the winner as part of BERT, the second best team solution directly), and the part of the system designed to choose sound label

---

[3]It can be argued that the second best system has high false positive rate relative to the frequency of gapping in natural language. However one should keep in mind that classes 0 and 1 had 2:1 distribution in the training set. Changing this balance in favour of negative examples may potentially increase the precision of the systems. Moreover, manual analysis of these false positives shows that some of these examples do in fact contain gapping while many others are borderline.

chains (FSA-based postprocessor for the winner, NCRF++ for the second best team; (Yang and Zhang, 2018)). The third element is necessary when solving the task as sequence labeling (and more task-specific FSA-postprocessing yields better results). We can assume the first two elements combined contain most syntactic and semantic information relevant to ellipsis resolution.

The top two systems share one additional feature that most other systems lack: both are joined models that simultaneously learn the sentence-level gapping class and token-level gapping element labels.

We assume that this feature is relevant because it allows systems to minimize false positive examples for the gap resolution and full annotation tasks. Since false positive examples receive a rather harsh score penalty, joint training could potentially offer a substantial score improvement for the whole system.

7 Conclusion

We have presented the AGRR-2019 gapping corpus for Russian. Our corpus contains 22.5k sentences, including 7.5k sentences with gapping and 15k relevant negative sentences. The corpus is multi-genre and social media texts form a quarter of it.

It should be noted that to the best of our knowledge no other publicly available corpus for any language contains a comparable number of gapping examples. We believe that theoretical studies may also benefit from this data.

We have developed an annotation scheme that identifies gapping elements - parts of the sentence most relevant for gapping resolution from the theoretical point of view (see analysis in section 2). Our annotation scheme allows for successful solution of gapping resolution tasks by modifying standard sequence labeling techniques.

An important property of the AGRR-2019 corpus is that the systems trained on this corpus yield low number of false positives. Given the fact that gapping is a naturally rare phenomenon, this feature is extremely important.

While our corpus has some inherent limitations (see Section 4), the evaluation of the top system on the SynTagRus gapping test set demonstrates that the AGRR-2019 corpus is not an artificial creation of Compreno parser, but rather covers a large subset of Russian language gapping (see

Section 6.1).

We hope that the size and diversity of our corpus will provide researchers interested in gapping with a valuable source of information that could bring the community closer to resolving ellipsis.

The corpus described in this paper can be utilized to improve parsing quality, possibly not only for Russian but for other Slavic languages as well.

Acknowledgments

We are grateful to Alexey Bogdanov for his help with linguistic analysis and useful advice. We are thankful to Ekaterina Lyutikova for her insightful comments on the SynTagRus gapping test set. We thank the anonymous reviewers for their valuable feedback.

The work was partially supported by the GA UK grant 794417.

References

Konstantin Anisimovich, Konstantin Druzhkin, Filipp Minlos, Maria Petrova, Vladimir Selegey, and Konstantin Zuev. 2012. Syntactic and semantic parser based on abbyy compreno linguistic technologies. In *Computational Linguistics and Intellectual Technologies: Proceedings of the International Conference "Dialog" [Komp'iuternaia Lingvistika i Intellektual'nye Tehnologii: Trudy Mezhdunarodnoj Konferentsii "Dialog"]*, volume 2, pages 90–103, Bekasovo, Russia.

Julia Bacskai-Atkari. 2018. *Deletion phenomena in comparative constructions: English comparatives in a cross-linguistic perspective.* Language Science Press, Berlin.

Alexey Bogdanov. 2012. Description of gapping in a system of automatic translation. In *Computational Linguistics and Intellectual Technologies: Proceedings of the International Conference "Dialog" [Komp'iuternaia Lingvistika i Intellektual'nye Tehnologii: Trudy Mezhdunarodnoj Konferentsii "Dialog"]*, volume 2, pages 61–70, Bekasovo, Russia.

Igor Boguslavsky, Leonid Iomdin, Svetlana Timoshenko, and Tatiana Frolova. 2009. Development of the russian tagged corpus with lexical and functional annotation. In *Metalanguage and Encoding Scheme Design for Digital Lexicography. MONDILEX Third Open Workshop. Proceedings. Bratislava, Slovakia*, pages 83–90.

Johan Bos and Jennifer Spenader. 2011. An annotated corpus for the analysis of vp ellipsis. *Language Resources and Evaluation*, 45(4):463–494.

Elizabeth Coppock. 2001. Gapping: In defense of deletion. In *Proceedings of the Chicago Linguistics Society*, volume 37, pages 133–148.

Jacob Devlin, Ming-Wei Chang, Kenton Lee, and Kristina Toutanova. 2018. Bert: Pre-training of deep bidirectional transformers for language understanding. In *arXiv preprint arXiv:1810.0480*.

Kira Droganova, Filip Ginter, Jenna Kanerva, and Daniel Zeman. 2018. Mind the gap: Data enrichment in dependency parsing of elliptical constructions. In *Proceedings of the Second Workshop on Universal Dependencies (UDW 2018)*, pages 47–54, Bruxelles, Belgium. Association for Computational Linguistics.

Pavel Dyachenko, Leonid Iomdin, Alexander Lazursky, Leonid Mityushin, Olga Podlesskaya, Victor Sizov, Tatiana Frolova, and Leonid Tsinman. 2015. Sovremennoe sostoyanie gluboko annotirovannogo korpusa tekstov russkogo yazyka (syntagrus). [the current state of the deeply annotated corpus of russian texts (syntagrus)]. *Trudy Instituta Russkogo Yazyka im. V. V. Vinogradova*, (6):272–300.

Jorge Hankamer and Ivan Sag. 1976. Deep and surface anaphora. *Linguistic inquiry*, 7(3):391–428.

Daniel Hardt. 1997. An empirical approach to vp ellipsis. *Computational Linguistics*, 23(4):525–541.

Jeremy Howard and Sebastian Ruder. 2018. Fine-tuned language models for text classification. Association for Computational Linguistics.

Leonid Iomdin and Victor Sizov. 2009. Structure editor: a powerful environment for tagged corpora. *Research Infrastructure for Digital Lexicography*, page 1.

Kyle Johnson. 2001. *What VP ellipsis can do, and what it can't, but not why*. Citeseer.

Konstantin Kazenin. 2007. O nekotoryh ogranicheniyah na ellipsis v russkov yazyke. [on some restrictions on ellipsis for russian]. *Voprosy Yazykoznaniya*, (2):92–107.

Chris Kennedy and Jason Merchant. 2000. Attributive comparative deletion. *Natural Language and Linguistic Theory*, 18.

Jonathan K Kummerfeld and Dan Klein. 2017. Parsing with traces: An o (n 4) algorithm and a structural representation. *Transactions of the Association for Computational Linguistics*, 5:441–454.

Guillaume Lample, Miguel Ballesteros, Sandeep Subramanian, Kazuya Kawakami, and Chris Dyer. 2016. Neural architectures for named entity recognition. In *NAACL-HLT*.

Xuezhe Ma and Eduard Hovy. 2016. End-to-end sequence labeling via bi-directional lstm-cnns-crf. In *ACL*.

Jason Merchant. 2001. *The syntax of silence: Sluicing, islands, and the theory of ellipsis*. Oxford University Press, Oxford.

Jason Merchant. 2016. *Ellipsis: A survey of analytical approaches*. University of Chicago, Chicago, IL.

Leif Arda Nielsen. 2005. *A corpus-based study of Verb Phrase Ellipsis Identification and Resolution*. Ph.D. thesis, King's College London.

Joakim Nivre, Paola Marongiu, Filip Ginter, Jenna Kanerva, Simonetta Montemagni, Sebastian Schuster, and Maria Simi. 2018. Enhancing universal dependency treebanks: A case study. In *Proceedings of the Second Workshop on Universal Dependencies (UDW 2018)*, pages 102–107.

Elena Paducheva. 1974. *O semantike sintaksisa. Materialy k transformacionnoj grammatike russkogo jazyka. [On the Semantics of Syntax: Materials toward the Transformational Grammar of Russian]*. Nauka, Moscow.

Matthew E Peters, Mark Neumann, Mohit Iyyer, Matt Gardner, Christopher Clark, Kenton Lee, and Luke Zettlemoyer. 2018. Deep contextualized word representations. In *Proceedings of NAACL*.

John Robert Ross. 1970. Gapping and the order of constituents. In *Manfred Bierwisch and Karl Erich Heidolph, editors, Progress in Linguistics, De Gruyter*, pages 249–259.

Sebastian Schuster, Joakim Nivre, and Christopher D Manning. 2018. Sentences with gapping: Parsing and reconstructing elided predicates. *arXiv preprint arXiv:1804.06922*.

Ivan Smurov, Maria Ponomareva, Tatiana Shavrina, and Kira Droganova. 2019. Agrr-2019: Automatic gapping resolution for russian. In *Computational Linguistics and Intellectual Technologies*, pages 561–575, Moscow, Russia. nakl. RGGU.

Yakov Testelets. 2011. Ellipsis in russian: theoretical and descriptive approaches. In *Tipologiya morfosintaksicheskih parametrov*, M.: MGGU.

Ashish Vaswani, Noam Shazeer, Niki Parmar, Jakob Uszkoreit, Llion Jones, Aidan N Gomez, Lukasz Kaiser, and Illia Polosukhin. 2017. Attention is all you need. In *Advances in Neural Information Processing Systems*, pages 5998–6008.

Susi Wurmbrand. 2013. Stripping and topless complements. *Ms., University of Connecticut*.

Jie Yang and Yue Zhang. 2018. Ncrf++: An open-source neural sequence labeling toolkit. In *Proceedings of the 56th Annual Meeting of the Association for Computational Linguistics*.

Creating a Corpus for Russian Data-to-Text Generation Using Neural Machine Translation and Post-Editing

Anastasia Shimorina
Lorraine University / LORIA
Nancy, France

Elena Khasanova
Lorraine University
Nancy, France

Claire Gardent
CNRS / LORIA
Nancy, France

{anastasia.shimorina,claire.gardent}@loria.fr
yelena.khas@gmail.com

Abstract

In this paper, we propose an approach for semi-automatically creating a data-to-text (D2T) corpus for Russian that can be used to learn a D2T natural language generation model. An error analysis of the output of an English-to-Russian neural machine translation system shows that 80% of the automatically translated sentences contain an error and that 53% of all translation errors bear on named entities (NE). We therefore focus on named entities and introduce two post-editing techniques for correcting wrongly translated NEs.

1 Introduction

Data-to-text (D2T) generation is a key task in Natural Language Generation (NLG) which focuses on transforming data into text and permits verbalising the data contained in data- or knowledge bases. However, creating the training data necessary to learn a D2T generation model is a major bottleneck as *(i)* naturally occurring parallel data-to-text data does not commonly exist and *(ii)* manually creating such data is highly complex. Moreover, the few parallel corpora that exist for D2T generation have been developed mainly for English. Methods that support the automatic creation of multi-lingual D2T corpora from these existing datasets would therefore be highly valuable.

In this paper, we introduce a semi-automatic method for deriving a parallel data-to-text corpus for Russian from the D2T WebNLG corpus whose texts are in English. Our method includes three main steps. First, we use neural machine translation (NMT) model to translate WebNLG English texts into Russian. Second, we perform a detailed error analysis on the output of the NMT model. Third, we exploit two techniques for automatically post-editing the automatic translations. As 53% of the translation errors bear on named entities, we

focus on these in the present paper and leave other error types for further research.

The new corpus, error classification and scripts are available at https://gitlab.com/shimorina/bsnlp-2019.

2 Related work

Our work is related to the domain of automatic post-editing (APE) of machine translation (MT) outputs. The task of APE consists in automatically correcting "black-box" MT output by learning from human corrections. Several WMT APE shared tasks were held focusing on English-German, German-English, and English-Spanish language pairs.[1]

Recent neural approaches to APE include, *inter alia*, multi-source training with original sentences and MT outputs (Junczys-Dowmunt and Grundkiewicz, 2018), encoding corrections by a sequence of post-edit operations (Libovický et al., 2016), as well as standard encoder-decoder architectures (Pal et al., 2016).

Submissions participating in the APE shared tasks extensively use large synthetic corpora (Negri et al., 2018). Despite that fact, a *"do-nothing"* baseline when MT outputs are kept unchanged is hard to beat according to the last year's results of the APE shared task (Chatterjee et al., 2018).

3 The WebNLG D2T Dataset

The WebNLG data-to-text corpus (Gardent et al., 2017) aligns knowledge graphs with textual descriptions verbalising the content of those graphs. The knowledge graphs are extracted from DBpedia (Lehmann et al., 2015) and consist of

---

[1] For this year round of the shared task, a new English-Russian language pair was added: http://www.statmt.org/wmt19/ape-task.html. We did not make use of the data, since our research started before this recent announcement.

Proceedings of the 7th Workshop on Balto-Slavic Natural Language Processing, pages 44–49,
Florence, Italy, 2 August 2019. ©2019 Association for Computational Linguistics

RDF triples	<Asterix, creator, René Goscinny> <René Goscinny, nationality, French people>
Original	Rene Goscinny is a French national and also the creator of the comics character Asterix.
MT	Рене Госкино - французский гражданин, а также создатель комического персонажа Астерикс. Rene Goskino French national and also creator $comic_{gen}$ $character_{gen}$ $Asterix_{inan}$
PE	Рене Госинни - французский гражданин, а также создатель персонажа комиксов Астерикса. Rene Goscinny French national and also creator $character_{gen}$ $comics_{gen}$ $Asterix_{anim}$
Errors	named entity, vocabulary, grammar
Links	<René Goscinny, sameAs, Рене Госинни> <French people, sameAs, Французы>

Table 1: WebNLG original instance in the ComicsCharacter category, its Russian translation (MT), and post-edited translation (PE) along with error annotation. Errors are highlighted in blue. Links are RDF triples of the form *<English entity, sameAs, Russian entity>*. However, such links are not available for all entities in DBpedia.

sets of (one to seven) RDF triples of the form *<subject, property, object>*. Textual descriptions are in English, and due to the nature of the knowledge graphs, they have an abundance of named entities. The first two lines of Table 1 show an example of a WebNLG instance.

WebNLG provides textual descriptions for entities in fifteen DBpedia categories (Airport, Artist, Astronaut, Athlete, Building, CelestialBody, City, ComicsCharacter, Food, MeanOfTransportation, Monument, Politician, SportsTeam, University, WrittenWork). The corpus possesses a hierarchical structure: if a set consisting of more than one triple is verbalised, then verbalisations of every single triple are to be found in the corpus. Given the example in Table 1, the pairs {*<Asterix, creator, René Goscinny>*: *René Goscinny created Asterix*} and {*<René Goscinny, nationality, French people>*: *René Goscinny is French*} are also present in the WebNLG data. That structure allows propagating post-edits made in texts describing one triple to those verbalising triple sets of larger sizes.

4 Creating a Russian Version of the WebNLG Dataset

4.1 Neural Machine Translation

Following Castro Ferreira et al. (2018), who created a silver-standard German version of WebNLG, we translated the WebNLG English texts into Russian using the English-Russian NMT system developed by the University of Edinburgh for the WMT17 translation shared task (Sennrich et al., 2017).[2] This system ranks first for the English-Russian News translation task both in

automatic metrics[3] and human assessment (Bojar et al., 2017). It is learned using Nematus, an encoder-decoder with attention, based on sub-word units (byte pair encoding). Since the Edinburgh model was trained on sentence-to-sentence data, we split WebNLG texts into sentences using the WebSplit sentence annotation (Narayan et al., 2017), input each sentence to the NMT system, and then concatenated translations to reconstruct the target texts.

4.2 Manual Post-Editing and Error Analysis

To determine the most common translation errors, we start by manually annotating error types in sentences verbalising one triple.

Error Classification The manual post-editing was done by two experts, native Russian speakers, on a part of the corpus for the categories Astronaut, ComicsCharacter, Monument, University for texts verbalising one triple only. Out of 1,076 machine translation outputs analysed, 856 texts (80%) were post-edited. The experts also classified errors that they identified in a translated text.

To define an error classification, we drew inspiration from various error typologies that were developed in the MT community and applied to different languages. See, for instance, Popović (2018) who provides an overview of different approaches to error classification. We also got some ideas from studies focused on errors made by language learners and non-experienced translators in the Russian-English and English-Russian translation directions (Kunilovskaya, 2013; Rakhilina et al., 2016; Komalova, 2017). That allowed us to extend the classification with some phenomena typical for Russian. Lastly, the classification

[2] http://data.statmt.org/wmt17_systems/
Specifically, we use their ensemble model consisting of four left-to-right models.

[3] http://matrix.statmt.org/matrix/
systems_list/1875

Category	Subcategory
Grammar	Case marking
	Copula
	Verbal aspect
	Preposition
	Possessive
	Part-of-speech
	Agreement
	Voice, intentionality
Vocabulary	Ambiguity
	Collocation
	Incorrect translation
Structure	Word Order
	Deletion
	Insertion
Named entity	
Punctuation	

Table 2: Main categories and subcategories of error classification.

was augmented with the notorious errors of the NMT systems: word repetitions, deletions, insertions (partly due to the subword-based nature of the applied NMT), untranslated common words, etc. Main error classes identified for the final classification are shown in Table 2. Named entities were treated as a separate category to highlight problems while applying the NMT system on WebNLG. If a text contained more than one mistake in a particular category, then each mistake was tagged as an error. If a spotted mistake concerned an NE, annotators were allowed to add other categories to specify the error.

Category	Proportion	Agreement
Grammar	17%	0.44
Vocabulary	14%	0.52
Structure	11%	0.32
Named entity	53%	0.67
Punctuation	4%	0.0

Table 3: Proportion of main error types in the manually post-edited data and Cohen's κ scores on the held-out category Athlete.

Error Analysis Table 3 shows the error type distribution in the post-edited texts. Named entities is the largest source of errors with 53% of all corrections. Grammatical and lexical mistakes constitute 17% and 14% of the identified errors respectively, while "Structure" (11%) ranks fourth. In fact, the majority of structural mistakes were spotted in named entities. For example, *the Baku Turkish Martyrs' Memorial* was translated as «Мемориал» «Мемориал» в Баку ('Memorial Memorial in Baku') with the following errors identified:

named entity, deletion, deletion, insertion.

The most common errors found in NE translations are:

- copying verbatim English entities into Russian translations (person names, locations);

- wrong transliteration, whereas a standard transliteration exists in Russian. E.g., *Lancashire* translated as Ланкассир ('Lancassir') instead of Ланкашир;

- misinterpretation of a named entity as a common noun. E.g., *Dane Whitman* translated as датчанин Уитмен ('inhabitant of Denmark Whitman') instead of Дейн Уитмен.

It should be noted that since the Edinburgh NMT system used subword units, there were also errors with copying named entities, e.g., *Visvesvaraya Technological University* became *Visvesvaraya Technical University*. In a similar vein, in the example from Table 1, the surname *Goscinny* was misinterpreted as the acronym *Goskino* meaning 'State Committee for Cinematography'.

Inter-annotator Agreement Erroneous words in translations can be attributed to several possible error types. To evaluate consistency between annotators and the appropriateness of the developed error classification, we calculated inter-annotator agreement (Cohen, 1960) on the 86 texts from the DBpedia category Athlete, to which annotators were not exposed before. Table 3 shows the kappa scores. The highest score (0.67) was reached for "Named entity", which corresponds to the substantial agreement. The main source of disagreement for named entities was a decision to perform transliteration or not, e.g., sport club names as *Tennessee Titans* can be kept 'as is' in a Russian text or can be put into Cyrillic. For other categories, agreements range from moderate to fair; as for "Punctuation", the agreement is zero due to the data sparseness in this category (there were two errors only identified by one annotator).

Overall, results show *(i)* consistency in correcting named entities, as well as *(ii)* the importance to perform more annotator training and/or establish clearer guidelines, especially for the "Structure" category.

5 Automatic Post-Editing

To improve the automatic translations, we experiment with two methods: a rule-based method based on the errors found during manual annotation and a neural approach.

5.1 Rule Based Post-Editing

Based on the manual corrections applied to the 1-triple data (WebNLG instances where the input graph consists of a single triple), we extract post-edit rules by building upon the operations used to compute the edit distance (Levenshtein, 1966). For example, given the neural translation (1a) and the manually edited correction (1b), the sequence of edit operations applied to compute the Levenshtein edit distance is (1c), i.e. replace 'Альба' by 'Алба-Юлия', delete 'Юлия', keep '–', keep 'город', keep 'в', keep 'Румынии'.

(1) a. 'Альба Юлия – город в Румынии'
    b. 'Алба-Юлия – город в Румынии'
    c. SUB DEL KEEP KEEP KEEP KEEP
    d. 'Alba Julia is a city in Romania'

Based on these edit sequences, we extracted sequences of substitution, deletion, and insertion rules along with the corresponding tokens (e.g., Альба Юлия → Алба-Юлия). We then checked these rules manually and excluded false positives. Lastly, we applied the validated rules to the automatic translations.

That method enabled us to increase the amount of post-edited data: after that procedure the total number of post-edited translations sums up to 4,188 (cf. Table 4).

	1 triple	2-7 triples	All triples
PE	856	3,332	4,188
Total	1,076	4,109	5,185

Table 4: Corpus statistics: number of post-edited (PE) texts. Total corresponds to both PE and non-PE texts.

5.2 Automatic Post-Editing Model

To see to which extent corrections can be learned automatically, we built a corpus of (MT, RPE) pairs where MT is an automatic translation and RPE is its correction using the rule-based system described in the preceding section and trained an APE model on it.

The baseline system is a *"do-nothing"* baseline where MT outputs are left unmodified. In our case, that baseline gives 82.4 BLEU between MT and RPE on the test set, which sets quite high standards for learning a new APE model.

The train/dev/test partition was 80/10/10. We used the OpenNMT-tf framework (Klein et al., 2017)[4] to train a bidirectional encoder-decoder model with attention (Luong et al., 2015). A single-layer LSTM (Hochreiter and Schmidhuber, 1997) is used for both encoder and decoder. We trained using full vocabulary and the maximal length in the source and target; all the hyperparameters were tuned on the development set. The APE model was trained with a mini-batch size of 32, a word embedding size of 512, and a hidden unit size of 512. It was optimised with Adam with a starting learning rate of 0.0005. We used early stopping based on BLEU on the development set, as a result of that, the model was trained for 23 epochs. Decoding was done using beam search with a beam size of 5. As an evaluation metric, we used BLEU-4 (Papineni et al., 2002) calculated between our model predictions and RPE. BLEU and statistical significance were calculated on tokenised texts using COMPARE-MT tool (Neubig et al., 2019), which, in turn, uses the NLTK implementation of BLEU. Results are shown in Table 5.

The APE model performance reached parity with the baseline on dev and test data. The difference between scores was not statistically significant via the bootstrap resampling (1000 samples, $p < 0.05$). On the training data, the model yielded 94 BLEU, which indicates a possible overfitting.

System	Train	Dev	Test
Baseline	81.11	81.25	82.85
Our APE model	94.45	83.00	83.65

Table 5: BLEU-4 scores.

Our results are in line with the last findings of WMT18 APE shared task that correcting NMT-based translations is a challenging task: gains were only up to 0.8 BLEU points in the NMT track (Chatterjee et al., 2018).

6 Evaluation of Rule-Based Post-Editing

Evaluation was carried out only on the rule-based method output, since it is more robust than the neural approach, and since the APE model did not yield better results.

We analysed a sample of total 66 lexicalisations in 4 categories: Astronaut, University, Monument (2-7 triples) and ComicsCharacter (2-5 triples). Around two thirds of analysed named entities were

---

[4]version 1.22.0, `https://github.com/OpenNMT/OpenNMT-tf`

replaced correctly. Below we analyse common sources of errors for the erroneous NEs.

The most frequent case is unrecognised named entities. In 62% of the cases the replacement was not performed, which includes 28% of Latin transcriptions kept, 27% of kept Cyrillic translations, and 7% of acronyms. For the majority of these NEs, the original translations include unaccounted elements (not covered by the extracted rules) such as missing or wrongly inserted prepositions or punctuation marks.

Another common error is lack of grammatical adaptation of the NE. Wrong case marking occurred in 23% of all NEs (cf. example 2), and gender and number agreement make about 6.5%. The less frequent but important error categories are spelling errors, such as missing capitalisation, insertions of quotation marks, and gender or number agreement with anaphors, especially in texts verbalising 5-7 triples.

(2) En: 'The dean of Accademia di Architettura'
MT: 'Декан Accademia di Projecttura'
RPE: 'Декан Академия$_{nomn}$ архитектуры'
Correct: 'Декан Академии$_{gen}$ архитектуры'

To conclude, many errors are caused by irregularities in the translations (which, in turn, are often caused by misspelled input) and can be eliminated by introducing more variation to the replacement algorithm. Grammatical adaptation of NEs, however, requires more careful further investigation.

7 Conclusion

In this study, we reported an ongoing effort to translate the data-to-text WebNLG corpus in Russian. A detailed error analysis showed that roughly 80% of the neural translations contained an error and that 53% of these errors were due to incorrectly translated named entities. We provided a rule-based method which permits correcting these errors and trained a neural post-editing model.

In future work, we plan to extend the approach to other error types and to investigate whether the neural model can be improved to help generalise post-editing to errors not captured by the rule-based method.

Another possible direction for future research will be to identify named entities before the translation phase, perform translation on the texts stripped of named entities (cf. WebNLG delexicalised version of Castro Ferreira et al. (2018)), and then insert named entities, which were translated and verified separately.

References

Ondřej Bojar, Rajen Chatterjee, Christian Federmann, Yvette Graham, Barry Haddow, Shujian Huang, Matthias Huck, Philipp Koehn, Qun Liu, Varvara Logacheva, Christof Monz, Matteo Negri, Matt Post, Raphael Rubino, Lucia Specia, and Marco Turchi. 2017. Findings of the 2017 conference on machine translation (wmt17). In *Proceedings of the Second Conference on Machine Translation, Volume 2: Shared Task Papers*, pages 169–214, Copenhagen, Denmark. Association for Computational Linguistics.

Thiago Castro Ferreira, Diego Moussallem, Emiel Krahmer, and Sander Wubben. 2018. Enriching the webnlg corpus. In *Proceedings of the 11th International Conference on Natural Language Generation*, pages 171–176, Tilburg University, The Netherlands. Association for Computational Linguistics.

Rajen Chatterjee, Matteo Negri, Raphael Rubino, and Marco Turchi. 2018. Findings of the wmt 2018 shared task on automatic post-editing. In *Proceedings of the Third Conference on Machine Translation: Shared Task Papers*, pages 710–725, Belgium, Brussels. Association for Computational Linguistics.

Jacob Cohen. 1960. A coefficient of agreement for nominal scales. *Educational and psychological measurement*, 20(1):37–46.

Claire Gardent, Anastasia Shimorina, Shashi Narayan, and Laura Perez-Beltrachini. 2017. Creating training corpora for nlg micro-planners. In *Proceedings of the 55th Annual Meeting of the Association for Computational Linguistics (Volume 1: Long Papers)*, pages 179–188, Vancouver, Canada. Association for Computational Linguistics.

Sepp Hochreiter and Jürgen Schmidhuber. 1997. Long short-term memory. *Neural computation*, 9(8):1735–1780.

Marcin Junczys-Dowmunt and Roman Grundkiewicz. 2018. Ms-uedin submission to the wmt2018 ape shared task: Dual-source transformer for automatic post-editing. In *Proceedings of the Third Conference on Machine Translation: Shared Task Papers*, pages 822–826, Belgium, Brussels. Association for Computational Linguistics.

Guillaume Klein, Yoon Kim, Yuntian Deng, Jean Senellart, and Alexander Rush. 2017. Opennmt: Open-source toolkit for neural machine translation. In *Proceedings of ACL 2017, System Demonstrations*, pages 67–72. Association for Computational Linguistics.

L. R. Komalova. 2017. Oshibki i netochnosti perevoda (svodnyj referat). *Social'nye i gumanitarnye nauki. Otechestvennaja i zarubezhnaja literatura. Ser. 6, Jazykoznanie: Referativnyj zhurnal*, (4):32–44.

M. A. Kunilovskaya. 2013. Klassifikacija perevodcheskih oshibok dlja sozdanija razmetki v uchebnom parallel'nom korpuse russian learner translator corpus. *Lingua mobilis*, (1 (40)):141–158.

Jens Lehmann, Robert Isele, Max Jakob, Anja Jentzsch, Dimitris Kontokostas, Pablo N Mendes, Sebastian Hellmann, Mohamed Morsey, Patrick Van Kleef, Sören Auer, et al. 2015. Dbpedia–a large-scale, multilingual knowledge base extracted from wikipedia. *Semantic Web*, 6(2):167–195.

V. I. Levenshtein. 1966. Binary Codes Capable of Correcting Deletions, Insertions and Reversals. *Soviet Physics Doklady*, 10:707.

Jindřich Libovický, Jindřich Helcl, Marek Tlustý, Ondřej Bojar, and Pavel Pecina. 2016. Cuni system for wmt16 automatic post-editing and multimodal translation tasks. In *Proceedings of the First Conference on Machine Translation*, pages 646–654, Berlin, Germany. Association for Computational Linguistics.

Thang Luong, Hieu Pham, and Christopher D. Manning. 2015. Effective approaches to attention-based neural machine translation. In *Proceedings of the 2015 Conference on Empirical Methods in Natural Language Processing*, pages 1412–1421. Association for Computational Linguistics.

Shashi Narayan, Claire Gardent, Shay B. Cohen, and Anastasia Shimorina. 2017. Split and rephrase. In *Proceedings of the 2017 Conference on Empirical Methods in Natural Language Processing*, pages 606–616, Copenhagen, Denmark. Association for Computational Linguistics.

Matteo Negri, Marco Turchi, Rajen Chatterjee, and Nicola Bertoldi. 2018. ESCAPE: a large-scale synthetic corpus for automatic post-editing. In *Proceedings of the 11th Language Resources and Evaluation Conference*, Miyazaki, Japan. European Language Resource Association.

Graham Neubig, Zi-Yi Dou, Junjie Hu, Paul Michel, Danish Pruthi, and Xinyi Wang. 2019. compare-mt: A tool for holistic comparison of language generation systems. In *Proceedings of the 2019 Conference of the North American Chapter of the Association for Computational Linguistics (Demonstrations)*, pages 35–41, Minneapolis, Minnesota. Association for Computational Linguistics.

Santanu Pal, Sudip Kumar Naskar, Mihaela Vela, and Josef van Genabith. 2016. A neural network based approach to automatic post-editing. In *Proceedings of the 54th Annual Meeting of the Association for Computational Linguistics (Volume 2: Short Papers)*, pages 281–286, Berlin, Germany. Association for Computational Linguistics.

Kishore Papineni, Salim Roukos, Todd Ward, and Wei-Jing Zhu. 2002. Bleu: a method for automatic evaluation of machine translation. In *Proceedings of the 40th Annual Meeting of the Association for Computational Linguistics*.

Maja Popović. 2018. *Error Classification and Analysis for Machine Translation Quality Assessment*, pages 129–158. Springer International Publishing, Cham.

Ekaterina Rakhilina, Anastasia Vyrenkova, Elmira Mustakimova, Alina Ladygina, and Ivan Smirnov. 2016. Building a learner corpus for Russian. In *Proceedings of the joint workshop on NLP for Computer Assisted Language Learning and NLP for Language Acquisition*, pages 66–75, Umeå, Sweden. LiU Electronic Press.

Rico Sennrich, Alexandra Birch, Anna Currey, Ulrich Germann, Barry Haddow, Kenneth Heafield, Antonio Valerio Miceli Barone, and Philip Williams. 2017. The University of Edinburgh's Neural MT Systems for WMT17. In *Proceedings of the Second Conference on Machine Translation, Volume 2: Shared Task Papers*, Copenhagen, Denmark.

Data Set for Stance and Sentiment Analysis from User Comments on Croatian News

Mihaela Bošnjak and Mladen Karan
Faculty of Electrical Engineering and Computing, University of Zagreb
`mihaella.bosnjak@protonmail.com, mladen.karan@fer.hr`

Abstract

Nowadays it is becoming more important than ever to find new ways of extracting useful information from the evergrowing amount of user-generated data available online. In this paper, we describe the creation of a data set that contains news articles and corresponding comments from Croatian news outlet *24 sata*. Our annotation scheme is specifically tailored for the task of detecting stances and sentiment from user comments as well as assessing if commentator claims are verifiable. Through this data, we hope to get a better understanding of the publics viewpoint on various events. In addition, we also explore the potential of applying supervised machine learning models to automate annotation of more data.

1 Introduction

In the world of unceasing connectedness there is a constant surge of user-generated data online. On news outlets a multitude of opinions and reactions are present. Such amounts of data are too large to analyze manually. On the other hand, automated analysis of this data is difficult due to its inherently unstructured nature. Models that could automatically and efficiently extract structured information from large amounts of data would save time, energy and yield valuable information. We propose a structured annotation scheme that labels claim verifiability, stance, and sentiment on news outlets.

Information about stance, can provide an overview of public opinions and information about currently favorable political movements. Furthermore, claim verifiability can help the fight against fake news, as automated verifiability detection could bring forth claims that are not verifiable and that could potentially be just a rumor or simply made up. Moreover, the data set could be analyzed in search of interactions between the labels. The contribution of this paper is twofold. First, we create a data set of user comments on news in Croatian annotated with claim verifiability, stance, and sentiment. Second, we perform preliminary experiments with several machine learning models on this data set. We present a general overview of the entire data set creation process with caveats and experimental results.

2 Related Work

For stance detection similar definitions of labels can be found in Mohammad et al. (2016) and Zhang et al. (2018). For claim detection we have strongly relied on Park and Cardie (2014) and Guggilla et al. (2016) when building our definitions of claim labels. An overview of approaches and labels for fake news detection can be found in Zhou and Zafarani (2018). For a good general overview of sentiment analysis or opinion mining we refer to Pang and Lee (2008).

3 Data Set

3.1 Data Source

To collect data we have turned to a Croatian news outlet *24 sata* (`www.24sata.hr`). We chose this outlet for practical reasons, as *24 sata* covers more shocking, diverse, and popular news. Thus, people commented more on this outlet. Most comments on this website contained noisy user-generated text expressing a wide range of stances and sentiment.

The data was scraped from three categories: *newest*, *trending*, and *news*. Articles were scraped and updated on a daily basis and new comments were added to articles old up to one month. We selected news articles for the annotation at random, ignoring those with less than five comments, as we wanted to focus on articles that peeked public interests. Furthermore, from each article, we select a random subset of comments for annotation. Comments that are considered are 'root' comments. These comments could have responses to them but

Proceedings of the 7th Workshop on Balto-Slavic Natural Language Processing, pages 50–55,
Florence, Italy, 2 August 2019. ©2019 Association for Computational Linguistics

they themselves are a response only to the article. Simply said they are the first comment in a thread. We didn't want to use comments that were in threads as that would additionally make the annotation process more complicated. Annotators would have to read the whole thread of comments and understand the main topic, arguments and the discussion that is lead. Also, a lot of labels such as *stance* should be revised to take into consideration former comments. We do understand that all comments may have some influence on the commentator and that they could be take into consideration. As we do not know the measure or significance of that influence we are not bringing any more complexity to an already complex process without knowing if we would reap any benefits.

3.2 Annotation Scheme

In a search for an adequate annotation system, we considered the reason people comment on these outlets and what we expected to gain. Most comments were not carefully curated sentences that were there to inform other readers. They were bursts of reactions, insults, compliments, opinions, etc. People commented because they were enticed by the news content enough that they had to express their inner opinions publicly. Some wrote sentences to inform, others to support or judge, but these are all speculations behind users motivation. Because of their spontaneous creation comments varied in size, structure, and purpose. The main question was how to structure something of this complexity without losing important details?

We have tried to answer that question with the following set of labels, motivated by similar schemes from Mohammad et al. (2016); Park and Cardie (2014). There are three main categories called *Claim*, *Stance*, and *Sentiment*. With these three groups, we are deconstructing a comment to three separate parts. There is a total of 8 labels, most of which are mutually non-exclusive. All annotations are made on the comment-level. We have taken into consideration EDU-level annotations. Considering the complexity of the labels and a limited time out annotators could dedicate we have for now opted for a comment-level annotations. Next we describe all label groups in detail.

3.3 Claim Label Group

Within the *Claim* group we wish to determine the type of the comment with respect to claims therein. Namely, whether it contains a claim. And if so, can

we verify it? We take interest in claims that can be objectively verified as we try to divide the claim domain mainly into two groups by standards that are appropriate for the given domain. This group contains 4 labels: *Spam*, *Non-Claim*, *Verifiable* and *Non-Verifiable*.

Verifiable – this label is assigned to comments that contain claims that can be objectively verified regardless of the subjective nature through which they are presented. E.g. *"I think the earth is flat."* Even though it is an opinion it can be objectively verified. Also, all quantifiable claims are considered verifiable regardless of the measure through which they are expressed as long as we know the metric under comparison (Park and Cardie, 2014). E.g. *"I had a lot of water."* A *lot* is subjective but it can be determined how much water you had or even if you had water. The term of degree is only something to be settled.

Non-Verifiable – comments that are labels this way contain claims that can't be verified objectively. Claims that talk about the future(E.g. *"In two moths it will rain"*), are simple sentences that only contain an adjective and are descriptive (E.g. *"That cat is boring"*) or are private facts (E.g. *"I have two sons"*) (Park and Cardie, 2014).

Spam – this label is here for everything that is unrelated to the news. If the news is talking about cheese then a comment about turtles is spam.

Non-claim – this label is added to cover everything that does pertain to the news article but is not a claim, i.e., does not belong in any of the groups above. This group contains mostly questions, imperative sentences and anything that is borderline. E.g., *"These crooks should be put in prison."* and we arent sure where to put it or if it even belongs to one group.

We point out that the concept of claim in the scope of this annotation does not denote exclusively claims in the classical sense as used in the literature (Aharoni et al., 2014), but also opinions as in Rosenthal and McKeown (2012). Moreover, a comment can contain sentences that fit into all categories. To address this we used the following annotation principle. The comment is first annotated as *Verifiable* and/or *Non-Verifiable* based on whether it contains at least one verifiable/non-verifiable claim. This annotation step is multi-label and the same comment can get both labels if it contains multiple claims of different types. If and only if no labels were assigned in the first step then the comment is

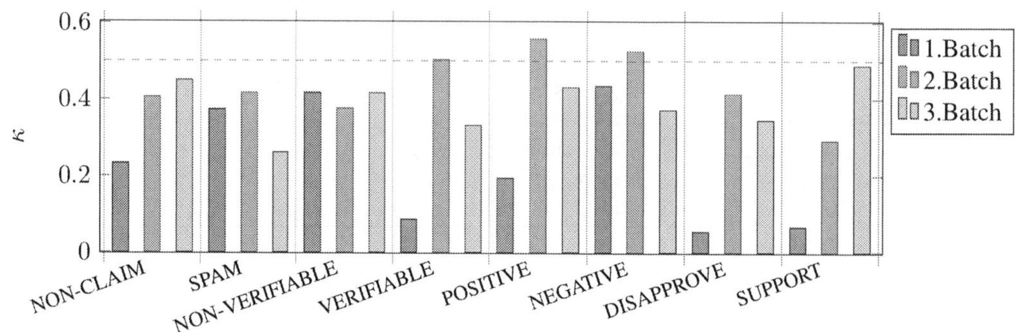

Figure 1: κ over first three batches for each label.

annotated as either only *Non-Claim* or only *Spam*. We acknowledge that some information is lost by this scheme. However, turning this entire group into multi-label would put an additional strain on annotators without much benefit. E.g., from a practical perspective, if a comment contains a sentence that is *Verifiable* it does not provide much additional information to know that it contains another sentence that is *Spam*.

3.4 Stance Group

The *Stance* group contains the *Support* and *Disapprove* labels and is determined *in respect to the title*. We have decided that the title is the target as it would be more difficult to determine stance with respect to the entire article. Also, it would present an additional problem for the annotators since that would make the task more subjective. As the comments on the outlet are not limited by length users often express a multitude of (often conflicting) stances. To allow for multiple stances in the same comment, and to differentiate annotations for comments that are neutral due to several conflicting stances from those truly neutral (with no stance expression), we decided to make this a multi-label task. This contrasts some previous work (Mohammad et al., 2016), where there was a single neutral stance class covering both cases. In our case, a neutral stance is one not containing favorability or interest towards a specific target.

3.5 Sentiment Group

The *Sentiment* group here refers to a manner of speaking. Namely, whether the commentator presents their comment in a positive or negative light. The annotators were instructed to disregard their own sentiment towards the topic of the comment, as this would bias annotations. There are

two labels: *Positive* and *Negative*. They are also multi-label for similar reasons as the *Stance* group.

3.6 Annotation Process

Annotators were given written instructions and detailed explanations of labels. Each annotator got an Excel table for each article with comments. For each label, they had to note if that label was present or not while abiding the rules regarding labels explained in the previous sections.

There were 5 annotators in total and 6 batches of data. They annotated independently. On first 3 batches, there were overlaps between all annotators in order to estimate inter-annotator agreement (IAA) and calibrate the annotators. For the first three batches, each batch had two groups and each group annotated one half of the batch. One of the annotators annotated all data of the first 3 batches (was in both groups). After the first three batches, the number of annotators had decreased, so we focused on collecting more data and occasionally checking IAA on some articles to ensure that annotators were still well aligned. In the final data set, we omit the first two batches as the labels have changed a bit during annotation and these batches were meant to calibrate the annotators.

During annotation, we faced two main challenges. First, we could not predict everything that could be in the comments, thus instructions were not perfect in the beginning and had to be revised during annotation. For the same reason, we revised the number of comments sampled per article, as we realized that it was better to take more articles and fewer comments. The revised approach covered a wider range of different topics and thus allowed us to get acquainted with the entire domain faster and made the data set more diverse.

	Claim				Sentiment		Stance	
	Non-Claim	Spam	Verifiable	Non-verifiable	Positive	Negative	Support	Dissaprove
Train	475 (124)	523 (20)	535 (257)	525 (250)	549 (61)	501 (193)	445 (69)	470 (68)
Train(b)	702 (351)	1006 (503)	556 (266)	548 (264)	976 (488)	616 (308)	752 (376)	804 (402)
Dev	205 (42)	162 (6)	172 (71)	215 (104)	131 (21)	148 (70)	222 (25)	224 (24)
Test	224 (42)	219 (6)	197 (91)	164 (75)	224 (21)	255 (88)	237 (32)	190 (30)

Table 1: Splits across labels for training and measuring results. Number of positive examples for each split and each label is in the parenthesis. Train(b) denotes the balanced version of the train set.

Second, because of a complicated annotation structure, it was challenging to calibrate the annotators, especially near the beginning of the annotation when our knowledge of the domain was limited. In the first batch, many annotators did not assign any class to many of the comments. Consequently, we strongly encouraged our annotators to label a comment with something, even if they were not sure of it or found the instructions pertaining to the specific situation unclear. This helped us to better calibrate the annotators as it provided insights into what was unclear and the reasons for disagreement. We did create additional noise with this approach but, we preferred recall over precision as positive examples in our data were generally scarce for most labels. We used Cohen-s κ as an IAA measure. For each label we calculated κ averaged over the annotator pairs as presented in Figure 1. On the graph, we can see the improvement of κ, especially in the stance category. The third batch is slightly worse. The likely cause of this small drop is a slight change in the meaning of labels introduced between the second and third batch. In the final data set, we included the last 4 batches out of 6. For the last 3 batches, we did not calculate total IAA because there were fewer annotators available. However, we did manual checks of agreement for some of the articles and further calibrated annotators through additional detailed explanations.

In total, the data set is comprised of 54 articles and 904 comments with 16.74 comments per article on average. The average lengths (in words) of articles and comments are 330.14 and 25.21, respectively. The least represented class is *spam* with only 32 positive examples. We make it publicly available.[1]

4 Models

There are 5 different models that we tested on this data set. The first is the baseline model which is a linear SVM (Vapnik, 2013). The input of the SVM is the concatenation of TF-IDF weighted vector representations of the news title, news body, and the comment, respectively. We also consider a second SVM model which is similar to the first one, but adds the following features: total word count in the comment (1 feature), and the count and presence in the comment of uppercase letters, question marks, exclamation marks, punctuation marks and negations (10 features total).

We also experiment with some deep learning based models. As the encoder for text we consider convolutional neural networks (Krizhevsky et al., 2012), gated recurrent units (GRU) (Cho et al., 2014), and long short-term memory networks (Hochreiter and Schmidhuber, 1997). We present the text to the encoder as a sequence of word2vec (Mikolov et al., 2013) word embeddings from a word2vec model trained on the HrWaC (Ljubešić and Erjavec, 2011; Šnajder et al., 2013) corpus. We have a separate encoder for (1) the concatenation of the article title and body and (2) for the comment. The outputs of both encoders are concatenated and passed through a linear classification layer. For regularization we perform early-stopping on the dev set. Hyperparameters for these models we considered are given in Table 3 and were also optimized on the dev set. As these are preliminary experiments, we did not perform exhaustive hyperparameter search for the deep learning models on all labels, but only for the more frequent ones, and reused those hyperparameter values for the models dealing with the rest of the labels. Admittedly, deep learning models could possibly yield better performance with more thorough hyperparameter tuning. We used the Adam (Kingma and Ba, 2015) algorithm with minibatch size 16 to train the models.

5 Experiments

For each label, we split the data into a train, dev, and test portions. The splits are disjunctive with respect to the articles, meaning that comments cor-

---

[1] http://takelab.fer.hr/crocomm/

	Claim				Sentiment		Stance	
	Non-Claim	Spam	Non-Verifiable	Verifiable	Positive	Negative	Support	Dissaprove
SVM	0.351	0.048	0.577	0.547	**0.194**	**0.519**	0.240	0.275
SVM + features	**0.367**	0.053	*0.627*	*0.678*	0.178	*0.471*	0.221	**0.296**
LSTM	*0.254*	*0.235*	0.591	*0.675*	0.167	*0.447*	**0.255**	0.247
GRU	0.337	***0.261***	0.577	0.553	0.152	*0.479*	0.194	0.290
CNN	0.300	0.000	***0.649***	***0.683***	0.154	0.515	0.251	0.231

Table 2: Results of classifiers across all labels. The best result for each label is given in bold. Entries in italic represent results that are statistically significantly better than the SVM baseline from the first row.

Model	Hyperparameter	Values
CNN	Number of kernels	5,**10**,25
	Kernel size	1,**3**,5
LSTM/GRU	Hidden/cell size	10,**25**,50
	Bidirectional	**Yes**, No

Table 3: Hyperparameters considered for the deep learning-based models. The values that were best performing in most experiments are given in bold.

responding to the same article are all in the same split. Furthermore, as the data set is highly imbalanced, we perform the splits in a stratified manner, ensuring the ratio of positive and negative examples is roughly equal for train, dev, and test. Through this, we have ensured that all of our splits contain positive examples. However, an imbalance that can hurt model performance was still present in the train data. To alleviate this issue we artificially balanced the train set by oversampling positive examples until the number of positive and negative examples was equal. This was done for all labels as positive examples were always the minority. For different labels, we had different splits. However, for each label, the same (artificially balanced) train, dev, and test sets were used for all models. In Table 1 we can see the split through the labels. For train we have counted in artificially examples thus the sum through columns isn't the same. We train all models on the train set, optimize hyperparameters on the dev set and report results on the test set.

Some preliminary results are given in Table 2 as F1 score for each label along with statistical significance tests (we used a permutation test on test set predictions). Performance on most labels is rather low, indicating the task is highly complex.

In most cases, adding features to the baseline model improved performance. For labels *Verifiable*, *Non-Verifiable* the differences are statistically significant. On the other hand, on the *Negative* label the SVM baseline is the overall best model.

The deep learning approaches were not expected to be very good, as the data set is small, but they do provide some respectable results, mostly for the classes from the *Claim* group.

6 Conclusion

In this paper, we presented a data set for Croatian news annotated with (1) claim verifiability, (2) sentiment, and (3) stance We have managed to calibrate annotators and achieved moderate Cohen κ agreement on this highly challenging task. We also present preliminary results of machine learning based prediction models.

A clear limitation of this work is the small size of the data set. Thus, we envision that in the future much more data could be annotated using the same methodology. This would enable a more meaningful analysis of user behavior and might reveal unobserved connections between labels. E.g., a comment with many claims may be more likely to also express a stance. In a related vein, transfer learning could be applied to such data, in order to exploit such relations between labels by jointly training the models. Another possibility for improving models is including information from other comments in the same thread as well as additional meta-data, Finally, the annotation scheme could be improved by annotating at the level of sentences, which would allow for even deeper further analysis.

Acknowledgments

We acknowledge Jan Šnajder nad Filip Boltužić for fruitful discussions and their input on this paper.

References

Ehud Aharoni, Anatoly Polnarov, Tamar Lavee, Daniel Hershcovich, Ran Levy, Ruty Rinott, Dan Gutfreund, and Noam Slonim. 2014. A benchmark dataset for automatic detection of claims and evidence in the context of controversial topics. In *Proceedings of the First Workshop on Argumentation Mining*, pages

64–68, Baltimore, Maryland. Association for Computational Linguistics.

Kyunghyun Cho, Bart van Merrienboer, Dzmitry Bahdanau, and Yoshua Bengio. 2014. On the properties of neural machine translation: Encoder–decoder approaches. In *Proceedings of SSST-8, Eighth Workshop on Syntax, Semantics and Structure in Statistical Translation*, pages 103–111.

Chinnappa Guggilla, Tristan Miller, and Iryna Gurevych. 2016. CNN- and LSTM-based claim classification in online user comments. In *Proceedings of COLING 2016, the 26th International Conference on Computational Linguistics: Technical Papers*, pages 2740–2751, Osaka, Japan. The COLING 2016 Organizing Committee.

Sepp Hochreiter and Jürgen Schmidhuber. 1997. Long short-term memory. *Neural computation*, 9(8):1735–1780.

Diederik P Kingma and Jimmy Ba. 2015. Adam: A method for stochastic optimization. pages 1–13.

Alex Krizhevsky, Ilya Sutskever, and Geoffrey E Hinton. 2012. Imagenet classification with deep convolutional neural networks. In *Advances in neural information processing systems*, pages 1097–1105.

Nikola Ljubešić and Tomaž Erjavec. 2011. hrWaC and slWaC: Compiling web corpora for croatian and slovene. In *International Conference on Text, Speech and Dialogue*, pages 395–402. Springer.

Tomas Mikolov, Kai Chen, Greg Corrado, and Jeffrey Dean. 2013. Efficient estimation of word representations in vector space. *arXiv preprint arXiv:1301.3781*.

Saif Mohammad, Svetlana Kiritchenko, Parinaz Sobhani, Xiaodan Zhu, and Colin Cherry. 2016. SemEval-2016 task 6: Detecting stance in tweets. In *Proceedings of the 10th International Workshop on Semantic Evaluation (SemEval-2016)*, pages 31–41, San Diego, California. Association for Computational Linguistics.

Bo Pang and Lillian Lee. 2008. Opinion mining and sentiment analysis. *Foundations and Trends in Information Retrieval*, 2(12):1–135.

Joonsuk Park and Claire Cardie. 2014. Identifying appropriate support for propositions in online user comments. In *Proceedings of the First Workshop on Argumentation Mining*, pages 29–38, Baltimore, Maryland. Association for Computational Linguistics.

S. Rosenthal and K. McKeown. 2012. Detecting opinionated claims in online discussions. In *2012 IEEE Sixth International Conference on Semantic Computing*, pages 30–37.

Jan Šnajder, Sebastian Padó, and Željko Agić. 2013. Building and evaluating a distributional memory for croatian. In *Proceedings of the 51st Annual Meeting of the Association for Computational Linguistics (Volume 2: Short Papers)*, volume 2, pages 784–789.

Vladimir Vapnik. 2013. *The nature of statistical learning theory*. Springer science & business media.

Qiang Zhang, Emine Yilmaz, and Shangsong Liang. 2018. Ranking-based method for news stance detection. In *Companion Proceedings of the The Web Conference 2018*, WWW '18, pages 41–42, Republic and Canton of Geneva, Switzerland. International World Wide Web Conferences Steering Committee.

Xinyi Zhou and Reza Zafarani. 2018. Fake news: A survey of research, detection methods, and opportunities. *CoRR*, abs/1812.00315.

A Dataset for Noun Compositionality Detection for a Slavic Language

Dmitry Puzyrev [†], **Artem Shelmanov**[‡], **Alexander Panchenko**[‡], and **Ekaterina Artemova**[†]

[†]National Research University Higher School of Economics, Moscow, Russia
[‡]Skolkovo Institute of Science and Technology, Moscow, Russia
dapuzyrev@edu.hse.ru, echernyak@hse.ru
a.{shelmanov, panchenko}@skoltech.ru

Abstract

This paper presents the first gold-standard resource for Russian annotated with compositionality information of noun compounds. The compound phrases are collected from the Universal Dependency treebanks according to part of speech patterns, such as ADJ+NOUN or NOUN+NOUN, using the gold-standard annotations. Each compound phrase is annotated by two experts and a moderator according to the following schema: the phrase can be either compositional, non-compositional, or ambiguous (i.e., depending on the context it can be interpreted both as compositional or non-compositional). We conduct an experimental evaluation of models and methods for predicting compositionality of noun compounds in unsupervised and supervised setups. We show that methods from previous work evaluated on the proposed Russian-language resource achieve the performance comparable with results on English corpora.

1 Introduction

The quality of many natural language processing applications is heavily dependent on the quality of vector representations of text elements. The streamline NLP research encompasses many works on building various distributional semantic models (DSMs), and on methods for combining vector representations of atomic elements like words into representations of bigger fragments: phrases, sentences, texts. A simple but strong baseline for this task suggests averaging word embeddings of a text fragment (sometimes weighted, e.g., according to IDF). Although the result vector representation is rough compared to results could be achieved by more elaborate neural network encoding methods, it was shown that this baseline has high performance in many tasks (Weston et al., 2013; Mikolov et al., 2013; Mitchell and Lapata, 2008; Anke and Schockaert, 2018).

The main advantages of such methods are computational efficiency and an ability to use them in an unsupervised setting, while neural encoders would commonly require heavy computational power, labeled datasets, and substantial time for training.

However, simple averaging of word embeddings often is too naïve. Idiomatic noun phrases are one of the cases where the averaging of the phrase parts would yield a wrong result since the meaning of such phrases is metaphorical and could not be directly "summed up" from meanings of its components. Therefore, it would be beneficial to have a DSM that tackles this problem, by having a distinct embedding for the whole phrase.

In this work, we focus on the task of predicting compositionality of noun phrases in Russian language texts. The goal is to develop a resource and methods for distinguishing compositional compounds, which meaning could be split into parts, from non-compositional ones that have a solid meaning, and for which we would like to have a dedicated embedding. The ability to detect compositionality for noun compounds is considered beneficial for many tasks including machine translation, semantic parsing, as well as word sense disambiguation.

The **contribution** of this paper is two-fold:

1. We present the first *gold-standard dataset* for Russian annotated with compositionality information of noun compounds.[1]

2. We provide an *experimental evaluation* of models and methods for predicting compositionality of noun compounds. We show that the methods from the previous work trained on the proposed Russian-language resource achieve the performance comparable with results on English corpora.

---

[1] https://github.com/slangtech/ru-comps

Proceedings of the 7th Workshop on Balto-Slavic Natural Language Processing, pages 56–62,
Florence, Italy, 2 August 2019. ©2019 Association for Computational Linguistics

2 Related Work

The construction of datasets presenting compositionality can be traced back to as early as the 2000s: Baldwin and Villavicencio (2002) proposed chunk-based extraction methods for English verb-prepositional combinations and gave some binary judgments on the subject of considering them as phrasal verbs. In the follow-up paper, Baldwin et al. (2003) used the same framework to retrieve 1,710 Noun-Noun compounds from 1996 Wall Street Journal corpus. The authors use LSA to calculate the similarity between a phrase and its components as one of the early compositionality prediction attempts. McCarthy et al. (2003) evaluated 116 candidates of English phrasal verbs using three annotators' predictions on a scale from 0 to 10. Venkatapathy and Joshi (2005) used 800 verb-object collocations obtained from British National Corpus to give annotations from 1 to 6 where one stands for total non-compositionality and 6 for complete compositionality.

The dataset developed by Reddy et al. (2011) contained 90 English noun compounds and used an average of 30 judgments to give each phrase compositionality scores. This work provided compositionality assessments for both the phrase and its constituents enabling the use of various operations with corresponding embeddings of a compound and its distinctive parts in the context of linking human validations with measurements of semantic distance.

Ramisch et al. (2016) extended this dataset to 180 phrases presenting two parallel sets for French and Portuguese languages. English Noun-Noun compounds were mapped with Noun-Prep-Noun and Noun-Adj constructions according to the grammar equivalents. Farahmand et al. (2015) presented considerably larger dataset, which has 1,042 Noun-Noun compounds annotated with the help of 4 experts.

We also should note some works on compositionality detection datasets for non-English languages. Gurrutxaga and Alegria (2013) studied 1,200 Basque Noun-Verb collocations and resolve classification task into three classes: idiom, collocation, and free combination. Roller et al. (2013) provides 244 German compounds with compositionality scores assigned from 1 to 7 as an average from 30 validations. PARSEME project (Savary et al., 2015) is devoted to the multilingual annotation of multiword expressions (MWE) of arbitrary length and syntactical structure. By design, PARSEME is more suited for MWE extraction tasks rather than compositionality evaluation. This dataet includes annotated verbal MWEs for several Slavic languages Jana et al. (2019) explored the use of hyperbolic embeddings for noun compositionality detection comparing it to the Euclidian embeddings.

Most of the experiments on noun compositionality were conducted for the English language and to the best of our knowledge, to date, there are no datasets for compositionality detection task for any Slavic language structurally similar to (Reddy et al., 2011) and (Farahmand et al., 2015).

Agreement Metric	Value
Pearson's correlation	0.541
Cronbach's alpha	0.700

Table 1: Annotation agreement metrics for our dataset.

3 Noun Compound Dataset

3.1 Data Collection

The compound phrases are collected from the Russian Universal Dependency (UD) treebanks (Nivre et al., 2016) according to part of speech patterns, such as adjectives (ADJ) + noun (NOUN) or noun + noun, based on gold-standard UD annotations, which guarantees that not only no preprocessing but also no POS tagging and no disambiguation is required. We use all Russian treebanks, available in the UD project. They consist of texts from the following genre: news, nonfiction, fiction. To extract nominal compounds, we loop over all nouns and select only those, which has noun or adjective dependant (i.e., are "head" of another noun or adjective). We filter out non-frequent compounds, and from the list of frequent compounds, we randomly select 1,000 compounds to be annotated. Note, that this procedure is coarse and does not rely on more precise compound definition such as the exact type of the dependency between the head and dependant tokens.

Each compound is lowercased and lemmatized. Stress characters are omitted. The head noun is provided in the nominal case and in singular number (if it exists), and the dependant adjectives are put in grammatical agreement with the head noun in case and gender, while dependant nouns remain unchanged.

Type of Compound	Compound Samples
Compositional (1)	*aviatsiannaya bomba* [aircraft bomb], *gimn strany* [national anthem], *gornolyzhnyi kurort* [ski resort], *dno okeana* [ocean bed], *federalnyi zakon* [federal law]
Non-compositional (0)	*goryachaya tochka* [trouble spot], *zheleznyi zanaves* [iron curtain], *kamennyi vek* [the Stone Age], *tsar gory* [king of the hill], *novaya volna* [new wave]
Ambiguous (2)	*novyi god* [New year celebration or new year], *krupnaya set'* [big net or big network], *ogromnaya massa* [big mass of or big amount of], *pozitsiya kompanii* [company place or company position], *drevnyaya professiya* [ancient profession or prostitution]

Table 2: Examples of non-compositional (0), compositional (1) and ambiguous (2) compounds.

3.2 Annotation Setup and Agreement

Each compound phrase in the selected list is annotated by two experts according to the following schema: (0) the phrase is non-compositional; (1) the phrase is compositional; (2) the phrase is ambiguous, which means that exact compositionality of the phrase is dependant on the corresponding context. After that, annotators' answers are reviewed by a moderator. Out of 1,000 randomly selected compounds, moderator samples 220 and resolves the ambiguity left from the first two annotators. We calculate the agreement metrics of the first two annotators on the dataset of 1,000 compounds. Annotators achieved a substantial agreement. We note that the typical problematic cases that are hard to annotate are compounds, which meaning tends to be compositional in a metaphorical way, e.g., *"otkrytoe more"* [open sea] and compounds, that contain polysemic words: *"hod dela"* [justicement or the course of business].

3.3 Dataset Description

The resulting dataset consists of 220 compound phrases with several full sentence contexts, collected from source texts. The number of contexts is not fixed. So far the contexts are not annotated. A few examples are provided in Table 2. Table 3 presents the cross-tabulation of compound pattern and compound compositionality. Each compound is provided with a sentence context. The number of contexts is not fixed as we extract all contexts that contain the compound from the UD treebanks. The contexts so far are not used in the experiments. However, one of the possible directions for the future work would be compound disambiguation, based on the contexts. Examples of the compound contexts are presented in Figure 1.

4 Experiments

We evaluate various methods for detection of compositionality presented in the previous work. For experiments, we train a distributional semantic model (DSM) that includes embeddings not just for single words but also for compounds. We achieve this by replacing in the training corpora all occurrences of compounds from the proposed resource with single tokens composed of their parts. We use two experimental setups in our work.

First, the **unsupervised setup** follows the method and evaluation pipeline presented in (Cordeiro et al., 2016). In this setting, we rely solely on a similarity between a compound embedding and an embedding composed from its parts using an additive function. The value of the similarity should correlate with annotators' judgments in the proposed resource.

Second, the **supervised setup** considers compositionality detection as a binary classification task. We train various supervised machine learning methods on vector representations of a compound and its parts to predict compositionality class. In this setup, we train an additional DSM that does not have any modifications (it does not contain embeddings for compounds). In this setup, embeddings of compound parts are obtained from this unmodified supplementary model.

We train DSMs using fastText (Bojanowski et al., 2016) and word2vec (Mikolov et al., 2013) models with CBOW architecture implemented in *gensim* package (Rehurek and Sojka, 2011). Russian Wikipedia dump is used as a training corpus (as of 02.05.2019, it consists of 1,542,621 articles), with Universal Dependencies raw texts as an enrichment, which helps to deal with cases of missing compounds. Both Wikipedia articles and compounds are lemmatized using MyStem

Под воздействием этого поля ядра	**атомов водорода**	в теле исследуемого , каждый со своим слабым магнитным полем , ориентируются определенным образом относительно сильного поля магнита .
Прозрачная жидкость , в которой на два	**атома водорода**	приходится один атом кислорода , может быть водой , а может быть и смесью жидких водорода и кислорода
Нам удалось сложить кучку из восьми атомов - двух атомов углерода и шести	**атомов водорода**	, изображенную на рисунке .
С чего начинать : сдвинуть два атома углерода или приставить	**атом водорода**	к атому углерода ?
Китайский	**Новый год**	и другие праздники , отмечаемые тайскими китайцами , отличаются в обоих случаях , так как они рассчитываются по китайскому календарю .
Перед самым	**Новым годом**	отключили поселок Никольское .
Речь , конечно же , идет об очередной заморозке до	**нового года**	цен на бензин .
В нашем рейтинге лучших подарков мужчине под	**Новый год**	пневматическая винтовка с ночным прицелом твердо заняла первое место .
Нынешнее заседание Госсовета - первое в	**новом году**	и последнее , на котором Владимир Путин выступит как президент страны .
Но это же был единственный русский фильм на	**Новый год**	, у него были все шансы на успех " .
А у нас политик	**второго эшелона**	ниже этого эшелона не опустится " , - говорит эксперт .
Несмотря на озабоченность Минобрнауки бесконтрольным размножением экономистов и недоверие солидных работодателей к дипломам вузов	**второго эшелона**	, молодой экономист сегодня вряд ли останется на обочине жизни .
Пока потребители	**второго эшелонов**	дожидаются сезона распродаж или приобретают подержанные вещи , лидеры консюмеризма переходят к следующей фазе потребления .
Опускаясь по стратификационной лестнице , они опережают по статусу тех , кто находится во	**втором эшелоне**	, то есть в предшествующей фазе потребительской гонки .

Figure 1: Compound contexts in KWIC format. The compounds and their compositionality classes are: *atom vodoroda* [hydrogen atom] (1), *novyi god* [New year celebration or new year] (2), *vtoroyi eshelon* [second tier] (0).

	Adjective-Noun	**Noun-Noun**	**Total**
Non-compositional (0)	23	10	33
Compositional (1)	71	96	167
Ambiguous (2)	9	11	20
Total	103	117	220

Table 3: The number of compositional and non-compositional compounds in our dataset.

(Segalovich, 2003). Minimal frequency count of 2 is used. We performed experiments on several sets of hyperparameters (dimensionality and amount of training epochs). We found that dimensionality of 300 and five epochs give good or the best results across all considered settings, therefore, we report results only for this set of hyperparameters.

To simplify the task, in experimental evaluation, we do not consider contextual information of compounds. It means that no ambiguity is under consideration and only phrases with compositionality classes of 1 and 0 are qualified for evaluation, which leaves 200 compounds. For three of them, models lack an embedding, which leaves 197 phrases for experiments: 164 are compositional, and 33 are non-compositional according to annotators (approximately 0.83 to 0.17 ratio).

4.1 Unsupervised Setup

For unsupervised setup, we calculate a metric from (Cordeiro et al., 2016) that measures similarity of an embedding of a compound as a whole and an additive embedding composed of its parts. Consider w_1, w_2 are words of a given compound and a function $v(\cdot)$ yielding vector representation of a word/compound. Then the similarity metric is equals to: $cos(v(w_1 w_2), v(w_1 + w_2))$, where $v(w_1 + w_2)$ is the normalized sum:

$$v(w_1 + w_2) = \frac{v(w_1)}{\|v(w_1)\|} + \frac{v(w_2)}{\|v(w_2)\|}.$$

In addition to cosine, we use similarity measures based on distance metrics between embeddings: Chebyshev distance (L_∞-norm), Manhattan distance (L_1-norm), and Euclidean distance (L_2-norm). When using these distances, instead

Supervised Model	Spearman's ρ	Precision	Recall	F-measure
Linear Support Vector classifier (LSVC)	**0.47**	0.37	**0.78**	0.48
Multi-layer Perceptron (MLP)	**0.46**	0.32	**0.82**	0.44
Desicion Tree (DT)	0.18	0.31	0.36	0.31
Naïve Bayes (NB)	**0.43**	**0.55**	0.52	**0.52**

Table 4: Performance of the classifiers in the supervised setup (classifier metrics presented for class 0).

Metric / Model	fastText	word2vec
cos (norm.)	**0.42**	0.37
L_∞ (avg.)	0.33	0.09
L_1 (avg.)	0.33	0.14
L_2 (avg.)	0.33	0.14

Table 5: Spearman correlation (ρ) of the metric with annotator judgments in the unsupervised setup.

of normalized sum, we use a simple averaging:

$$v(w_1 + w_2) = \frac{1}{2}(w_1 + w_2).$$

We evaluate the performance of these metrics to predict compositionality based on Spearman rank correlation (Spearman's ρ) between them and the compositionality class in the annotated dataset as considered in (Cordeiro et al., 2016).

4.2 Supervised Setup

In supervised setup, we access average performance on 25 stratified randomized splits of the selected dataset into 75% for training and 25% for testing with the following machine learning algorithms: linear support vector machine (LSVC) with $C = 1$ (Platt, 1999); three-layer perceptron (MLP) with α=1, solver='lbfgs', sizes of layers=200/20/20 (Hinton, 1989); decision tree (DT) with maximum depth=10, max features=20 (Breiman, 2017); Naïve Bayes (NB) (Zhang, 2004). For feature representation, we use a concatenation of compound embedding with embeddings of compound parts. We evaluate the Spearman correlation with the annotation class, as well as precision, recall, and F_1-score.

4.3 Results and Discussion

The results of the experimental evaluation for unsupervised setup are presented in Table 5, for supervised setup – in Table 4. Of presented metrics, L_1, L_2, and L_∞ present substantial negative correlation. That can be explained by the nature of embedding vectors. The bigger the distance value, the further compound is from its components in a semantic sense. If the sense of the compound widely differs from corresponding senses of its components, it is deemed as non-compositional. To be comparable with previous papers, we present a positive correlation bringing minus of a distance instead. Taking this into consideration, all metrics perform comparably on the dataset. We can see a not strong, yet stable and substantial correlation between similarity and compositionality class.

Considering the supervised classification task, precision, recall, and F_1 metrics are presented alongside Spearman rank correlation. As non-compositional compounds are in the minority in this dataset, and detecting idiomatic phrases provides more interest practice-wise, we report on zero-class quality metrics to access algorithm performance. LSVC, MLP, and NB present higher ρ than the unsupervised counterpart. LSVC and MLP also give relatively high recall on non-compositional examples. Overall, linear SVC and multi-layer perceptron perform better than the other models across all metrics.

5 Conclusion

We presented the first Russian-language dataset of noun compounds annotated, where each compound follows one of the noun compound patterns (noun+noun or adjective+noun) and is annotated with as non-compositional, compositional or ambiguous compounds. The latter can be either compositional or not, depending on the context. Each compound is provided along with the sentence contexts. The inter-annotator agreement metrics show that annotator judgments on the scores agree well. We investigated the performance of various algorithms from previous work and showed that the achieved evaluation metrics correspond with other state-of-the-art results for English. We hope that our resource will foster the research in the area of compositionality detection for Russian and other Slavic languages.

Acknowledgements

Dmitry Puzyrev and Ekaterina Artemova were supported by the framework of the HSE University Basic Research Program and Russian Academic Excellence Project "5-100".

References

Luis Espinosa Anke and Steven Schockaert. 2018. Seven: Augmenting word embeddings with unsupervised relation vectors. In *Proceedings of the 27th International Conference on Computational Linguistics*, pages 2653–2665.

Timothy Baldwin, Colin Bannard, Takaaki Tanaka, and Dominic Widdows. 2003. An empirical model of multiword expression decomposability. In *Proceedings of the ACL 2003 Workshop on Multiword Expressions: Analysis, Acquisition and Treatment - Volume 18*, pages 89–96.

Timothy Baldwin and Aline Villavicencio. 2002. Extracting the unextractable: A case study on verb-particles. In *Proceedings of CoNLL*, pages 1–7.

Piotr Bojanowski, Edouard Grave, Armand Joulin, and Tomas Mikolov. 2016. Enriching word vectors with subword information. *CoRR*, abs/1607.04606.

Leo Breiman. 2017. *Classification and regression trees*. Routledge.

Silvio Cordeiro, Carlos Ramisch, Marco Idiart, and Aline Villavicencio. 2016. Predicting the compositionality of nominal compounds: Giving word embeddings a hard time. In *Proceedings of the 54th Annual Meeting of the Association for Computational Linguistics (Volume 1: Long Papers)*, volume 1, pages 1986–1997.

Meghdad Farahmand, Aaron Smith, and Joakim Nivre. 2015. A multiword expression data set: Annotating non-compositionality and conventionalization for english noun compounds. In *Proceedings of the 11th Workshop on Multiword Expressions*, pages 29–33.

Antton Gurrutxaga and Iñaki Alegria. 2013. Combining different features of idiomaticity for the automatic classification of noun+verb expressions in Basque. In *Proceedings of the 9th Workshop on Multiword Expressions*, pages 116–125.

Geoffrey E. Hinton. 1989. Connectionist learning procedures. *Artif. Intell.*, 40(1-3):185–234.

Abhik Jana, Dmitry Puzyrev, Alexander Panchenko, Pawan Goyal, Chris Biemann, and Animesh Mukherjee. 2019. On the compositionality prediction of noun phrases using poincaré embeddings. In *The 57th Annual Meeting of the Association for Computational Linguistics (ACL)*, Florence, Italy.

Diana McCarthy, Bill Keller, and John Carroll. 2003. Detecting a continuum of compositionality in phrasal verbs. In *Proceedings of the ACL 2003 Workshop on Multiword Expressions: Analysis, Acquisition and Treatment - Volume 18*, MWE '03, pages 73–80.

Tomas Mikolov, Ilya Sutskever, Kai Chen, Greg S Corrado, and Jeff Dean. 2013. Distributed representations of words and phrases and their compositionality. In *Advances in neural information processing systems*, pages 3111–3119.

Jeff Mitchell and Mirella Lapata. 2008. Vector-based models of semantic composition. In *proceedings of ACL-08: HLT*, pages 236–244.

Joakim Nivre, Marie-Catherine De Marneffe, Filip Ginter, Yoav Goldberg, Jan Hajic, Christopher D Manning, Ryan McDonald, Slav Petrov, Sampo Pyysalo, Natalia Silveira, et al. 2016. Universal dependencies v1: A multilingual treebank collection. In *Proceedings of the Tenth International Conference on Language Resources and Evaluation (LREC 2016)*, pages 1659–1666.

John C. Platt. 1999. Probabilistic outputs for support vector machines and comparisons to regularized likelihood methods. In *Advances in large margin classifiers*, pages 61–74.

Carlos Ramisch, Silvio Cordeiro, Leonardo Zilio, Marco Idiart, and Aline Villavicencio. 2016. How naked is the naked truth? a multilingual lexicon of nominal compound compositionality. In *Proceedings of the 54th Annual Meeting of the Association for Computational Linguistics (Volume 2: Short Papers)*, pages 156–161.

Siva Reddy, Diana McCarthy, and Suresh Manandhar. 2011. An empirical study on compositionality in compound nouns. In *Proceedings of the 5th International Joint Conference on Natural Language Processing*, pages 210–218.

Radim Rehurek and Petr Sojka. 2011. Gensim–python framework for vector space modelling. *NLP Centre, Faculty of Informatics, Masaryk University, Brno, Czech Republic*, 3(2).

Stephen Roller, Sabine Schulte im Walde, and Silke Scheible. 2013. The (un)expected effects of applying standard cleansing models to human ratings on compositionality. In *Proceedings of the 9th Workshop on Multiword Expressions*, pages 32–41.

Agata Savary, Manfred Sailer, Yannick Parmentier, Michael Rosner, Victoria Rosén, Adam Przepiórkowski, Cvetana Krstev, Veronika Vincze, Beata Wójtowicz, Gyri Smørdal Losnegaard, Carla Parra Escartín, Jakub Waszczuk, Matthieu Constant, Petya Osenova, and Federico Sangati. 2015. PARSEME – PARSing and Multiword Expressions within a European multilingual network. In *7th Language & Technology Conference: Human Language*

Technologies as a Challenge for Computer Science and Linguistics (LTC 2015).

Ilya Segalovich. 2003. A fast morphological algorithm with unknown word guessing induced by a dictionary for a web search engine. In *MLMTA*.

Sriram Venkatapathy and Aravind K. Joshi. 2005. Measuring the relative compositionality of verb-noun (v-n) collocations by integrating features. In *Proceedings of the Conference on Human Language Technology and Empirical Methods in Natural Language Processing*, HLT '05, pages 899–906.

Jason Weston, Antoine Bordes, Oksana Yakhnenko, and Nicolas Usunier. 2013. Connecting language and knowledge bases with embedding models for relation extraction. In *Proceedings of the 2013 Conference on Empirical Methods in Natural Language Processing*, pages 1366–1371.

Harry Zhang. 2004. The optimality of naive bayes. In *Proceedings of the Seventeenth International Florida Artificial Intelligence Research Society Conference, FLAIRS 2004*, volume 2.

The Second Cross-Lingual Challenge on Recognition, Normalization, Classification, and Linking of Named Entities across Slavic Languages

Jakub Piskorski,[1] Laska Laskova,[5] Michał Marcińczuk,[4]
Lidia Pivovarova,[2] Pavel Přibáň,[3] Josef Steinberger,[3] Roman Yangarber[2]

[1]Joint Research Centre, Ispra, Italy `first.last@ec.europa.eu`
[2]University of Helsinki, Finland `first.last@cs.helsinki.fi`
[3]University of West Bohemia, Czech Republic `{pribanp, jstein}@kiv.zcu.cz`
[4]Wrocław University of Science and Technology, Poland `michal.marcinczuk@pwr.edu.pl`
[5]Bulgarian Academy of Sciences, Bulgaria `laska@bultreebank.org`

Abstract

We describe the Second Multilingual Named Entity Challenge in Slavic languages. The task is recognizing mentions of named entities in Web documents, their normalization, and cross-lingual linking. The Challenge was organized as part of the 7th Balto-Slavic Natural Language Processing Workshop, co-located with the ACL-2019 conference. Eight teams participated in the competition, which covered four languages and five entity types. Performance for the named entity recognition task reached 90% F-measure, much higher than reported in the first edition of the Challenge. Seven teams covered all four languages, and five teams participated in the cross-lingual entity linking task. Detailed evaluation information is available on the shared task web page.

1 Introduction

Due to rich inflection and derivation, free word order, and other morphological and syntactic phenomena exhibited by Slavic languages, analysis of named entities (NEs) in these languages poses a challenging problem (Przepiórkowski, 2007; Piskorski et al., 2009). Fostering research on detection and normalization of NEs—and on the closely related problem of cross-lingual, cross-document *entity linking*—is of paramount importance for improving multilingual and cross-lingual information access in these languages.

This paper describes the Second Shared Task on multilingual NE recognition (NER), which aims at addressing these problems in a systematic way. The shared task was organized in the context of the 7th Balto-Slavic Natural Language Processing Workshop co-located with the ACL 2019 conference. The task covers four languages—Bulgarian, Czech, Polish and Russian—and five types of NE: person, location, organization, product, and event. The input text collection consists of doc-uments collected from the Web, each collection centered on a certain "focal" entity. The rationale of such a setup is to foster the development of "all-round" NER and cross-lingual entity linking solutions, which are not tailored to specific, narrow domains. This paper also serves as an introduction and a guide for researchers wishing to explore these problems using the training and test data.[1]

This paper is organized as follows. Section 3 describes the task; Section 4 describes the annotation of the dataset. The evaluation methodology is introduced in Section 5. Participant systems are described in Section 6 and the results obtained by these systems are presented in Section 7. Conclusions and lessons learned are discussed in Section 8.

2 Prior Work

The work we describe here builds on the First Shared Task on Multilingual Named Entity Recognition, Normalization and cross-lingual Matching for Slavic Languages, (Piskorski et al., 2017), which, to the best of our knowledge, was the first attempt at such a shared task covering several Slavic languages.

Similar shared tasks have been organized previously. The first *non-English* monolingual NER evaluations—covering Chinese, Japanese, Spanish, and Arabic—were carried out in the context of the Message Understanding Conferences (MUCs) (Chinchor, 1998) and the ACE Programme (Doddington et al., 2004). The first shared task focusing on *multilingual* named entity recognition, which covered several European languages, including Spanish, German, and Dutch, was organized in the context of CoNLL conferences (Tjong Kim Sang, 2002; Tjong Kim Sang

---

[1]`bsnlp.cs.helsinki.fi/shared_task.html`

Proceedings of the 7th Workshop on Balto-Slavic Natural Language Processing, pages 63–74,
Florence, Italy, 2 August 2019. ©2019 Association for Computational Linguistics

and De Meulder, 2003). The NE types covered in these campaigns were similar to the NE types covered in our Challenge. Also related to our task is Entity Discovery and Linking (EDL), (Ji et al., 2014, 2015), a track of the NIST Text Analysis Conferences (TAC). EDL aimed to extract entity mentions from a collection of documents in multiple languages (English, Chinese, and Spanish), and to partition the entities into cross-document equivalence classes, by either linking mentions to a knowledge base or directly clustering them. An important difference between EDL and our task is that we do not link entities to a knowledge base.

Related to cross-lingual NE recognition is NE transliteration, i.e., linking NEs across languages that use different scripts. A series of NE Transliteration Shared Tasks were organized as a part of NEWS—Named Entity Workshops—(Duan et al., 2016), focusing mostly on Indian and Asian languages. In 2010, the NEWS Workshop included a shared task on Transliteration Mining (Kumaran et al., 2010), i.e., mining of names from parallel corpora. This task included corpora in English, Chinese, Tamil, Russian, and Arabic.

Prior work targeting NEs specifically for Slavic languages includes tools for NE recognition for Croatian (Karan et al., 2013; Ljubešić et al., 2013), a tool tailored for NE recognition in Croatian tweets (Baksa et al., 2017), a manually annotated NE corpus for Croatian (Agić and Ljubešić, 2014), tools for NE recognition in Slovene (Štajner et al., 2013; Ljubešić et al., 2013), a Czech corpus of 11,000 manually annotated NEs (Ševčíková et al., 2007), NER tools for Czech (Konkol and Konopík, 2013), tools and resources for fine-grained annotation of NEs in the National Corpus of Polish (Waszczuk et al., 2010; Savary and Piskorski, 2011) and a recent shared task on NE Recognition in Russian (Alexeeva et al., 2016).

3 Task Description

The data for the shared task consists of sets of documents in four Slavic languages: Czech, Polish, Russian, and Bulgarian. To accommodate entity linking, each set of documents is chosen to focus around one certain entity—e.g., a person, an organization or an event. The documents were obtained from the Web, by posing a keyword query to a search engine and extracting the textual content from the Web pages.

The task is to recognize, classify, and "normal-ize" all named-entity mentions in each of the documents, and to link across languages all named mentions referring to the same real-world entity. Formally, the Multilingual Named Entity Recognition task includes three sub-tasks:

- **Named Entity Mention Detection and Classification:** Recognizing all named mentions of entities of five types: persons (PER), organizations (ORG), locations (LOC), products (PRO), and events (EVT).

- **Name Normalization:** Mapping each named mention of an entity to its corresponding *base form*. By "base form" we generally mean the lemma ("dictionary form") of the inflected word-form. In some cases normalization should go beyond inflection and transform a derived word into a base word's lemma, e.g., in case of personal possessives (see below). Multi-word names should be normalized to the *canonical multi-word expression*—rather than a sequence of lemmas of the words making up the multi-word expression.

- **Entity Linking.** Assigning a unique identifier (ID) to each detected named mention of an entity, in such a way that mentions referring to the same real-world entity should be assigned the same ID—referred to as the cross-lingual ID.

The task does not require positional information of the name entity mentions. Thus, for all occurrences of the same form of a NE mention (e.g., an inflected variant, an acronym or abbreviation) within a given document, no more than one annotation should be produced.[2] Furthermore, distinguishing typographical case is not necessary since the evaluation is case-insensitive. If the text includes lowercase, uppercase or mixed-case variants of the same entity, the system should produce only one annotation for all of these mentions. For instance, for "*BREXIT*" and "*Brexit*" (provided that they refer to the same NE type), only one annotation should be produced. Note that recognition of common-noun or pronominal references to named entities is not part of the task.

3.1 Named Entity Classes

The task defines the following five NE classes.

---

[2]Unless the different occurrences have different entity types (different *readings*) assigned to them, which is rare.

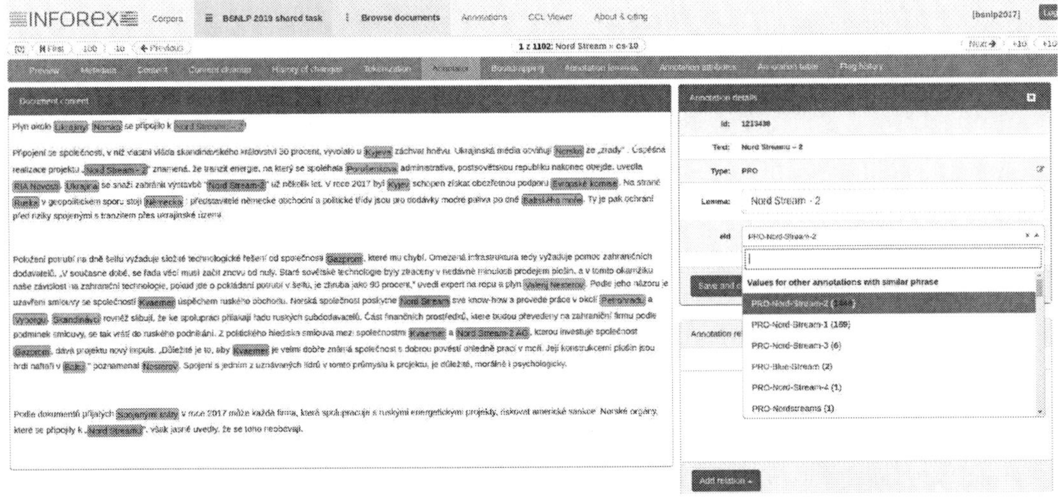

Figure 1: Screenshot of the Inforex Web interface, the tool used for data annotation

Person names (PER): Names of real (or fictional) persons. Person names should not include titles, honorifics, and functions/positions. For example, in the text fragment "...*CEO Dr. Jan Kowalski*...", only "*Jan Kowalski*" is recognized as a person name. Initials and pseudonyms are considered named mentions of persons and should be recognized. Similarly, named references to groups of people (that do not have a formal organization unifying them) should also be recognized, e.g., "*Ukrainians.*" In this context, mentions of a single member belonging to such groups, e.g., "*Ukrainian,*" should be assigned the same cross-lingual ID as plural mentions, i.e., "*Ukrainians*" and "*Ukrainian*" when referring to the nation receive the same cross-lingual ID.

Personal possessives derived from a person's name should be classified as a Person, and the base form of the corresponding name should be extracted. For instance, in "*Trumpov tweet*" (Croatian) one is expected to classify "*Trumpov*" as PER, with the base form "*Trump.*"

Locations (LOC): All toponyms and geopolitical entities—cities, counties, provinces, countries, regions, bodies of water, land formations, etc.— including named mentions of *facilities*—e.g., stadiums, parks, museums, theaters, hotels, hospitals, transportation hubs, churches, railroads, bridges, and similar facilities.

In case named mentions of facilities *also* refer to an organization, the LOC tag should be used. For example, from the text "*The Schipol Airport has acquired new electronic gates*" the mention "*The Schipol Airport*" should be classified as LOC.

Organizations (ORG): All organizations, including companies, public institutions, political parties, international organizations, religious organizations, sport organizations, educational and research institutions, etc.

Organization designators and potential mentions of the seat of the organization are considered to be part of the organization name. For instance, from the text "*...Citi Handlowy w Poznaniu...*" (a bank in Poznań), the full phrase "*Citi Handlowy w Poznaniu*" should be extracted.

Products (PRO): All names of *products and services*, such as electronics ("*Motorola Moto Z Play*"), cars ("*Subaru Forester XT*"), newspapers ("*The New York Times*"), web-services ("*Twitter*").

When a company name is used to refer to a *service* (e.g., "*na Twiterze*" (Polish for "on Twitter"), the mention of "*Twitter*" is considered to refer to a service/product and should be tagged as PRO. However, when a company name refers to a service, expressing an opinion of the company, e.g., "*Fox News*", it should be tagged as ORG.

This category also includes legal documents and treaties, e.g., "*Traktat Lizboński*" (Polish: "Treaty of Lisbon").

Events (EVT): This category covers named mentions, including conferences, e.g. "24.

Japonci se ptají na czexit, říká Špicar ze Svazu průmyslu. "Odešli bychom z Česka," varovali ho Případné vystoupení České republiky z Evropské unie by bylo podle ekonomů, Hospodářské komory i Svazu průmyslu a dopravy ekonomickou sebevraždou. Odchod z EU by znamenal ztrátu stovek tisíc pracovních míst a česká ekonomika by se podle některých dostala na úroveň Běloruska. Praha 21:18 7. února 2018

cs-10

Japonci	Japonci	PER	GPE-Japan
czexit	czexit	EVT	EVT-Czexit
Špicar	Špicar	PER	PER-Radek-Spicar
Svazu průmyslu	Svaz průmyslu	ORG	ORG-Svaz-Prumyslu
Česka	Česko	LOC	GPE-Czech-Republic
České republiky	Česká republika	LOC	GPE-Czech-Republic
Evropské unie	Evropská unie	ORG	ORG-European-Union
Hospodářské komory	Hospodářská komora	ORG	ORG-Hospodarska-Komora
Svazu průmyslu a dopravy	Svaz průmyslu a dopravy	ORG	ORG-Svaz-Prumyslu
EU	EU	ORG	ORG-European-Union
Běloruska	Bělorusko	LOC	GPE-Belarus
Praha	Praha	LOC	GPE-Prague

Figure 2: Example input and output formats.

Konference Žárovného Zinkování" (Czech: "Hot Galvanizing Conference"), concerts, festivals, holidays, e.g., "*Vánoce*" (Polish: "Christmas"), wars, battles, disasters, e.g., "*Katastrofa Czernobylska*" (Polish: "the Chernobyl catastrophe"). Future, speculative, and fictive events— e.g., "Czexit" or "Polexit"—are considered as event mentions as well.

3.2 Complex and Ambiguous Entities

In case of complex named entities, consisting of nested named entities, only the *top-most* entity should be recognized. For example, from the text "*George Washington University*" one should not extract "*George Washington*", but only the top-level entity.

In case one word-form (e.g., "*Washington*") is used to refer to more than one different real-world entities in different contexts in the same document (e.g., a person and a location), the system should return two annotations, associated with different cross-lingual IDs.

In case of coordinated phrases, like "*European and British Parliament*," two names should be extracted (as ORG). The lemmas would be "*European*" and "*British Parliament*", and the IDs should refer to "*European Parliament*" and "*British Parliament*" respectively.

In rare cases, plural forms might have two annotations—e.g., in the phrase "*a border between Irelands*"—"*Irelands*" should be extracted twice with identical lemmas but different IDs.

3.3 System Input and Response

Input Document Format: Documents in the collection are represented in the following format. The first five lines contain meta-data:

```
<DOCUMENT-ID>
<LANGUAGE>
<CREATION-DATE>
<URL>
<TITLE>
<TEXT>
```

The text to be processed begins from the sixth line and runs till the end of file. The `<URL>` field stores the origin from which the text document was retrieved. The values of the meta-data fields were computed automatically (see Section 4 for details). The values of `<CREATION-DATE>` and `<TITLE>` were not provided for all documents, due to unavailability of such data or due to errors in parsing during data collection.

System Response. For each input file, the system should return one output file as follows. The first line should contain only the `<DOCUMENT-ID>`, which corresponds to the input. Each subsequent line contains one annotation, as tab-separated fields:

```
<MENTION> TAB <BASE> TAB <CAT> TAB <ID>
```

The `<MENTION>` field should be the NE as it appears in text. The `<BASE>` field should be the base form of the entity. The `<CAT>` field stores the category of the entity (ORG, PER, LOC, PROD, or EVT) and `<ID>` is the cross-lingual identifier. The cross-lingual identifiers may consist of an arbitrary sequence of alphanumeric characters. An example document in Czech and the corresponding response is shown in Figure 2.

For detailed descriptions of the tasks and guidelines, please refer to the web page of the shared task.[3]

4 Data

The data consist of four sets of documents extracted from the Web, each related to a given *focus*

---

[3]bsnlp.cs.helsinki.fi/Guidelines_ 20190122.pdf

	Brexit				Asia Bibi				Nord Stream				Ryanair			
	PL	CS	RU	BG	PL	CS	RU	BG	PL	CS	RU	BG	PL	CS	RU	BG
Documents	500	284	153	600	88	89	118	99	151	153	137	130	146	149	149	87
PER	2 650	1 108	1 308	2 515	683	570	643	565	538	543	334	335	136	157	71	147
LOC	3 525	1 279	666	2 407	403	366	567	379	1 430	1 566	1 144	910	822	774	888	343
ORG	3 080	1 036	828	2 454	286	214	419	244	837	446	658	540	529	634	494	237
EVT	1 072	471	261	776	14	3	1	8	15	9	3	6	7	12	0	4
PRO	667	232	137	489	55	42	47	63	405	350	445	331	114	65	73	79
Total	10 994	4 126	3 200	8 641	1 441	1 195	1 677	1 259	3 225	2 914	2 584	2 122	1 608	1 642	1 526	810
Distinct																
Surface forms	2 813	1 110	771	1 200	507	303	406	403	843	769	850	500	514	475	394	322
Lemmas	2 133	839	568	1 092	412	248	317	359	634	549	568	448	420	400	327	314
Entity IDs	1 508	582	269	777	273	160	178	231	444	393	314	305	322	306	247	246

Table 1: Overview of the training and test datasets.

entity. We tried to choose entities related to current events covered in news in various languages. Asia Bibi, which relates to a Pakistani woman involved in a blasphemy case, Brexit, Ryanair, which faced a massive strike, and Nord Stream, a controversial Russian-European project.

Each dataset was created as follows. For the focus entity, we posed a search query to Google, in each of the target languages. The query returned documents in the target language. We removed duplicates, downloaded the HTML—mainly news articles—and converted them into plain text. This process was done semi-automatically using the tool described in (Crawley and Wagner, 2010). In particular, some of the meta-data—i.e., creation date, title, URL—were automatically extracted using this tool.

HTML parsing results may include not only the main text of a Web page, but also some additional text, e.g., labels from menus, user comments, etc., which may not constitute well-formed utterances in the target language.[4] The resulting set of partially "cleaned" documents were used to manually select documents for each language and topic, for the final datasets.

Documents were annotated using the Inforex[5] web-based system for annotation of text corpora (Marcinczuk et al., 2017). Inforex allows parallel access and resource sharing by multiple annotators. It let us share a common list of entities, and perform entity-linking semi-automatically: for a given entity, an annotator sees a list of entities of the same type inserted by all annotators and can select an entity ID from the list. A snapshot of the Inforex interface is in Figure 1.

In addition, Inforex keeps track of all lemmas and IDs inserted for each surface form, and inserts them automatically, so in many cases the annotator only confirms the proposed values, which speeds up the annotation process a great deal. All annotations were made by native speakers. After annotation, we performed automatic and manual consistency checks, to reduce annotation errors, especially in entity linking.

Using Inforex allowed us to annotate data much faster than in the first edition of the shared task. Thus we were able to annotated larger datasets and provide participants with training data. (In the first edition participants received only test data.) Data statistics are presented in Table 1.

Documents about Asia Bibi and Brexit were used for training and distributed to the participating teams with annotations. The testing datasets—Ryanair and Nord Stream—were released to the participants 2 days before the submission deadline. The participants did not know the topics in advance, and did not receive the annotations. Thus, we push participants to build a general solution for Slavic NER, rather than to optimize their models toward a particular set of names.

5 Evaluation Methodology

The NER task (exact case-insensitive matching) and Name Normalization (or "lemmatization") were evaluated in terms of precision, recall, and F1-measure. For NER, two types of evaluations were carried out:

- **Relaxed:** An entity mentioned in a given

---

[4]This occurred in a small fraction of texts processed. Some of these texts were included in the test dataset in order to maintain the flavor of "real-data." However, obvious HTML parser failure (e.g., extraction of JavaScript code, extraction of empty texts, etc.) were removed from the data sets. Some of the documents were polished further by removing erroneously extracted boilerplate content.

[5]github.com/CLARIN-PL/Inforex

document is considered to be extracted correctly if the system response includes *at least one* annotation of a named mention of this entity (regardless of whether the extracted mention is in base form);

- **Strict:** The system response should include exactly one annotation *for each* unique form of a named mention of an entity in a given document, i.e., identifying all variants of an entity is required.

In relaxed evaluation we additionally distinguish between *exact* and *partial matching*: in the latter case, an entity mentioned in a given document is considered to be extracted correctly if the system response includes at least one partial match of a named mention of this entity.

We evaluate systems at several levels of granularity: we measure performance for (a) all NE types and all languages, (b) each given NE type and all languages, (c) all NE types for each language, and (d) each given NE type per language.

In the name normalization task, we take into account only correctly recognized entity mentions and only those that were normalized (on both the annotation and system's sides). Formally, let $N_{correct}$ denote the number of all correctly recognized entity mentions for which the system returned a correct base form. Let N_{key} denote the number of all normalized entity mentions in the gold-standard answer key and $N_{response}$ denote the number of all normalized entity mentions in the system's response. We define precision and recall for the name normalization task as:

$$Recall = \frac{N_{corrrect}}{N_{key}} \qquad Precision = \frac{N_{corrrect}}{N_{response}}$$

In evaluating document-level, single-language and cross-lingual entity linking we adopted the Link-Based Entity-Aware metric (LEA) (Moosavi and Strube, 2016), which considers how important the entity is and how well it is resolved. LEA is defined as follows. Let $K = \{k_1, k_2, \ldots, k_{|K|}\}$ denote the set of key entities and $R = \{r_1, r_2, \ldots, r_{|R|}\}$ the set of response entities, i.e., $k_i \in K$ ($r_i \in R$) stand for set of mentions of the same entity in the key entity set (response entity set). LEA recall and precision are then defined as follows:

$$Recall_{LEA} = \frac{\sum_{k_i \in K}(imp(k_i) \times res(k_i))}{\sum_{k_z \in K} imp(k_z)}$$

$$Precision_{LEA} = \frac{\sum_{r_i \in R}(imp(r_i) \times res(r_i))}{\sum_{r_z \in R} imp(r_z)}$$

where imp and res denote the measure of importance and the resolution score for an entity, respectively. In our setting, we define $imp(e) = \log_2 |e|$ for an entity e (in K or R), $|e|$ is the number of mentions of e—i.e., the more mentions an entity has the more important it is. To avoid biasing the importance of the more frequent entities log is used. The resolution score of key entity k_i is computed as the fraction of correctly resolved co-reference links of k_i:

$$res(k_i) = \sum_{r_j \in R} \frac{link(k_i \cap r_j)}{link(k_i)}$$

where $link(e) = (|e| \times (|e| - 1))/2$ is the number of unique co-reference links in e. For each k_i, LEA checks all response entities to check whether they are partial matches for k_i. Analogously, the resolution score of response entity r_i is computed as the fraction of co-reference links in r_i that are extracted correctly:

$$res(r_i) = \sum_{k_j \in K} \frac{link(r_i \cap k_j)}{link(r_i)}$$

LEA brings several benefits. For example, LEA considers resolved co-reference relations instead of resolved mentions and has more discriminative power than other metrics for co-reference resolution (Moosavi and Strube, 2016).

It is important to note at this stage that the evaluation was carried out in "case-insensitive" mode: all named mentions in system response and test corpora were lower-cased.

6 Participant Systems

Sixteen teams from eight countries registered for the shared task. Half of the registered teams submitted results by the deadline. Five teams submitted description of their systems in the form of a Workshop paper. The remaining teams submitted a short description of their systems.

We briefly review the systems; complete descriptions appear in the corresponding papers.

CogComp used multi-source BiLSTM-CRF models, using solely the BERT multilingual embeddings, (Devlin et al., 2019), which directly allows the model to train on datasets in multiple languages. The team submitted several models trained on different combinations of input languages. They found that multi-source training with multilingual BERT outperforms single-source. Cross-lingual (even cross-script) training worked remarkably well. Multilingual BERT can handle train/test sets with mismatching tagsets in certain situations. The best performing models were trained on a combination of data in four languages, while adding English into training data worsen the overall performance, (Tsygankova et al., 2019).

CTC-NER is a baseline prototype of a NER component of an entity recognition system currently under development at the Cognitive Technologies Center, Russia. The system has a hybrid architecture, combining rule-based and ML techniques, where the ML-component is loosely related to (Antonova and Soloviev, 2013). As the system processes Russian, English and Ukrainian, the team submitted output only for Russian.

IIUWR.PL combines Flair[6], Polyglot[7] and BERT.[8] Additional training corpora were used: KPWr[9] for Polish, CNEC[10] for Czech, and data extracted using heuristics from Wikipedia. Lemmatization is partially trained on Wikipedia and PolEval corpora,[11] and partially rule-based. Entity linking is rule-based, and uses WikiData and FastText (Bojanowski et al., 2017).

JRC-TMA-CC is a hybrid system combining a rule-based approach and machine learning techniques. It is a corpus-driven system, lightweight and highly multilingual, exploiting both automatically created lexical resources, such as JRC-Names (Ehrmann et al., 2017), and external resources, such as BabelNet (Jacquet et al., 2019a). The main focus of the approach is on generating the possible inflected variants for known names (Jacquet et al., 2019b).

NLP Cube[12] is an open-source NLP framework that handles sentence segmentation, POS Tagging and lemmatization. The low-level features obtained from the framework, such as part of speech tags, were used as input for an LSTM model. Each

---

[6] github.com/zalandoresearch/flair

[7] polyglot.readthedocs.io

[8] github.com/huggingface/pytorch-pretrained-BERT, github.com/sberbank-ai/ner-bert

[9] clarin-pl.eu/dspace/handle/11321/270

[10] ufal.mff.cuni.cz/cnec/cnec2.0

[11] poleval.pl/tasks/task2

[12] github.com/adobe/NLP-Cube

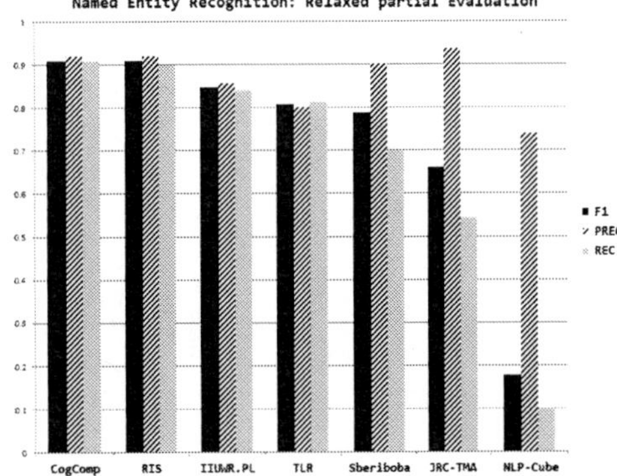

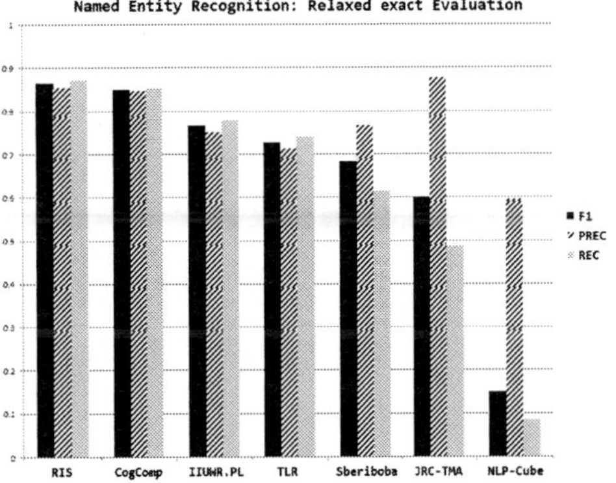

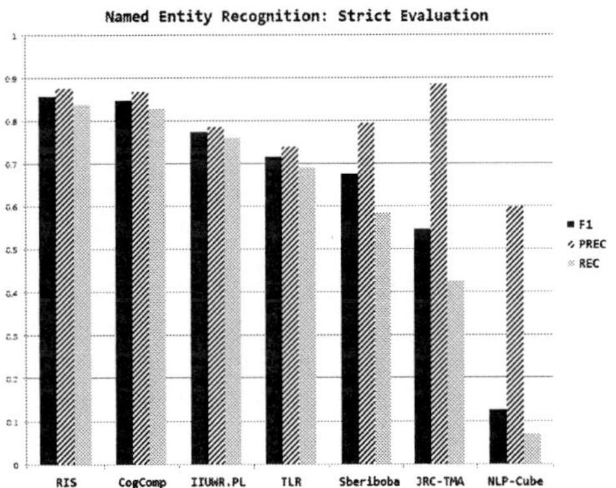

Figure 3: Average system performances on the test data

language was trained individually, producing four models. The models were trained using DyNet[13].

RIS is a modified BERT model, which uses CRF as the top-most layer (Arkhipov et al., 2019). The model was initialized with an existing BERT model trained on 100 languages.

Sberiboba uses multilingual BERT embeddings, summed with learned weights and followed by BiLSTM, attention layers and NCRF++ on the top (Emelianov and Artemova, 2019). Multilin-

---

[13] dynet.io

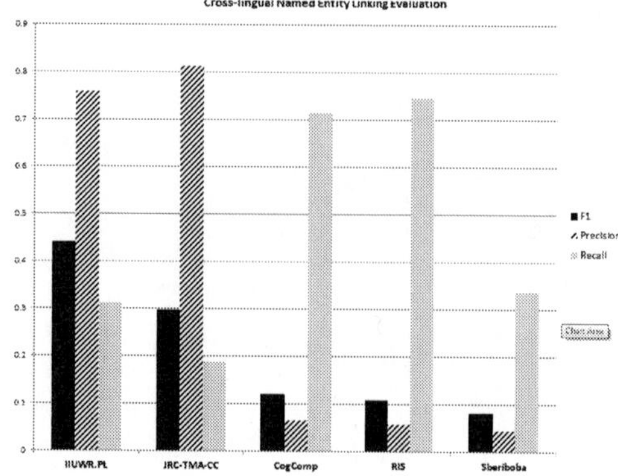

Figure 4: Evaluation results for closs-lingual entity linking. Averaged across two corpora.

Nord Stream		Ryanair	
System	F1	System	F1
IIUWR.PL	41.5	IIUWR.PL	48.7
JRC-TMA	31.0	JRC-TMA	27.0
RIS	11.1	CogComp	13.0
CogComp	11.1	RIS	10.3
Sberiboba	05.6	Sberiboba	10.2

Table 2: Cross-lingual entity linking.

gual BERT is used only for the embeddings, with no fine-tuning for the tasks.

TLR used a standard end-to-end architecture for sequence labeling, namely: LSTM-CNN-CRF, (Ma and Hovy, 2016). It was combined with contextual embeddings using a weighted average (Reimers and Gurevych, 2019) of a BERT model pre-trained for multiple languages (including all of the languages of the Task).

As seen from these descriptions, most of the teams use the BERT model, except NLP Cube, which uses another deep learning model (LSTM), and JRC, which uses rule-based processing of Slavic inflection.

7 Evaluation Results

Figure 3 shows system performance averaged across all languages and two test corpora. We present results for seven teams, since CTC-NER submitted results only for Russian. For each team, we present their best-performing model.[14]

As the plots show, the best performing model, CogComp, yields F-measure 91% according to the relaxed partial evaluation, and 85.6% according to the strict evaluation. Also, the only hybrid model, JRC-TMA-CC, reaches the highest precision— 93.7% relaxed partial, and 88.6% strict—but lower recall—54.4% relaxed partial, 42.7% strict.

Five teams submitted results for *cross-lingual entity linking*. The best results for each team, averaged across two corpora, are presented in Figure 4, and in Table 2. The plots show that this task is much more difficult than entity extraction.

The best performing model, IIUWR.PL, yields F-measure 45%. As seen from the plot, for this task it is harder to balance recall and precision: the first two models obtain much higher precision, while the last three obtain much higher recall. The two best-performing models used rule-based entity linking.

Note that in our setting the performance on entity linking depends on performance on name recognition and normalization: a system had to link entities that it extracted from documents upstream, rather than link a correct set of entities.

Tables 3 and 4 present the F-measure for all tasks, split by language, for the Ryanair and Nord Stream datasets; Table 2 shows performance on the final phase—cross-lingual entity linking. We show one top-performing model for each team. For recognition, we present only the *relaxed* evaluation, since results obtained on the three evaluation schemes are correlated, as can be seen from Figure 3.

The tables indicate that the test corpora present approximately the same level of difficulty for the participating systems, since the values in both tables are similar. The only exception is *single-language* document linking, which seems to be much harder for the Ryanair dataset, especially for Russian. This needs to be investigated further.

In Table 5 we present the results of the evaluation by entity type. As seen in the table, performance was higher overall for Loc and Per, and substantially lower for Org and Pro, which corresponds with our findings from the First shared task, where Org and Misc were the most problematic categories (Piskorski et al., 2017). The Pro category also exhibits higher variation across languages and corpora than other categories, which might point to some annotation artefacts. The results for the Evt category are less informative, since there are few examples of this category in the dataset, as seen in Table 1.

---

[14]Complete results available on the Workshop's Web page: `bsnlp.cs.helsinki.fi/final_ranking.pdf`

RYANAIR									
		Language							
Phase	*Metric*	bg		cz		pl		ru	
Recognition	Relaxed Partial	CogComp	87.5	CogComp	94.2	RIS	92.1	CogComp	94.3
		RIS	85.8	RIS	93.5	CogComp	91.4	RIS	92.5
		IIUWR.PL	75.9	IIUWR.PL	84.1	IIUWR.PL	84.1	CTC-NER	91.0
		TLR	75.9	TLR	82.2	TLR	82.2	TLR	83.4
		JRC-TMA	64.2	Sberiboba	80.5	Sberiboba	80.5	IIUWR.PL	78.9
		Sberiboba	64.6	JRC-TMA	53.6	JRC-TMA	53.6	JRC-TMA	63.7
		NLP Cube	14.7	NLP Cube	18.8	NLP Cube	18.0	Sberiboba	76.9
								NLP Cube	16.4
Normalization		CogComp	83.4	CogComp	88.7	RIS	87.4	RIS	91.3
		RIS	78.1	RIS	87.4	CogComp	86.3	CogComp	90.3
		TLR	68.3	IIUWR.PL	80.7	IIUWR.PL	78.9	CTC	85.9
		IIUWR.PL	68.0	Sberiboba	74.9	TLR	75.1	TLR	78.0
		JRC-TMA	61.3	TLR	72.5	Sberiboba	73.1	JRC-TMA	74.2
		Sberiboba	55.9	JRC-TMA	50.2	JRC-TMA	52.6	IIUWR.PL	73.5
		NLPCube	11.2	NLPCube	11.0	NLPCube	15.2	Sberiboba	66.9
								NLPCube	14.8
Entity linking	Document level	IIUWR.PL-5	35.5	IIUWR.PL	51.8	IIUWR.PL	58.6	IIUWR.PL	29.4
		JRC-TMA	15.8	JRC-TMA	51.7	JRC-TMA	54.6	CogComp	09.4
		CogComp	10.5	CogComp	16.7	CogComp	25.7	RIS	09.3
		RIS	07.1	Sberiboba	16.2	Sberiboba	23.2	CTC-NER	05.4
		Sberiboba	03.1	RIS	13.9	RIS	22.3	Sberiboba	05.4
								JRC-TMA	02.7
	Single language	IIUWR.PL	60.2	IIUWR.PL	70.0	IIUWR.PL	61.9	IIUWR.PL	55.9
		JRC-TMA	48.8	JRC-TMA	36.3	JRC-TMA	28.3	JRC-TMA	49.6
		CogComp	13.9	RIS	13.4	RIS	23.3	RIS	14.8
		RIS	07.4	Sberiboba	12.7	CogComp	23.1	CogComp	12.6
		Sberiboba	05.2	CogComp	11.3	Sberiboba	16.9	CTC-NER	12.4
		NLP Cube	02.0	NLP Cube	00.7	NLP Cube	02.0	Sberiboba	11.9
								NLP Cube	03.1

Table 3: F-measure results for the RYANAIR corpus

8 Conclusion

This paper reports on the Second Multilingual Named Entity Challenge, which focuses on recognizing mentions of NEs in Web documents in Slavic languages, normalization/lemmatization of NEs, and cross-lingual entity linking. The Challenge attracted much wider interest compared to the First Challenge in 2017, with 16 teams registering for the competition and eight teams submitting results from working systems, many with multiple systems variants. Many of the systems used state-of-the-art neural network models. Overall, the results of the best-performing systems are quite strong for extraction and normalization, while cross-lingual linking appears to be substantially more challenging.

We show summary results for the main aspects of the challenge and the best-performing model for each team. For detailed, in-depth evaluations of all submissions systems and their performance figures please consult the Shared Task's Web page. To stimulate further research into NER for Slavic languages, including cross-lingual entity linking, our training and test datasets, the detailed annotations, and scripts used for evaluations are made available to the public on the Shared Task's Web page.[15] The annotation interface is released by the Inforex team, to support annotation of additional data for expanded future tests.

This challenge covered four Slavic languages. For future editions of the Challenge, we plan to expand the training and test datasets, covering a wider range of entity types, and supporting cross-lingual entity linking. We also plan to cover a wider set of languages, including *non-Slavic* ones, and recruit more annotators as the SIGSLAV community expands. We will also undertake further refinement of the underlying annotation guidelines—always a highly complex task in a real-world setting. More complex phenomena also need to addressed, e.g., coordinated NEs, contracted versions of multiple NEs, etc.

We hope that this work will stimulate research into robust, end-to-end NER solutions for processing real-world texts in Slavic languages.

---

[15]bsnlp.cs.helsinki.fi/shared_task.html

| Nord Stream 2 | | Language | | | | | | | |
Phase	Metric	bg		cz		pl		ru	
Recognition	Relaxed Partial	RIS	89.6	CogComp	94.4	RIS	93.7	CTC-NER	86.1
		CogComp	89.4	RIS	94.1	CogComp	93.2	CogComp	85.9
		IIUWR.PL	84.5	IIUWR.PL	88.1	IIUWR.PL	91.3	RIS	84.8
		TLR	83.3	Sberiboba	84.3	Sberiboba	84.4	IIUWR.PL	76.5
		JRC-TMA	77.9	TLR	82.1	TLR	80.6	Sberiboba	73.5
		Sberiboba	73.3	JRC-TMA	65.9	JRC-TMA	59.3	TLR	73.1
		NLP Cube	16.4	NLP Cube	23.8	NLP Cube	15.2	JRC-TMA	69.5
								NLP Cube	17.1
Normalization		RIS	84.9	CogComp	89.3	RIS	89.2	RIS	78.0
		CogComp	84.3	RIS	89.1	CogComp	86.4	CogComp	72.5
		TLR	73.3	IIUWR.PL	83.3	IIUWR.PL	85.9	CTC-NER	69.4
		IIUWR.PL	70.7	TLR	74.4	TLR	72.0	IIUWR.PL	65.0
		JRC-TMA	66.7	Sberiboba	71.1	Sberiboba	67.9	Sberiboba	60.3
		Sberiboba	63.3	JRC-TMA	50.3	JRC-TMA	42.4	TLR	59.6
		NLP Cube	13.5	NLP Cube	15.6	NLP Cube	09.0	JRC-TMA	53.0
								NLP Cube	10.5
Entity linking	Document level	IIUWR.PL	46.8	IIUWR.PL	71.9	IIUWR.PL	74.3	IIUWR.PL	52.8
		JRC-TMA	17.0	CogComp	20.1	JRC-TMA	18.8	RIS	18.2
		RIS	11.3	RIS	19.0	CogComp	15.4	Sberiboba	14.6
		CogComp	10.3	Sberiboba	14.2	RIS	14.4	CogComp	12.3
		Sberiboba	08.6	JRC-TMA	11.5	Sberiboba	12.2	JRC-TMA	11.3
								CTC-NER	06.7
	Single language	IIUWR.PL	58.9	IIUWR.PL	67.2	IIUWR.PL	68.6	IIUWR.PL	48.8
		JRC-TMA	54.8	JRC-TMA	35.3	JRC-TMA	31.5	JRC-TMA	38.0
		RIS	12.1	RIS	20.1	RIS	15.5	RIS	08.8
		CogComp	10.6	CogComp	18.6	CogComp	14.4	CTC-NER	06.8
		Sberiboba	07.8	Sberiboba	08.7	Sberiboba	06.0	Sberiboba	05.9
		NLP Cube	01.0	NLP Cube	01.0	NLP Cube	01.3	CogComp	05.6
								NLP Cube	00.7

Table 4: Evaluation results (F-measure) for the Nord Stream 2 corpus

	Nord Stream				Ryanair			
	bg	cs	pl	ru	bg	cs	pl	ru
Per	93.9	95.7	93.0	93.3	97.8	96.3	97.7	97.4
Loc	94.8	98.3	95.5	98.7	98.3	97.1	97.6	96.6
Org	85.1	95.0	95.5	92.5	90.1	90.1	89.9	83.4
Pro	59.5	79.6	54.1	65.1	72.8	92.3	90.4	57.1
Evt	0.50	0.55	100.0	-	50.0	18.2	50.0	40.0

Table 5: Recognition F-measure (relaxed partial) by entity type—best-performing systems for each language.

Acknowledgments

We thank Tomek Bernaś, Anastasia Golovina, Natalia Novikova, Elena Shukshina, Yana Vorobieva, and Alina Zaharova and many others for contributing to data annotation. We also thank Petya Osenova and Kiril Simov for their assistance.

The shared task was supported in part by the Europe Media Monitoring Project (EMM), carried out by the Text and Data Mining Unit of the Joint Research Centre of the European Commission.

Work was supported in part by investment in the CLARIN-PL research infrastructure funded by the Polish Ministry of Science and Higher Education.

Work was supported in part by ERDF "Research and Development of Intelligent Components of Advanced Technologies for the Pilsen Metropolitan Area (InteCom)" (no. CZ.02.1.01 / 0.0 / 0.0 / 17_048/0007267), and by Grant No. SGS-2019-018 "Processing of heterogeneous data and its specialized applications."

References

Željko Agić and Nikola Ljubešić. 2014. The SE-Times.HR linguistically annotated corpus of Croatian. In *Ninth International Conference on Language Resources and Evaluation (LREC 2014)*, pages 1724–1727, Reykjavík, Iceland.

S. Alexeeva, S.Y. Toldova, A.S. Starostin, V.V. Bocharov, A.A. Bodrova, A.S. Chuchunkov, S.S. Dzhumaev, I.V. Efimenko, D.V. Granovsky, V.F. Khoroshevsky, et al. 2016. FactRuEval 2016: Evaluation of named entity recognition and fact extraction systems for Russian. In *Computational Linguistics and Intellectual Technologies. Proceedings of the Annual International Conference "Dialogue"*, pages 688–705.

AY Antonova and AN Soloviev. 2013. Conditional random field models for the processing of Russian. In *Computational Linguistics and Intellectual Technologies: Papers From the Annual Conference "Dialogue"(Bekasovo, 29 May–2 June 2013)*, volume 1, pages 27–44.

Mikhail Arkhipov, MAria Trofimova, Yuri Kuratov, and Alexey Sorokin. 2019. Tuning multilingual transformers for language-specific named entity recognition. In *Proceedings of the 7th Workshop on Balto-Slavic Natural Language Processing*. Association for Computational Linguistics.

Krešimir Baksa, Dino Golović, Goran Glavaš, and Jan Šnajder. 2017. Tagging named entities in Croatian tweets. *Slovenščina 2.0: empirical, applied and interdisciplinary research*, 4(1):20–41.

Piotr Bojanowski, Edouard Grave, Armand Joulin, and Tomas Mikolov. 2017. Enriching word vectors with subword information. *Transactions of the Association for Computational Linguistics*, 5:135–146.

Nancy Chinchor. 1998. Overview of MUC-7/MET-2. In *Proceedings of Seventh Message Understanding Conference (MUC-7)*.

Jonathan B. Crawley and Gerhard Wagner. 2010. Desktop Text Mining for Law Enforcement. In *Proceedings of IEEE International Conference on Intelligence and Security Informatics (ISI 2010)*, pages 23–26, Vancouver, BC, Canada.

Jacob Devlin, Ming-Wei Chang, Kenton Lee, and Kristina Toutanova. 2019. Bert: Pre-training of deep bidirectional transformers for language understanding. In *NAACL-HLT*.

George R. Doddington, Alexis Mitchell, Mark A. Przybocki, Lance A. Ramshaw, Stephanie Strassel, and Ralph M. Weischedel. 2004. The Automatic Content Extraction (ACE) program—tasks, data, and evaluation. In *Fourth International Conference on Language Resources and Evaluation (LREC 2004)*, pages 837–840, Lisbon, Portugal.

Xiangyu Duan, Rafael E. Banchs, Min Zhang, Haizhou Li, and A. Kumaran. 2016. Report of NEWS 2016 machine transliteration shared task. In *Proceedings of The Sixth Named Entities Workshop*, pages 58–72, Berlin, Germany.

Maud Ehrmann, Guillaume Jacquet, and Ralf Steinberger. 2017. Jrc-names: Multilingual entity name variants and titles as linked data. *Semantic Web*, 8(2):283–295.

Anton Emelianov and Ekaterina Artemova. 2019. Multilingual named entity recognition using pretrained embeddings, attention mechanism and NCRF. In *Proceedings of the 7th Workshop on Balto-Slavic Natural Language Processing*. Association for Computational Linguistics.

Guillaume Jacquet, Jakub Piskorski, and Sophie Chesney. 2019a. Out-of-context fine-grained multi-word entity classification: exploring token, character N-gram and NN-based models for multilingual entity classification. In *Proceedings of the 34th ACM/SIGAPP Symposium on Applied Computing*, pages 1001–1010. ACM.

Guillaume Jacquet, Jakub Piskorski, Hristo Tanev, and Ralf Steinberger. 2019b. JRC TMA-CC: Slavic named entity recognition and linking. participation in the BSNLP-2019 shared task. In *Proceedings of the 7th Workshop on Balto-Slavic Natural Language Processing*. Association for Computational Linguistics.

Heng Ji, Joel Nothman, and Ben Hachey. 2014. Overview of TAC-KBP2014 entity discovery and linking tasks. In *Proceedings of Text Analysis Conference (TAC2014)*, pages 1333–1339.

Heng Ji, Joel Nothman, and Ben Hachey. 2015. Overview of TAC-KBP2015 tri-lingual entity discovery and linking. In *Proceedings of Text Analysis Conference (TAC2015)*.

Mladen Karan, Goran Glavaš, Frane Šarić, Jan Šnajder, Jure Mijić, Artur Šilić, and Bojana Dalbelo Bašić. 2013. CroNER: Recognizing named entities in Croatian using conditional random fields. *Informatica*, 37(2):165.

Michal Konkol and Miloslav Konopík. 2013. CRF-based Czech named entity recognizer and consolidation of Czech NER research. In *Text, Speech and Dialogue*, volume 8082 of *Lecture Notes in Computer Science*, pages 153–160. Springer Berlin Heidelberg.

A Kumaran, Mitesh M. Khapra, and Haizhou Li. 2010. Report of NEWS 2010 transliteration mining shared task. In *Proceedings of the 2010 Named Entities Workshop*, pages 21–28, Uppsala, Sweden.

Nikola Ljubešić, Marija Stupar, Tereza Jurić, and Željko Agić. 2013. Combining available datasets for building named entity recognition models of Croatian and Slovene. *Slovenščina 2.0: empirical, applied and interdisciplinary research*, 1(2):35–57.

Xuezhe Ma and Eduard Hovy. 2016. End-to-end sequence labeling via bi-directional LSTM-CNNs-CRF. In *Proceedings of the 54th Annual Meeting of the Association for Computational Linguistics (Volume 1: Long Papers)*, volume 1, pages 1064–1074.

Michal Marcinczuk, Marcin Oleksy, and Jan Kocon. 2017. Inforex - a collaborative system for text corpora annotation and analysis. In *Proceedings of the International Conference Recent Advances in Natural Language Processing, RANLP 2017, Varna, Bulgaria, September 2-8, 2017*, pages 473–482. INCOMA Ltd.

Nafise Sadat Moosavi and Michael Strube. 2016. Which coreference evaluation metric do you trust? A proposal for a link-based entity aware metric. In *Proceedings of the 54th Annual Meeting of the Association for Computational Linguistics (ACL 2016)*, pages 632–642, Berlin, Germany.

Jakub Piskorski, Lidia Pivovarova, Jan Šnajder, Josef Steinberger, and Roman Yangarber. 2017. The first cross-lingual challenge on recognition, normalization and matching of named entities in Slavic languages. In *Proceedings of the 6th Workshop on Balto-Slavic Natural Language Processing*. Association for Computational Linguistics.

Jakub Piskorski, Karol Wieloch, and Marcin Sydow. 2009. On knowledge-poor methods for person name matching and lemmatization for highly inflectional languages. *Information retrieval*, 12(3):275–299.

Adam Przepiórkowski. 2007. Slavonic information extraction and partial parsing. In *Proceedings of the Workshop on Balto-Slavonic Natural Language Processing: Information Extraction and Enabling Technologies*, ACL '07, pages 1–10, Stroudsburg, PA, USA. Association for Computational Linguistics.

Nils Reimers and Iryna Gurevych. 2019. Alternative weighting schemes for elmo embeddings. *arXiv preprint arXiv:1904.02954*.

Agata Savary and Jakub Piskorski. 2011. Language Resources for Named Entity Annotation in the National Corpus of Polish. *Control and Cybernetics*, 40(2):361–391.

Magda Ševčíková, Zdeněk Žabokrtský, and Oldřich Kruza. 2007. Named entities in Czech: annotating data and developing NE tagger. In *International Conference on Text, Speech and Dialogue*, pages 188–195. Springer.

Tadej Štajner, Tomaž Erjavec, and Simon Krek. 2013. Razpoznavanje imenskih entitet v slovenskem besedilu. *Slovenščina 2.0: empirical, applied and interdisciplinary research*, 1(2):58–81.

Erik Tjong Kim Sang. 2002. Introduction to the CoNLL-2002 shared task: Language-independent named entity recognition. In *Proceedings of the 6th Conference on Natural Language Learning - Volume 20*, COLING-02, pages 1–4, Stroudsburg, PA, USA. Association for Computational Linguistics.

Erik Tjong Kim Sang and Fien De Meulder. 2003. Introduction to the CoNLL-2003 shared task: Language-independent named entity recognition. In *Proceedings of the Seventh Conference on Natural Language Learning at HLT-NAACL 2003 - Volume 4*, CONLL '03, pages 142–147, Stroudsburg, PA, USA. Association for Computational Linguistics.

Tatiana Tsygankova, Stephen Mayhew, and Dan Roth. 2019. BSNLP2019 shared task submission: Multisource neural NER transfer. In *Proceedings of the 7th Workshop on Balto-Slavic Natural Language Processing*. Association for Computational Linguistics.

Jakub Waszczuk, Katarzyna Głowińska, Agata Savary, and Adam Przepiórkowski. 2010. Tools and methodologies for annotating syntax and named entities in the National Corpus of Polish. In *Proceedings of the International Multiconference on Computer Science and Information Technology (IMCSIT 2010): Computational Linguistics – Applications (CLA'10)*, pages 531–539, Wisła, Poland. PTI.

BSNLP2019 Shared Task Submission: Multisource Neural NER Transfer

Tatiana Tsygankova, Stephen Mayhew, Dan Roth
University of Pennsylvania
Philadelphia, PA, 19104
`{ttasya, mayhew, danroth}@seas.upenn.edu`

Abstract

This paper describes the Cognitive Computation (CogComp) Group's submissions to the multilingual named entity recognition shared task at the Balto-Slavic Natural Language Processing (BSNLP) Workshop (Piskorski et al., 2019). The final model submitted is a multi-source neural NER system with multilingual BERT embeddings, trained on the concatenation of training data in various Slavic languages (as well as English). The performance of our system on the official testing data suggests that multi-source approaches consistently outperform single-source approaches for this task, even with the noise of mismatching tagsets.

1 Introduction

This paper describes the Cognitive Computation (CogComp) Group's submission to the shared task of the Balto-Slavic Natural Language Processing (BSNLP) Workshop at ACL 2019 (Piskorski et al., 2019). This shared task centers around multilingual named entity recognition (NER) in Slavic languages, and is composed of recognition, lemmatization, and entity linking subtasks. The niche focus of this task on Slavic languages makes it both interesting and challenging. The languages used in the shared task (Bulgarian, Czech, Polish, and Russian) belong to the same language family and share complex grammatical and morphological features which may be understudied in an English-focused research community. Further, they encompass both Latin and Cyrillic scripts, complicating the multilingual nature of the problem. In addition to the language specific challenges, there are varying sizes of training data, somewhat non-standard named entity types (making finding additional data challenging), and differing domains – the training and test sets are composed of newswire documents collected around domain-specific topics, with different topics in train and test.

This year's shared task is the second edition of the multilingual named entity recognition task on Slavic languages organized for the BSNLP workshop. A similar shared task was previously held in 2017 (BSNLP2017), and was composed of the same subtasks, but was evaluated on seven Slavic languages. It had a slightly different format, in that training data was not provided to the participants, so the majority of the submissions relied on cross-lingual or rule-based approaches.

Our overarching research goal for this project was to experiment with multisource neural NER transfer, leveraging recent advances in multilingual contextual embeddings (Devlin et al., 2019). Ultimately, we aimed to maximize parameter-sharing by training a single model on the concatenation of training data from sources (languages). Such *multi-source* systems have seen success in machine translation (Zoph and Knight, 2016), and to some extent in non-neural NER systems (Mayhew et al., 2017), and neural systems (Rahimi et al., 2019). Given that training data is available in this iteration of the shared task, we purposefully chose to not include rule-based components into our model in order to focus on getting the most out of the given training data.

Our results on the official test data show that multi-source models using multilingual contextual embeddings produce strong performance, and incorporating a greater variety of languages within the same language family further boosts the results. We also observe that combining training data from distinct tagsets often improves performance, and generalizes to the intended tagset better than expected. Finally, our experiments using cross-lingual NER trained on English showed results inferior to monolingual experiments, but surprisingly high nonetheless.

Proceedings of the 7th Workshop on Balto-Slavic Natural Language Processing, pages 75–82,
Florence, Italy, 2 August 2019. ©2019 Association for Computational Linguistics

2   Related Work

The first shared task in Balto-slavic NLP was held in 2017, and reported in Piskorski et al. (2017). The task was somewhat different from the 2019 task in that training data was not provided to participants. Approaches submitted to this task included a model based on parallel projection (Mayfield et al., 2017) and a model with language-specific features trained on found data (Marcińczuk et al., 2017). There has also been follow-up work on this dataset using cross-lingual embeddings (Sharoff, 2018).

Named Entity Recognition (NER), the task of detecting and classifying named entities in text, has been studied for many years. Early models proposed were averaged perceptron (Ratinov and Roth, 2009), and conditional random field (Manning et al., 2014). In recent years, neural models have proved successful, with the BiLSTM-CRF model dominant (Chiu and Nichols, 2016; Lample et al., 2016). A further increase in performance has come with contextual embeddings (Devlin et al., 2019; Peters et al., 2018; Akbik et al., 2018), which are based on large language models trained over massive corpora.

Of particular interest is the multilingual BERT model (Devlin et al., 2019), which is trained over the concatenation of the Wikipedias in over 100 languages.[1] Although BERT is not trained with explicit cross-lingual objectives, it has been shown to have emergent cross-lingual properties, as well as language identification capabilities (Wu and Dredze, 2019).

Several models have been proposed for multi-source learning, in which multiple languages are used to train a model, including for machine translation (Zoph and Knight, 2016; Johnson et al., 2017; Currey and Heafield, 2018), and NER (Täckström, 2012; Tsai et al., 2016; Mayhew et al., 2017; Rahimi et al., 2019).

3   Task

We first describe the details of the shared task, including the data, the evaluation metrics, and the subtasks.

3.1   Data

The BSNLP 2019 training set contained four Slavic languages: Bulgarian, Czech, Polish and

Lang.	Docs	Tokens
English (CoNLL)	964	203,621
Bulgarian (BG)	699	226,728
Czech (CS)	373	84,636
Polish (PL)	586	237,333
Russian (RU)	271	67,495

Table 1: Training data sizes in CoNLL and BSNLP19 datasets. Of the BSNLP19 sets, the largest (Polish) is nearly 3 times the size of the smallest (Russian).

Tag	Total	Unique	Ratio
PER	9986	2851	3.5
LOC	9563	1540	6.2
ORG	8520	1923	4.4
EVT	2601	235	11.0
PRO	1699	739	2.3

Table 2: Entity distribution statistics across all languages in the BSNLP19 training set, where the "Ratio" column refers to the proportion of the "Total" number of entity type annotations to the "Unique" annotations.

Russian. Of these, Czech and Polish are written in Latin script, and Russian and Bulgarian are written in Cyrillic script, a property that we will later explore in our experiments. Table 1 summarizes the size of the datasets. There is a large disparity in the amount of training data by language, with the largest (Polish), containing almost 3 times as many tokens as the smallest (Russian). The training data is in the form of newswire articles and contains document-level annotations of five different entity types: persons (PER), locations (LOC), organizations (ORG), events (EVT) and products (PRO). In document-level supervision, the entity annotations are given for each document as a list of unique surface forms of entities and their corresponding tags, but with no span information. Although this is quite different from the token-level annotations used more commonly for NER data, we argue later that it's possible to convert between the two formats in a (mostly) lossless fashion.

The training documents are divided into two topics: one set containing news articles relating to Brexit, and the other with news articles about a Pakistani woman named Asia Bibi. These focused domains suggest that the set of unique entities will be relatively small within each topic. Table 2 supports this hypothesis and shows the distribution of total and unique entity tags for the entire training set. The high ratio of total to unique mentions for certain tags such as event (EVT) means that

---

[1] github.com/google-research/bert/blob/ master/multilingual.md

the training data contains a small variety of distinct surface forms labeled as "EVT", which could lead to potential overfitting to these entities. Given that the test set used for evaluation of our models contains news articles surrounding two distinct topics (containing documents about Nord Stream, an offshore gas pipeline in Russia, and Ryanair, an Irish low-cost airline), it's also likely that the small number of unique entities could lead to poor domain generalization results for those tags.

3.2 Evaluation Metrics

Since the shared task annotations are created on the document level, the evaluation metrics are somewhat different from standard NER. They are similarly based on precision, recall, and F1 measure of retrieved entities, but are based on matching surface forms between sets of entities instead of matching spans. When matching surface forms, two types of evaluation are used. These are described in the official documentation[2] as:

- **Relaxed evaluation**: an entity mentioned in a given document is considered to be extracted correctly if the system response includes at least one annotation of a named mention of this entity (regardless whether the extracted mention is base form); This is evaluated in two ways:
    - **Partial match**: partial matches count.
    - **Exact match**: full string must match.
- **Strict evaluation**: the system response should include exactly one annotation for each unique form of a named mention of an entity that is referred to in a given document, i.e., capturing and listing all variants of an entity is required. There is no partial score given for this metric.

In our analysis below, we chose to report Strict evaluation as being the most similar to the span-based F1 commonly used in NER.

3.3 Subtasks

Within this shared task there are three distinct subtasks: Recognition, Lemmatization, and Linking. We focus only on the Recognition task.

4 Experimental Setup

4.1 Annotation Conversion

Given that the annotations for the training data were provided at the document-level, we decided

to simply convert these to token-level annotations in order to use standard token-level NER tools. We performed the conversion by traversing each of the annotated entities in the list of document-level annotations and extrapolating the named entity tags to matching surface level forms in the original document. For example, if the list of document-level annotations for some document X contained an annotation for "Brexit" as event (EVT), we would tag all instances of "Brexit" in document X as event at the token-level, and assign "O" to everything that does not have an annotation.

This conversion is susceptible to two types of annotation errors: tagging a token as a named entity when it should be tagged as "O", and tagging a token as an incorrect named entity type.

Although we have no sure way of estimating the error from the first type aside from inspection, experience suggests that such situations are relatively rare in Slavic languages.[3] For example, an entity like *Nunzio Galantino* (a person) is virtually always a person.

As for the second type of error, we found that only 15 documents contained a surface form with multiple entity tags. We decided that this small number of errors is insignificant, and would add very little noise.

For the official evaluation, we made token-level predictions on the test data and converted them to the document level submission format.

4.2 Additional Data

In our experiments, we included two additional datasets – the testing data from the previous iteration of the BSNLP Multilingual NER Shared Task composed of document-level annotations for 7 Balto-Slavic languages, and the English CoNLL 2003 data. What made the use of these datasets challenging was that both were labeled with the CoNLL 2003 entity types – PER, LOC, ORG and MISC – a set not identical to that of the BSNLP19 data. In theory, such a mismatch would be prohibitive, since it would result in unwanted MISC tags, and missed EVT and PRO tags in our output. However, in our preliminary experiments, we were surprised to learn that tagset mismatch across languages seemed to not be a problem (see more discussion of this phenomenon in Section 6). Models trained on data with MISC tags occasionally pro-

---

[2]bsnlp.cs.helsinki.fi/shared_task.html

[3]This may be more of a problem in Semitic languages, for example.

duced MISC tags in the output (less than 10 times in the test data), but we simply removed these predictions at post-processing time.

We hypothesized that the model is able to associate language with tagset, and accordingly only used BSNLP 2017 languages that were not present in our training set, that is: Croatian, Slovak, Slovene, and Ukrainian.

4.3 Preliminary Experiments

In our preliminary experiments, we created a development set to measure the relative improvement of each idea. Given that our training set was composed of documents surrounding two distinct topics, our initial approach was to create a multi-topic validation split, where the development set contained documents from both topics. However, our models reached nearly perfect scores on this split due to the small variation of entities within a given topic. This split was not representative of the official test set evaluation, since the testing data contains entirely new topics, and a lot more generalization would be needed. To better imitate testing conditions, we split the training data by topic, using one topic for training, and the other for development. Our preliminary experiments (not reported here) showed that using off-the-shelf multilingual FastText embeddings[4] (Joulin et al., 2018) resulted in significantly worse performance than BERT, and so omitted them from our submissions.

4.4 Model

For our model, we use a standard BiLSTM-CRF (Lample et al., 2016) implemented in AllenNLP (Gardner et al., 2018). The model used character embeddings with a single layer Convolutional Neural Network (CNN) with 128 filters, and word embeddings from multilingual BERT (Devlin et al., 2019). We used the bert-base-multilingual-cased model from huggingface[5] which uses a shared wordpiece vocabulary among all languages, meaning that we can share models even across Cyrillic and Latin scripts. We did not fine-tune BERT during training, but learned a scalar mix of the 12 layers. For each word, we use the first wordpiece to be representative of the entire word, as done in Devlin et al. (2019).

---

[4]`fasttext.cc/docs/en/aligned-vectors.html`
[5]`github.com/huggingface/pytorch-pretrained-BERT`

5 Results

Our main results are shown in Table 3, as F1 scores from the Strict evaluation (results from all metrics can be seen in the Appendix). We made a total of 8 submissions to the shared task, with each row in the table denoting a separate submission, with the exception of the first 4 rows. Those together composed one submission, since we tested each single-source model only on the same target language. Each submission in the table is also given a name (e.g. *LatinScript*) that is descriptive of the training data used. The columns are divided into two sections: training data on the left, and testing data on the right, both separated into various languages. The checkmarks denote which datasets were included in training. The rows of the table are divided into two sections, with the upper section representing single-source systems (using only one language in training), and the lower section representing multi-source models.

BSNLP17 training corpus refers to the testing data from the BSNLP shared task in 2017, as described in Section 4.2. **EN** refers to the CoNLL 2003 English training set.

6 Analysis

There are several interesting lessons in our results. First, multi-source training with BERT is a success, as evidenced by the 2.7 F1 improvement between the single-source experiments and the best experiment (*AllLangs*).

Surprisingly, these results hold even in the face of tagset mismatches. Recall from Section 4.2 that English CoNLL (EN) and the BSNLP17 datasets use a tagset somewhat different from the BSNLP19 test data. Despite this, we see an overall improvement from *AllTrain* (which does not use additional data from the BSNLP17 languages) to *AllLangs* (which does), and similarly from *AllTrainEng* to *AllLangsEng*. We believe that two factors contributed to this success:

Factor 1. The large overlap in the tagset distributions. PER, LOC, and ORG tags made up the majority of annotations in all datasets. Thus, most information required to learn a model is present in the training data regardless of tagset. Furthermore, PRO and EVT entities are rare enough in the test data that even small scores shouldn't hurt the micro-average. In fact, Table 4 shows that when going from *AllTrain*, which uses only the BSNLP19 tagset, to *AllLangsEng*, which includes

	Submission	Training Data						Testing Data				
		BG	**CS**	**PL**	**RU**	**EN**	**BSNLP17**	**BG**	**CS**	**PL**	**RU**	**ALL**
Single-source	Bulgarian	✓						80.9	–	–	–	82.0
	Czech		✓					–	84.0	–	–	82.0
	Polish			✓				–	–	85.2	–	82.0
	Russian				✓			–	–	–	76.8	82.0
	English					✓		74.3	76.0	72.2	73.3	73.9
Multi-source	LatinScript		✓	✓				78.1	87.8	85.2	77.0	82.6
	LatinScriptEng		✓	✓		✓		77.9	87.8	85.6	77.2	82.8
	AllTrain	✓	✓	✓	✓			82.7	88.0	85.9	**79.4**	84.3
	AllTrainEng	✓	✓	✓	✓	✓		82.8	87.8	85.6	78.5	84.0
	AllLangs	✓	✓	✓	✓		✓	**84.1**	88.3	86.1	79.3	**84.7**
	AllLangsEng	✓	✓	✓	✓	✓	✓	83.0	**88.5**	**86.3**	78.3	84.4

Table 3: Official results on the Recognition task of BSNLP19, measured as F1 with Strict evaluation. The training languages used are: Bulgarian (BG), Czech (CS), Polish (PL), Russian (RU), English (EN, CoNLL2003) and the BSNLP17 languages (Croatian, Slovak, Slovene and Ukrainian). The top section of the table shows single-source experiments, in which each model is trained on a single language. The bottom section shows multi-source experiments. The rightmost column, **ALL**, is a micro-average of the test results over the 4 test languages.

Method	PER	LOC	ORG	PRO	EVT
P. AllTrain	90.9	94.1	90.6	77.6	48.1
P. AllLangsEng	92.3	95.1	90.9	75.2	32.7
R. AllTrain	94.2	97.8	89.2	54.2	27.8
R. AllLangsEng	95.8	97.7	86.8	60.6	31.5
F1. AllTrain	92.5	95.9	89.9	63.9	35.3
F1. AllLangsEng	94.0	96.3	88.9	67.1	32.1

Table 4: Precision (P), Recall (R), and F1 scores by tag across all languages. *AllTrain* is the largest set of training data that uses solely the target tagset, and *AllLangsEng* includes training data with the tagset with MISC and without PRO or EVT.

data with the divergent tagset, the recall on EVT and PRO actually improves.

Factor 2. The power of multilingual BERT. We know that multilingual BERT can detect language (Wu and Dredze, 2019), and we hypothesize that multilingual BERT is able to associate language with tagset.

While we show that multi-source training data helps, our results also show that choosing the right languages for inclusion is important. Naturally, scores are better if the target language is present in the training data, with the exception of Single-source Russian compared with *LatinScript* Russian. This could be attributed to the fact that there is relatively little Russian training data, and the model is powerful enough that a large amount of Polish and Czech data is better than a small

amount Russian data. Even so, scores further improve when Russian is added again (*AllTrain*).

Finally, there are some interesting observations on the model trained only on English data. It performs well both across tagsets, and across scripts (on Bulgarian and Russian). Although one might expect that this approach would perform best on Latin script languages, such a correlation is not present. Further, scores across languages are within 4 points of each other, compared to individual monolingual systems that range over 10 points.

7 Conclusion

This paper has described our submission the BSNLP19 shared task on named entity recognition. Our approach is based on multi-source neural NER transfer, with experiments contrasting single-source and cross-lingual approaches. We found that using more data almost always helps, at least when in the same family.

Acknowledgement

This work was supported by Contracts HR0011-15-2-0025 and HR0011-18-2-0052 with the US Defense Advanced Research Projects Agency (DARPA). Approved for Public Release, Distribution Unlimited. The views expressed are those of the authors and do not reflect the official policy or position of the Department of Defense or the U.S. Government.

References

Alan Akbik, Duncan Blythe, and Roland Vollgraf. 2018. Contextual string embeddings for sequence labeling. In *Proceedings of the 27th International Conference on Computational Linguistics*, pages 1638–1649, Santa Fe, New Mexico, USA. Association for Computational Linguistics.

Jason P.C. Chiu and Eric Nichols. 2016. Named entity recognition with bidirectional LSTM-CNNs. *Transactions of the Association for Computational Linguistics*, 4:357–370.

Anna Currey and Kenneth Heafield. 2018. Multi-source syntactic neural machine translation. In *Proceedings of the 2018 Conference on Empirical Methods in Natural Language Processing*, pages 2961–2966, Brussels, Belgium. Association for Computational Linguistics.

Jacob Devlin, Ming-Wei Chang, Kenton Lee, and Kristina Toutanova. 2019. BERT: Pre-training of deep bidirectional transformers for language understanding. In *Proceedings of the 2019 Conference of the North American Chapter of the Association for Computational Linguistics: Human Language Technologies, Volume 1 (Long and Short Papers)*, pages 4171–4186, Minneapolis, Minnesota. Association for Computational Linguistics.

Matt Gardner, Joel Grus, Mark Neumann, Oyvind Tafjord, Pradeep Dasigi, Nelson F. Liu, Matthew Peters, Michael Schmitz, and Luke Zettlemoyer. 2018. AllenNLP: A deep semantic natural language processing platform. In *Proceedings of Workshop for NLP Open Source Software (NLP-OSS)*, pages 1–6, Melbourne, Australia. Association for Computational Linguistics.

Melvin Johnson, Mike Schuster, Quoc V. Le, Maxim Krikun, Yonghui Wu, Zhifeng Chen, Nikhil Thorat, Fernanda Viégas, Martin Wattenberg, Greg Corrado, Macduff Hughes, and Jeffrey Dean. 2017. Google's multilingual neural machine translation system: Enabling zero-shot translation. *Transactions of the Association for Computational Linguistics*, 5:339–351.

Armand Joulin, Piotr Bojanowski, Tomas Mikolov, Hervé Jégou, and Edouard Grave. 2018. Loss in translation: Learning bilingual word mapping with a retrieval criterion. In *Proceedings of the 2018 Conference on Empirical Methods in Natural Language Processing*, pages 2979–2984, Brussels, Belgium. Association for Computational Linguistics.

Guillaume Lample, Miguel Ballesteros, Sandeep Subramanian, Kazuya Kawakami, and Chris Dyer. 2016. Neural architectures for named entity recognition. In *Proceedings of the 2016 Conference of the North American Chapter of the Association for Computational Linguistics: Human Language Technologies*, pages 260–270, San Diego, California. Association for Computational Linguistics.

Christopher Manning, Mihai Surdeanu, John Bauer, Jenny Finkel, Steven Bethard, and David McClosky. 2014. The Stanford CoreNLP natural language processing toolkit. In *Proceedings of 52nd Annual Meeting of the Association for Computational Linguistics: System Demonstrations*, pages 55–60, Baltimore, Maryland. Association for Computational Linguistics.

Michał Marcińczuk, Jan Kocoń, and Marcin Oleksy. 2017. Liner2 — a generic framework for named entity recognition. In *Proceedings of the 6th Workshop on Balto-Slavic Natural Language Processing*, pages 86–91, Valencia, Spain. Association for Computational Linguistics.

James Mayfield, Paul McNamee, and Cash Costello. 2017. Language-independent named entity analysis using parallel projection and rule-based disambiguation. In *Proceedings of the 6th Workshop on Balto-Slavic Natural Language Processing*, pages 92–96, Valencia, Spain. Association for Computational Linguistics.

Stephen Mayhew, Chen-Tse Tsai, and Dan Roth. 2017. Cheap translation for cross-lingual named entity recognition. In *Proceedings of the 2017 Conference on Empirical Methods in Natural Language Processing*, pages 2536–2545, Copenhagen, Denmark. Association for Computational Linguistics.

Matthew Peters, Mark Neumann, Mohit Iyyer, Matt Gardner, Christopher Clark, Kenton Lee, and Luke Zettlemoyer. 2018. Deep contextualized word representations. In *Proceedings of the 2018 Conference of the North American Chapter of the Association for Computational Linguistics: Human Language Technologies, Volume 1 (Long Papers)*, pages 2227–2237, New Orleans, Louisiana. Association for Computational Linguistics.

Jakub Piskorski, Laska Laskova, Michał Marcińczuk, Lidia Pivovarova, Pavel Přibáň, Josef Steinberger, and Roman Yangarber. 2019. The second cross-lingual challenge on recognition, classification, lemmatization, and linking of named entities across Slavic languages. In *Proceedings of the 7th Workshop on Balto-Slavic Natural Language Processing*, Florence, Italy. Association for Computational Linguistics.

Jakub Piskorski, Lidia Pivovarova, Jan Šnajder, Josef Steinberger, and Roman Yangarber. 2017. The first cross-lingual challenge on recognition, normalization, and matching of named entities in Slavic languages. In *Proceedings of the 6th Workshop on Balto-Slavic Natural Language Processing*, pages 76–85, Valencia, Spain. Association for Computational Linguistics.

Afshin Rahimi, Yuan Li, and Trevor Cohn. 2019. Massively multilingual transfer for NER. In *Proceedings of the 57th Annual Meeting of the Association for Computational Linguistics*, Florence, Italy.

Lev Ratinov and Dan Roth. 2009. Design challenges and misconceptions in named entity recognition. In *Proceedings of the Thirteenth Conference on Computational Natural Language Learning (CoNLL-2009)*, pages 147–155, Boulder, Colorado. Association for Computational Linguistics.

Serge Sharoff. 2018. Language adaptation experiments via cross-lingual embeddings for related languages. In *Proceedings of the 11th Language Resources and Evaluation Conference*, Miyazaki, Japan. European Language Resource Association.

Oscar Täckström. 2012. Nudging the envelope of direct transfer methods for multilingual named entity recognition. In *Proceedings of the NAACL-HLT Workshop on the Induction of Linguistic Structure*, pages 55–63, Montréal, Canada. Association for Computational Linguistics.

Chen-Tse Tsai, Stephen Mayhew, and Dan Roth. 2016. Cross-lingual named entity recognition via wikification. In *Proceedings of The 20th SIGNLL Conference on Computational Natural Language Learning*, pages 219–228, Berlin, Germany. Association for Computational Linguistics.

Shijie Wu and Mark Dredze. 2019. Beto, Bentz, Becas: The surprising cross-lingual effectiveness of BERT. *arXiv preprint arXiv:1904.09077.*

Barret Zoph and Kevin Knight. 2016. Multi-source neural translation. In *Proceedings of the 2016 Conference of the North American Chapter of the Association for Computational Linguistics: Human Language Technologies*, pages 30–34, San Diego, California. Association for Computational Linguistics.

A Detailed Results

The full summary of our results with all submissions and all evaluation metrics is shown in Table 6. Table 1 has the key that maps between submission ID and name used in the main paper.

Model	Submission Key
Bulgarian	ccg-2
Czech	ccg-2
Polish	ccg-2
Russian	ccg-2
English	ccg-8
LatinScript	ccg-3
LatinScriptEng	ccg-4
AllTrain	ccg-1
AllTrainEng	ccg-5
AllLangs	ccg-6
AllLangsEng	ccg-7

Table 5: Key matching the descriptive submission names used throughout the paper with the submission numbers referenced in our results section.

ALL CORPORA	Language							
Metric	bg		cs		pl		ru	
Relaxed Partial	ccg-1	86.9	ccg-1	93.5	ccg-1	92.1	ccg-1	**88.6**
	ccg-2	85.1	ccg-2	92.0	ccg-2	92.0	ccg-2	86.0
	ccg-3	84.3	ccg-3	93.2	ccg-3	91.9	ccg-3	88.0
	ccg-4	84.3	ccg-4	93.6	ccg-4	**92.4**	ccg-4	87.7
	ccg-5	88.1	ccg-5	93.5	ccg-5	91.9	ccg-5	88.0
	ccg-6	**88.9**	ccg-6	93.5	ccg-6	92.0	ccg-6	88.5
	ccg-7	87.6	ccg-7	**94.0**	ccg-7	92.3	ccg-7	88.3
	ccg-8	81.0	ccg-8	83.4	ccg-8	78.6	ccg-8	83.5
Relaxed Exact	ccg-1	83.8	ccg-1	87.3	ccg-1	85.0	ccg-1	**81.4**
	ccg-2	82.0	ccg-2	83.2	ccg-2	84.3	ccg-2	78.3
	ccg-3	79.1	ccg-3	87.0	ccg-3	84.1	ccg-3	78.2
	ccg-4	78.7	ccg-4	87.0	ccg-4	84.7	ccg-4	78.3
	ccg-5	84.0	ccg-5	87.0	ccg-5	84.7	ccg-5	80.1
	ccg-6	**85.3**	ccg-6	87.9	ccg-6	**85.4**	ccg-6	81.0
	ccg-7	84.0	ccg-7	**88.0**	ccg-7	**85.4**	ccg-7	80.4
	ccg-8	75.5	ccg-8	74.5	ccg-8	70.1	ccg-8	74.1
Strict	ccg-1	82.7	ccg-1	88.0	ccg-1	85.9	ccg-1	**79.4**
	ccg-2	80.9	ccg-2	84.0	ccg-2	85.2	ccg-2	76.8
	ccg-3	78.1	ccg-3	87.8	ccg-3	85.2	ccg-3	77.0
	ccg-4	77.9	ccg-4	87.8	ccg-4	85.6	ccg-4	77.2
	ccg-5	82.8	ccg-5	87.8	ccg-5	85.6	ccg-5	78.5
	ccg-6	**84.1**	ccg-6	88.3	ccg-6	86.1	ccg-6	79.3
	ccg-7	83.0	ccg-7	**88.5**	ccg-7	**86.3**	ccg-7	78.3
	ccg-8	74.3	ccg-8	76.0	ccg-8	72.2	ccg-8	73.3

Table 6: Evaluation results (topics combined)

TLR at BSNLP2019: A Multilingual Named Entity Recognition System

Jose G. Moreno   **Elvys Linhares Pontes**[1,2] **Mickaël Coustaty**[1]   **Antoine Doucet**[1]

University of Toulouse   1 - L3i laboratory, University of La Rochelle, La Rochelle, France
IRIT, UMR 5505 CNRS   {firstname.lastname}@univ-lr.fr
jose.moreno@irit.fr   2 - University of Avignon, Avignon, France

Abstract

This paper presents our participation at the shared task on multilingual named entity recognition at BSNLP2019. Our strategy is based on a standard neural architecture for sequence labeling. In particular, we use a mixed model which combines multilingual-contextual and language-specific embeddings. Our only submitted run is based on a voting schema using multiple models, one for each of the four languages of the task (Bulgarian, Czech, Polish, and Russian) and another for English. Results for named entity recognition are encouraging for all languages, varying from 60% to 83% in terms of Strict and Relaxed metrics, respectively.

1 Introduction

Correctly detecting mentions of entities in text documents in multiple languages is a challenging task (Ji et al., 2014, 2015; Ji and Nothman, 2016; Ji et al., 2017). This is especially true when documents relate to news because of the huge range of topics covered by newspapers. In this context, the shared task on multilingual named entity recognition (NER) proposes to participants to test their system under a multilingual setup. Four languages are addressed in BSNLP2019: Bulgarian (bg), Czech (cz), Polish (pl), and Russian (ru). Similarly to the first edition of this task in 2017 (Piskorski et al., 2017), participants are required to recognize, normalize, and link entities from raw texts written in multiple languages. Our participation is focused on the sole recognition of entities while other steps will be covered in our future work.

In order to build a unique NER system for multiple languages, we decided to contribute a solution based on an end-to-end system without (or almost without) language specific pre-processing. We explored an existing neural architecture, the LSTM-CNNs-CRF (Ma and Hovy, 2016), initially proposed for NER in English. This neural model is based on word embeddings to represent each token in a sentence. In order to have a unique embedding space, we propose to use a transformer-based (Vaswani et al., 2017) contextual embedding called BERT (Devlin et al., 2019). This pre-trained model includes multilingual representations that are context-aware. However, as noted by Reimers and Gurevych (2019), contextual embeddings provide multiple layers that are challenging to combine together. To overcome this problem, we used the weighted average strategy they successfully tested using (Peters et al., 2018).

The results of our participation are quite encouraging. Regarding the *Relaxed Partial* metric, our run achieves 80.26% in average for the four languages and the two topics that compose the test collection. In order to present comparative results against the state of the art, we run experiments using two extra datasets under the standard CoNLL evaluation setup. The remainder of this paper is organized as follows: Section 2 introduces the related work while Section 3 presents the proposed multi-lingual model. Section 4 presents the results while conclusions are drawn in Section 5.

2 Related Work

Named entity recognition has been largely studied through the organization of shared tasks in the last two decades (Nadeau and Sekine, 2007; Yadav and Bethard, 2018). The large variety of models can be grouped into three types: rule-based (Chiticariu et al., 2010), gazetteers-based (Sundheim, 1995), and statistically-based models (Florian et al., 2003). The latter type is a current hot topic in research, in particular with the return of neural based models[1]. Two main contributions

---

[1] In all their flavors, including attention.

Proceedings of the 7th Workshop on Balto-Slavic Natural Language Processing, pages 83–88,
Florence, Italy, 2 August 2019. ©2019 Association for Computational Linguistics

have recently redrawn the landscape of models for sequence labelling such as NER: the proposal of new architectures (Ma and Hovy, 2016; Lample et al., 2016), the use of contextualized embeddings (Peters et al., 2018; Reimers and Gurevych, 2019), or even, the use of both of them (Devlin et al., 2019). The use of contextualized embeddings is a clear advantage for several kinds of neural-based NER systems, however as pointed out by Reimers and Gurevych (2019) the combination of multiples vectors proposed by these models is computationally expensive.

3 TLR System: A Neural-based Multilingual NER Tagger

This section describes our model which is based on a standard end-to-end architecture for sequence labeling, namely LSTM-CNNs-CRF (Ma and Hovy, 2016). We have combined this architecture with contextual embeddings using a weighted average strategy (Reimers and Gurevych, 2019) applied to a pre-trained model for multiple languages (Devlin et al., 2019) (including all languages of the task). We trained a NER model for each of the four languages and predict labels based on a classical voting strategy. As an example, the overall architecture of our model for Polish using the sentence *"Wielka Brytania z zadowoleniem przyjeła porozumienie z Unia Europejska"* (or "United Kingdom welcomes agreement with the European Union" in English) is depicted in Figure 1.

3.1 FastText Embedding

In this layer, we used pre-trained embeddings for each language trained on Common Crawl and Wikipedia using fastText (Bojanowski et al., 2017; Grave et al., 2018). These models were trained using the continuous bag-of-words (CBOW) strategy with position weights. A total of 300 dimensions were used with character n-grams of length 5, a window of size 5 and 10 negatives. The four languages of the task are included in this publicly available[2] pre-trained embedding (Grave et al., 2018). We have used the fastText library to ensure that every token (also in other alphabets) has a corresponding vector avoiding out of vocabulary tokens.

3.2 Case Encoding

This layer allows to encode each token based on the case information as proposed by (Reimers and Gurevych, 2017). We have used a one-hot encoding of the following seven classes: {'other', 'numeric', 'mainly_numeric', 'allLower', 'allUpper', 'initialUpper', 'contains_digit'}.

3.3 Multilingual BERT

We used the multilingual pre-trained embedding of BERT[3]. In particular, we used the model learned for 104 languages including the four of this task. This model is composed of 12 layers and 768 dimensions in each layer for a total of 110M parameters. Directly using the 12 layers can be hard to compute in a desktop computer. To cope with this problem, we used the weighted strategy proposed by Reimers and Gurevych (2019) and combined only the first two layers. When a token was composed of multiple BERT tokens, we averaged them to obtain a unique vector per token.

3.4 Char Representation

We used the char representation strategy proposed by Ma and Hovy (2016) where char embeddings are combined using a convolutional neural network (CNN). Thus, an embedding vector is learned for each character by iterating trough the entire collection. Note that the four languages include unique characters which make harder the sharing of patterns between languages. To deal with this problem, we transliterated each token to the Latin alphabet using the unidecode library[4] as a preprocessing step. This conversion is only applied at this layer and is not used elsewhere.

3.5 Language-Dependent and Independent Features

In Figure 1, we observe that the "char representation", "multilingual BERT", and "case encoding" layers are language-independent features[5] So, all the processing steps are applied without considering the language, including the transliteration to the Latin alphabet. It means that some tokens are translated even knowing that they are already in a

---

[2]https://fasttext.cc/docs/en/crawl-vectors.html

[3]https://github.com/google-research/bert/blob/master/multilingual.md

[4]https://pypi.org/project/Unidecode/

[5]We mean that as the four languages follow exactly the same process, those steps become completely independent in this specific context.

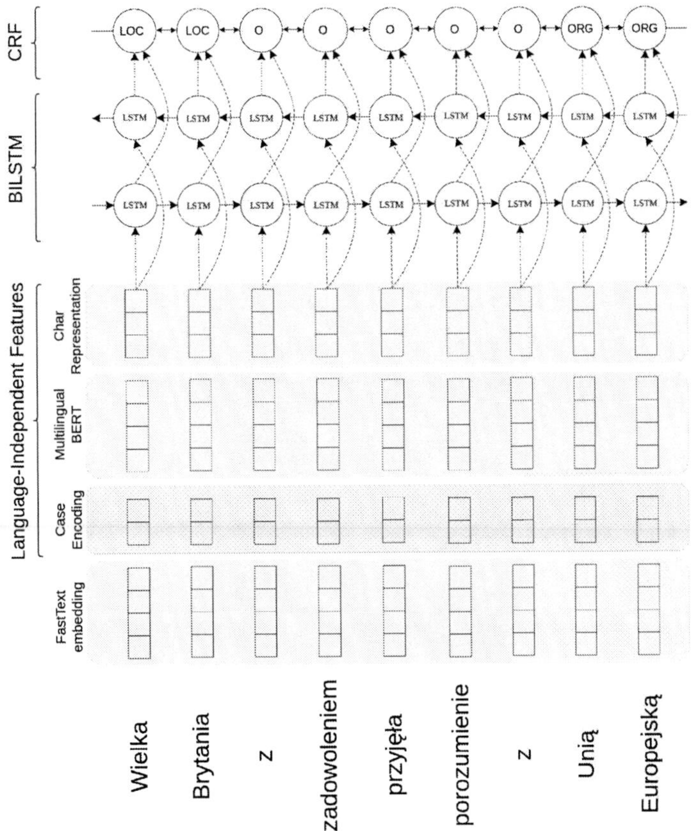

Figure 1: Architecture of a single-language model of our system. Note that for each token we provide a unique NER prediction.

Latin alphabet. On the other hand, "fastText embedding" is clearly a language-dependent feature. However, we intentionally reduce the language dependency by using the architecture in Figure 1 as many times as the number of languages involved in the task, e.g. four times. Each time we switched the "fastText embedding" model for the one corresponding to each language, this make a total of four different NER models. Our final prediction is obtained by applying a simple majority voting schema between these four NER models.

4 Experiments

4.1 Experimental Setup

We follow the configuration setup proposed by the task organizers. Two topics, "nord_stream" and "ryanair", were used to test our models. These topics include 1100 documents in the four languages. Further details can be found in the 2019 shared task overview paper (Piskorski et al.,

2019). For training, we have used the documents provided for the task but also the ones in Czech, Polish, and Russian from the previous round of same task in 2017 (Piskorski et al., 2017). We additionally added the training example form the CoNLL2003 (Sang and De Meulder, 1837) collection in English (13879 train, 3235 dev, and 3422 test sentences). Used metrics include the officially proposed metrics and standard metrics for the CoNLL2003 dataset (F1 metric).

4.2 Official Results

The official results of our unique run are presented in Table 1 and identified as TLR-1. Note that only NER metrics are presented for the four languages. We have added the results for each language model using the partial annotations provided by the organizers[6]. Each result is identified with the language used for the "fastText embed-

---

[6]We were able to calculate "Recognition Strict" for these unofficial results.

NORD_STREAM		Language						
Phase	*Metric*	bg		cz		pl		ru	
Recognition	Relaxed Partial	TLR-1	83.384	TLR-1	82.124	TLR-1	80.665	TLR-1	73.145
	Relaxed Exact	TLR-1	76.114	TLR-1	74.106	TLR-1	71.423	TLR-1	62.168
	Strict	TLR-1	73.312	TLR-1	74.475	TLR-1	72.026	TLR-1	59.627
		bg	**72.873**	bg	67.841	bg	68.281	bg	54.922
		cz	68.821	cz	**78.225**	cz	71.509	cz	52.590
		pl	69.892	pl	73.636	pl	**75.820**	pl	53.939
		ru	72.661	ru	71.522	ru	70.356	ru	**58.399**

RYANAIR		Language						
Phase	*Metric*	bg		cz		pl		ru	
Recognition	Relaxed Partial	TLR-1	75.861	TLR-1	82.865	TLR-1	82.182	TLR-1	83.419
	Relaxed Exact	TLR-1	69.824	TLR-1	73.493	TLR-1	77.463	TLR-1	78.303
	Strict	TLR-1	68.377	TLR-1	72.509	TLR-1	75.118	TLR-1	78.028
		bg	**76.152**	bg	77.533	bg	79.168	bg	78.518
		cz	61.755	cz	**78.549**	cz	76.863	cz	75.280
		pl	67.876	pl	77.907	pl	**82.242**	pl	76.864
		ru	70.288	ru	74.805	ru	76.135	ru	**79.784**

Table 1: Evaluation results of our TLR submission. We have added extra results for the strict metric using each single model based on one of the four languages.

ding" layer in Figure 1. Based on strict recognition, most of the cases[7], the use of the correct language embedding improves the recognition of the respective language. However, the voting schema outperforms the individual models on average. This suggest that a system aware of the language of the input sentence could provide better results that our voting schema.

4.3 Unofficial Results

In order to compare our system to the state-of-the-art, we have evaluated our architecture using the CoNLL2003 dataset. Our results using two and six layers are presented in Table 2. Note that English is not part of our target languages. So, an underperformance of 2.5 is acceptable in our system[8]. It is also worth nothing that the use of more BERT layers increases our results. However, the amount of memory used is also increased manifold. We set the number of layers (hyperparameter) to two layers due to our computation constraints despite the downgrading in performances for English.

The number of epochs (hyperparameter) was set using the BSNLP2017 dataset (for ru, cs, and

Method		Metric		
	Set	P	R	F1
BRNN-CNN-CRF	Dev	94.8	94.6	94.7
(Ma and Hovy, 2016)	Test	91.3	91.0	91.2
BiLSTM + ElMo	Dev	95.1	95.7	95.4
(Reimers and Gurevych, 2019)	Test	90.9	92.1	91.5
BiLSTM + MultiBERT2L	Dev	92.3	93.0	92.7
(ours)	Test	88.2	89.7	89.0
BiLSTM + MultiBERT6L	Dev	93.2	93.8	93.5
(ours)	Test	89.3	90.3	89.8

Table 2: Evaluation results on the CoNLL 2003 dataset, an English only dataset.

---

[7] 6 out of 8, with differences smaller than 0.4 points.

[8] More experiments using BERT English-only model will be performed in our future work.

Language	BSNLP2017+CoNLL2003			
	P	R	F1	Epochs
en	78.9	82.8	80.8	10
bg	77.1	79.3	78.2	6
cz	78.7	82.2	80.4	24
pl	79.7	83.6	81.6	16
ru	79.1	83.4	81.2	21

Table 3: Evaluation results on the BSNLP2017 and CoNLL 2003 datasets, a multilingual dataset. Each row represents a model learned with a fastText language specific embedding.

pl) combined with CoNLL2003 as a validation set of our final models. Results for these combined datasets are presented in Table 3. Surprisingly, our results seem very similar independently of the fastText embedding. It suggests that our architecture is able to generalize the prediction for several target languages. Note that the worst results are obtained by the Bulgarian model, but no test examples were included for this language. In contrast, we believe that the examples provided in other languages were rich enough to help the predictions (also in English).

5 Conclusion

This paper presents the TLR participation at the shared task on multilingual named entity recognition at BSNLP2019. Our system is a combination of multiple representation including character information, multilingual embedding, and language specific embedding. However, we combine them in such a way that it can be seen as a generic multilingual NER system for a large number of languages (104 in total). Although top participants outperform our average score of 80.26% of "Relaxed Partial" (Piskorski et al., 2019), the strengths of the proposed strategy relays on the fact that it can be easily adapted to new languages and topics without extra effort.

Acknowledgements

This paper is supported by European Union's Horizon 2020 research and innovation programme under grant agreement No 825153, project EM-BEDDIA (Cross-Lingual Embeddings for Less-Represented Languages in European News Media).

References

Piotr Bojanowski, Edouard Grave, Armand Joulin, and Tomas Mikolov. 2017. Enriching Word Vectors with Subword Information. *Transactions of the Association for Computational Linguistics*, 5:135–146.

Laura Chiticariu, Rajasekar Krishnamurthy, Yunyao Li, Frederick Reiss, and Shivakumar Vaithyanathan. 2010. Domain Adaptation of Rule-based Annotators for Named-Entity Recognition Tasks. In *Proceedings of the 2010 conference on empirical methods in natural language processing*, pages 1002–1012. Association for Computational Linguistics.

Jacob Devlin, Ming-Wei Chang, Kenton Lee, and Kristina Toutanova. 2019. Bert: Pre-training of Deep Bidirectional Transformers for Language Understanding. In *2019 Annual Conference of the North American Chapter of the Association for Computational Linguistics (NAACL-HLT)*.

Radu Florian, Abe Ittycheriah, Hongyan Jing, and Tong Zhang. 2003. Named Entity Recognition through Classifier Combination. In *Proceedings of the seventh conference on Natural language learning at HLT-NAACL 2003-Volume 4*, pages 168–171. Association for Computational Linguistics.

Edouard Grave, Piotr Bojanowski, Prakhar Gupta, Armand Joulin, and Tomas Mikolov. 2018. Learning Word Vectors for 157 Languages. In *Proceedings of the International Conference on Language Resources and Evaluation (LREC 2018)*.

Heng Ji and Joel Nothman. 2016. Overview of TAC-KBP2016 Tri-lingual EDL and its impact on end-to-end Cold-Start KBP. In *Proc. Text Analysis Conference (TAC2016)*.

Heng Ji, Joel Nothman, Ben Hachey, and Radu Florian. 2015. Overview of TAC-KBP2015 Tri-lingual Entity Discovery and Linking. In *Proc. Text Analysis Conference (TAC2015)*.

Heng Ji, Joel Nothman, Ben Hachey, et al. 2014. Overview of TAC-KBP2014 Entity Discovery and Linking Tasks. In *Proc. Text Analysis Conference (TAC2014)*, pages 1333–1339.

Heng Ji, Xiaoman Pan, Boliang Zhang, Joel Nothman, James Mayfield, Paul McNamee, Cash Costello, and Sydney Informatics Hub. 2017. Overview of TAC-KBP2017 13 Languages Entity Discovery and Linking. In *Proc. Text Analysis Conference (TAC2017)*.

Guillaume Lample, Miguel Ballesteros, Sandeep Subramanian, Kazuya Kawakami, and Chris Dyer. 2016. Neural Architectures for Named Entity Recognition. In *2016 Annual Conference of the North American Chapter of the Association for Computational Linguistics (NAACL-HLT)*, pages 260–270.

Xuezhe Ma and Eduard Hovy. 2016. End-to-end Sequence Labeling via Bi-directional LSTM-CNNs-CRF. In *Proceedings of the 54th Annual Meeting of the Association for Computational Linguistics (Volume 1: Long Papers)*, pages 1064–1074, Berlin, Germany. Association for Computational Linguistics.

David Nadeau and Satoshi Sekine. 2007. A Survey of Named Entity Recognition and Classification. *Lingvisticae Investigationes*, 30(1):3–26.

Matthew Peters, Mark Neumann, Mohit Iyyer, Matt Gardner, Christopher Clark, Kenton Lee, and Luke Zettlemoyer. 2018. Deep Contextualized Word Representations. In *Proceedings of the 2018 Conference of the North American Chapter of the Association for Computational Linguistics: Human Language Technologies, Volume 1 (Long Papers)*, pages 2227–2237.

Jakub Piskorski, Laska Laskova, Michał Marcińczuk, Lidia Pivovarova, Pavel Přibáň, Josef Steinberger, and Roman Yangarber. 2019. The Second Cross-Lingual Challenge on Recognition, Classification, Lemmatization, and Linking of Named Entities across Slavic Languages. In *Proceedings of the 7th Workshop on Balto-Slavic Natural Language Processing*, Florence, Italy. Association for Computational Linguistics.

Jakub Piskorski, Lidia Pivovarova, Jan Šnajder, Josef Steinberger, Roman Yangarber, et al. 2017. The First Cross-Lingual Challenge on Recognition, Normalization and Matching of Named Entities in Slavic Languages. In *Proceedings of the 6th Workshop on Balto-Slavic Natural Language Processing*. Association for Computational Linguistics.

Nils Reimers and Iryna Gurevych. 2017. Reporting Score Distributions Makes a Difference: Performance Study of LSTM-networks for Sequence Tagging. In *Proceedings of the 2017 Conference on Empirical Methods in Natural Language Processing (EMNLP)*, pages 338–348, Copenhagen, Denmark.

Nils Reimers and Iryna Gurevych. 2019. Alternative Weighting Schemes for ELMo Embeddings. *arXiv preprint arXiv:1904.02954*.

Erik F Tjong Kim Sang and Fien De Meulder. 1837. Introduction to the CoNLL-2003 Shared Task: Language-Independent Named Entity Recognition. In *Development*, volume 922, page 1341.

Beth M. Sundheim. 1995. Overview of Results of the MUC-6 Evaluation. In *Proceedings of the 6th Conference on Message Understanding*, MUC6 '95, pages 13–31, Stroudsburg, PA, USA. Association for Computational Linguistics.

Ashish Vaswani, Noam Shazeer, Niki Parmar, Jakob Uszkoreit, Llion Jones, Aidan N Gomez, Łukasz Kaiser, and Illia Polosukhin. 2017. Attention is all you need. In *Advances in neural information processing systems*, pages 5998–6008.

Vikas Yadav and Steven Bethard. 2018. A Survey on Recent Advances in Named Entity Recognition from Deep Learning Models. In *Proceedings of the 27th International Conference on Computational Linguistics*, pages 2145–2158.

Tuning Multilingual Transformers for Named Entity Recognition on Slavic Languages

Mikhail Arkhipov[*,1] **Maria Trofimova**[*,2] **Yuri Kuratov**[*,3] **Alexey Sorokin**[*,◇,4]

[*]Neural Networks and Deep Learning Laboratory, Moscow Institute of Physics and Technology
[◇]Faculty of Mathematics and Mechanics, Moscow State University
[1]arkhipov.mu@mipt.ru
[2]mary.vikhreva@gmail.com
[3]yurii.kuratov@phystech.edu
[4]alexey.sorokin@list.ru

Abstract

Our paper addresses the problem of multilingual named entity recognition on the material of 4 languages: Russian, Bulgarian, Czech and Polish. We solve this task using the BERT model. We use a hundred languages multilingual model as base for transfer to the mentioned Slavic languages. Unsupervised pre-training of the BERT model on these 4 languages allows to significantly outperform baseline neural approaches and multilingual BERT. Additional improvement is achieved by extending BERT with a word-level CRF layer. Our system was submitted to BSNLP 2019 Shared Task on Multilingual Named Entity Recognition and took the 1st place in 3 competition metrics out of 4 we participated in. We open-sourced NER models and BERT model pre-trained on the four Slavic languages.

1 Introduction

Named Entity Recognition (further, NER) is a task of recognizing named entities in running text, as well as detecting their type. For example, in the sentence *Asia Bibi is from Pakistan*, the following NER classes can be detected: [*Asia Bibi*]PER *is from* [*Pakistan*]LOC. The commonly used BIO-annotation for this sentence is shown in Figure 1.

The recognizer of named entities can be trained on a single target task dataset as any other sequence tagging model. However, it often benefits from additional data from a different source, either labeled or unlabeled, which is known as transfer learning. To enrich the model one can either train it on several tasks simultaneously (Collobert et al., 2011), which makes its word representations more flexible and robust, or pretrain on large amounts of unlabeled data to utilize unlimited sources available in the Web and then fine-tune them on a specific task (Dai and Le, 2015; Howard and Ruder, 2018).

One of the most powerful unsupervised models is BERT (Devlin et al., 2018), which is a multi-layer Transformer trained on the objective of masked words recovery and on the task of next sentence prediction (known also as Natural Language Inference (NLI) task). The original model was trained on vast amounts of data for more than 104 languages which makes its representations useful for almost any task. Our contribution is three-fold: first, multilingual BERT embeddings with a dense layer on the top clearly beat BiLSTM-CRF over FastText embeddings trained on the four target languages. Second, language-specific BERT, trained only on the target languages from Wikipedia and news dump, significantly outperforms the multilingual BERT. Third, we adapt a CRF layer as a a top module over the outputs of the BERT-based model and demonstrate that it improves performance even further.

2 Model Architecture

Our model extends the recently introduced BERT (Devlin et al., 2018) model. BERT itself is a multilayer transformer (Vaswani et al., 2017) which takes as input a sequence of subtokens, obtained using WordPiece tokenization (Wu et al., 2016), and produces a sequence of context-based embeddings of these subtokens. When a word-level task, such as NER, is being solved, the embeddings of word-initial subtokens are passed through a dense layer with softmax activation to produce a probability distribution over output labels. We refer the reader to the original paper, see also Figure 2.

We modify BERT by adding a CRF layer instead of the dense one, which was commonly used in other works on neural sequence labeling (Lample et al., 2016) to ensure output consistency. It also transforms a sequence of word-initial subtoken embeddings to a sequence of probability dis-

89

Proceedings of the 7th Workshop on Balto-Slavic Natural Language Processing, pages 89–93,
Florence, Italy, 2 August 2019. ©2019 Association for Computational Linguistics

$$\begin{array}{cccccc}
\text{Asia} & \text{Bibi} & \text{is} & \text{from} & \text{Pakistan} & . \\
\text{B-PER} & \text{I-PER} & \text{O} & \text{O} & \text{B-LOC} & \text{O}
\end{array}$$

Figure 1: An example of BIO-annotation for tokens.

tributions, however, each prediction depends not only on the current input, but also from the previous one.

3 Transfer from Multilingual Language Model

There are two basic options for building multilingual system: to train a separate model for each language or to use a single multilingual model for all languages. We follow the second approach since it enriches the model with the data from related languages, which was shown to be beneficial in recent studies (Mulcaire et al., 2018).

The original BERT embedder itself is essentially multilingual since it was trained on 104 languages with largest Wikipedias[1]. However, for our four Slavic languages (Polish, Czech, Russian, and Bulgarian) we do not need the full inventory of multilingual subtokens. Moreover, the original WordPiece tokenization may lack Slavic-specific ngrams, which makes the input sequence longer and the training process more problematic and computationally expensive.

Hence we retrain the Slavic BERT on stratified Wikipedia data for Czech, Polish and Bulgarian and News data for Russian. Our main innovation is the training procedure: training BERT from scratch is extremely expensive computationally so we initialize our model with the multilingual one. We rebuild the vocabulary of subword tokens using subword-nmt[2]. When a single Slavic subtoken may consist of multiple multilingual subtokens, we initilalize it as an average of their vectors, resembling (Bojanowski et al., 2016). All weights of transformer layers are initialized using the multilingual weights.

4 Experiment Details

4.1 Target Task and Dataset

The 2019 edition of the Balto-Slavic Natural Language Processing (BSNLP) (Piskorski et al., 2019) shared task aims at recognizing mentions of named entities in web documents in Slavic languages. The input text collection consists of sets of news articles from online media, each collection revolving around a certain entity or an event. The corpus was obtained by crawling the web and parsing the HTML of relevant documents. The 2019 edition of the shared task covers 4 languages (Bulgarian, Czech, Polish, Russian) and focuses on recognition of five types of named entities including persons (`PER`), locations (`LOC`), organizations (`ORG`), events (`EVT`) and products (`PRO`).

The dataset consists of pairs of files: news text and a file with mentions of entities with corresponding tags. There are two groups of documents in the train part of the dataset. Namely, news about Asia Bibi and Brexit. Brexit part is substantially bigger, therefore, we used it for training and Asia Bibi for validation.

4.2 Pre- and Post-processing

We use NLTK (Loper and Bird, 2002) sentence tokenizers for Bulgarian, Polish, and Czech. Due to the absence of Bulgarian sentence tokenizer we apply the English NLTK one instead. For Russian language we use DeepMIPT sentence tokenizer[3]. We replace all UTF separators and space characters with regular spaces. Due to mismatch of BSNLP 2019 data format and common format for tagging tasks we first convert the dataset to BIO format to obtain training data. After getting predictions in BIO format we transform them back to the labeling scheme proposed by Shared Task organizers. This step probably causes extra errors, so we partially correct them using post-processing.

We found that sometimes the model predicts a single opening quote without closing one. So we filter out all single quotation marks in the predicted entities. At the prediction stage we perform inference for a sliding window of two sentences with overlaps to reduce sentence tokenization errors.

The Shared Task also included the entity normalization subtask: for example, the phrase

---

[1] `https://github.com/google-research/bert`

[2] `https://github.com/rsennrich/subword-nmt`

[3] `https://github.com/deepmipt/ru_sentence_tokenizer`

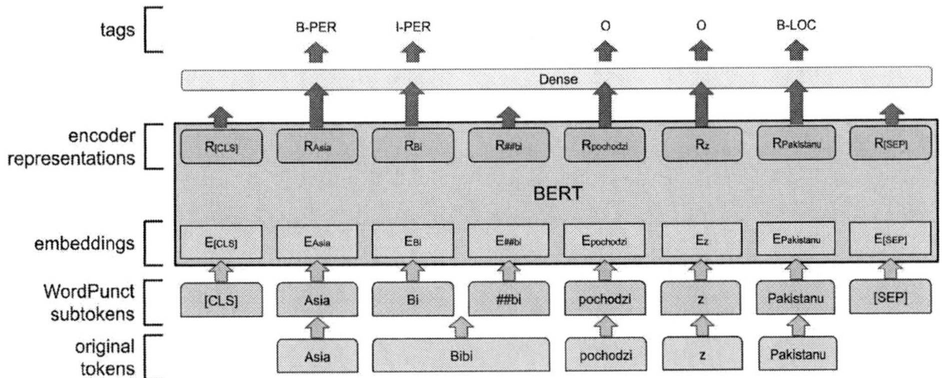

Figure 2: In the figure, E_s and R_s represent the input embedding and the contextual representation of subtoken s, $[CLS]$ is the special symbol to get full input representation, and $[SEP]$ is the special symbol to separate non-consecutive token sequences.

"Верховным судом Пакистана" (Supreme+Ins Court+Ins of Pakistan+Gen) should be "Верховный суд Пакистана". We used the UDPipe 2.3 (Straka et al., 2016) lemmatizers whose output was corrected using language-specific rules. For example, "Пакистана" (Pakistan+Gen) should not be lemmatized because in Russian noun modifiers remain in Genitive.

4.3 Model Parameters

See below parameters of transferring multilingual BERT from to Slavic languages. The training took 9 days with DGX-1 comprising of eight P-100 16Gb GPUs. We train BERT in two stages: train full BERT on sequences with 128 subtokens length and then train only positional embeddings on 512 length sequences. We found that both initialization from multilingual BERT and reassembling of embeddings speed up convergence of the model.

- **Batch size**: `256`
- **Learning rate**: `2e-5`
- **Iterations of full BERT training**: `1M`
- **Iterations of positional embeddings training**: `300k`

Parameters of all BERT-based NER models are:

- **Batch size**: `16`
- **BERT layers learning rate**: `1e-5`
- **Top layers learning rate**: `3e-4`
- **Optimizer**: `AdamOptimizer`
- **Epochs**: `3`

In contrast to original BERT paper (Devlin et al., 2018), we use different learning rates for the task-specific top layers and BERT layers when training BERT-based NER models. We found that this modification leads to faster convergence and higher scores.

We evaluate the model every 10 batches on the whole validation set and chose the one that performed best on it. Despite this strategy being very time consuming, we found it crucial to get extra couple of points. For all experiments we used the span F_1 score for validation.

Our best model used CRF layer and performed moving averages of variables by employing an exponential decay to model parameters.

5 Results

We evaluated Slavic BERT NER model on the BSNLP 2019 Shared Task dataset. The model is compared with two baselines: Bi-LSTM-CRF (Lample et al., 2016) and NER model based on multilingual BERT. For Bi-LSTM-CRF we use FastText word embeddings trained on the same data as Slavic BERT.

Table 1 presents the scores of our model on development set (Asia Bibi documents) when training on Brexit documents. We report a standard span-level F1-score based on the CONLL-2003 evaluation script (Sang and De Meulder, 2003) and three official evaluation metrics(Piskorski et al., 2019)[4]: Relaxed Partial Matching (RPM), Relaxed Exact Matching (REM), and Strict

---

[4] `http://bsnlp.cs.helsinki.fi/` `BSNLP-NER-Evaluator-19.0.1.zip`

Matching (SM). Our system showed top performance in multilingual setting for all mentioned metrics except RPM.

Even without CRF the multilingual BERT model significantly outperforms Bi-LSTM-CRF model. Adding a CRF layer strongly increases performance both for multilingual and Slavic BERT models. Slavic BERT is the top performing model. The error rate of Slavic BERT-CRF is more than one third less than the one of Multilingual BERT baseline.

We experimented with transfer learning from other NER corpora. We used three corpora as source for transfer: Russian NER corpus (Mozharova and Loukachevitch, 2016), Bulgarian BulTreeBank (Simov et al., 2004; Georgiev et al., 2009), and BSNLP 2017 Shared Task dataset(Piskorski et al., 2017)[6] with Czech, Russian, and Polish data. For pre-training we use stratified sample from the concatenated dataset. The set of tags for the task-specific layer includes all tags that occur in at least one dataset. After pre-training we replace the task-specific layer with the one suited for the BSNLP 2019 dataset and train until convergence. We find this approach to be beneficial for models without CRF, however, the CRF-enhanced model without NER pretraining demonstrates slightly higher scores.

Table 2 presents a detailed evaluation report across 4 languages for the top performing Slavic BERT-CRF model. Note that the languages with Latin script (Polish and Czech) demonstrate higher scores than Cyrillic-based ones (Russian and Bulgarian). Low scores for Russian might be caused by the dataset imbalance, since it covers only 7.7% of the whole BSNLP dataset, however, Bulgarian includes 39% but shows even lower quality, especially in terms of recall. We have two explanations: first, incorrect sentence tokenization since we used English sentence tokenizer for Bulgarian (this may explain the skew towards precision). Second, Russian and Bulgarian are much less related than Czech and Polish so they obtain less gain from having additional multilingual data.

5.1 Releasing the Models

We release the best BERT based NER model along with the BERT model pre-trained on the four competition languages[7]. We provide the code for the inference of our NER model as well as for using the pretrained BERT. The BERT model is fully compatible with original BERT repository.

6 Conclusion

We have established that BERT models pretrained on task-specific languages and initialized using the multilingual model, significantly outperform multilingual baselines on the task of Named Entity Recognition. We also demonstrate that adding a word-level CRF layer on the top improves the quality of both extended models. We hope our approach will be useful to fine-tune language-specific BERTs not only for Named Entity Recognition but for other NLP tasks as well.

Acknowledgements

The research was conducted under support of National Technological Initiative Foundation and Sberbank of Russia. Project identifier 0000000007417F630002.

References

Piotr Bojanowski, Edouard Grave, Armand Joulin, and Tomas Mikolov. 2016. Enriching word vectors with subword information. *arXiv preprint arXiv:1607.04606*.

Ronan Collobert, Jason Weston, Léon Bottou, Michael Karlen, Koray Kavukcuoglu, and Pavel Kuksa. 2011. Natural language processing (almost) from scratch. *Journal of machine learning research*, 12(Aug):2493–2537.

Andrew M Dai and Quoc V Le. 2015. Semi-supervised sequence learning. In *Advances in neural information processing systems*, pages 3079–3087.

Jacob Devlin, Ming-Wei Chang, Kenton Lee, and Kristina Toutanova. 2018. Bert: Pre-training of deep bidirectional transformers for language understanding. *arXiv preprint arXiv:1810.04805*.

Georgi Georgiev, Preslav Nakov, Kuzman Ganchev, Petya Osenova, and Kiril Ivanov Simov. 2009. Feature-rich named entity recognition for Bulgarian using conditional random fields. In *RANLP*.

Jeremy Howard and Sebastian Ruder. 2018. Universal language model fine-tuning for text classification. *arXiv preprint arXiv:1801.06146*.

---

[6] `http://bsnlp-2017.cs.helsinki.fi/shared_task.html`

[7] `https://github.com/deepmipt/Slavic-BERT-NER`

Model	Span F_1	RPM	REM	SM
Bi-LSTM-CRF (Lample et al., 2016)	75.8	73.9	72.1	72.3
Multilingual BERT [5]	79.6	77.8	76.1	77.2
Multilingual BERT-CRF	81.4	80.9	79.2	79.6
Slavic BERT	83.5	83.8	82.0	82.2
Slavic BERT-CRF	87.9	85.7 (90.9)	84.3 (86.4)	84.1 (85.7)

Table 1: Metrics for BSNLP on validation set (Asia Bibi documents). Metrics on the test set are in the brackets.

Language	P	R	F_1
cs	93.6	94.7	93.9
ru	88.2	86.6	87.3
bg	90.3	84.3	87.2
pl	93.4	93.1	93.2

Table 2: Precision (P), Recall (R), and F_1 RPM scores of Slavic BERT-CRF model for Czech (cs), Russian (ru), Bulgarian (bg) and Polish (pl) languages.

Guillaume Lample, Miguel Ballesteros, Sandeep Subramanian, Kazuya Kawakami, and Chris Dyer. 2016. Neural architectures for named entity recognition. *arXiv preprint arXiv:1603.01360*.

Edward Loper and Steven Bird. 2002. NLTK: the natural language toolkit. *arXiv preprint cs/0205028*.

Valerie Mozharova and Natalia Loukachevitch. 2016. Two-stage approach in Russian named entity recognition. In *2016 International FRUCT Conference on Intelligence, Social Media and Web (ISMW FRUCT)*, pages 1–6. IEEE.

Phoebe Mulcaire, Swabha Swayamdipta, and Noah Smith. 2018. Polyglot semantic role labeling. *arXiv preprint arXiv:1805.11598*.

Jakub Piskorski, Laska Laskova, Michał Marcińczuk, Lidia Pivovarova, Pavel Přibáň, Josef Steinberger, and Roman Yangarber. 2019. The second cross-lingual challenge on recognition, classification, lemmatization, and linking of named entities across Slavic languages. In *Proceedings of the 7th Workshop on Balto-Slavic Natural Language Processing*, Florence, Italy. Association for Computational Linguistics.

Jakub Piskorski, Lidia Pivovarova, Jan Šnajder, Josef Steinberger, and Roman Yangarber. 2017. The first cross-lingual challenge on recognition, normalization, and matching of named entities in Slavic languages. In *Proceedings of the 6th Workshop on Balto-Slavic Natural Language Processing*, pages 76–85, Valencia, Spain. Association for Computational Linguistics.

Erik F Sang and Fien De Meulder. 2003. Introduction to the CoNLL-2003 shared task: Language-independent named entity recognition. *arXiv preprint cs/0306050*.

Kiril Simov, Petya Osenova, Sia Kolkovska, Elisaveta Balabanova, and Dimitar Doikoff. 2004. A language resources infrastructure for Bulgarian. In *Proceedings of the Fourth International Conference on Language Resources and Evaluation (LREC'04)*, Lisbon, Portugal. European Language Resources Association (ELRA).

Milan Straka, Jan Hajic, and Jana Straková. 2016. UDPipe: Trainable pipeline for processing CoNLL-U files performing tokenization, morphological analysis, POS tagging and parsing. In *LREC*.

Ashish Vaswani, Noam Shazeer, Niki Parmar, Jakob Uszkoreit, Llion Jones, Aidan N Gomez, Łukasz Kaiser, and Illia Polosukhin. 2017. Attention is all you need. In *Advances in neural information processing systems*, pages 5998–6008.

Yonghui Wu, Mike Schuster, Zhifeng Chen, Quoc V. Le, Mohammad Norouzi, Wolfgang Macherey, Maxim Krikun, Yuan Cao, Qin Gao, Klaus Macherey, Jeff Klingner, Apurva Shah, Melvin Johnson, Xiaobing Liu, Lukasz Kaiser, Stephan Gouws, Yoshikiyo Kato, Taku Kudo, Hideto Kazawa, Keith Stevens, George Kurian, Nishant Patil, Wei Wang, Cliff Young, Jason Smith, Jason Riesa, Alex Rudnick, Oriol Vinyals, Greg Corrado, Macduff Hughes, and Jeffrey Dean. 2016. Google's neural machine translation system: Bridging the gap between human and machine translation. *CoRR*, abs/1609.08144.

Multilingual Named Entity Recognition Using Pretrained Embeddings, Attention Mechanism and NCRF

Anton A. Emelyanov
MIPT, Sberbank
Moscow, Russia
`login-const@mail.ru`

Ekaterina Artemova
National Research University
Higher School of Economics
echernyak@hse.ru
`echernyak@hse.ru`

Abstract

In this paper we tackle multilingual named entity recognition task. We use the BERT Language Model as embeddings with bidirectional recurrent network, attention, and NCRF on the top. We apply multilingual BERT only as embedder without any fine-tuning. We test out model on the dataset of the BSNLP shared task, which consists of texts in Bulgarian, Czech, Polish and Russian languages.

1 Introduction

Sequence labeling is one of the most fundamental NLP models, which is used for many tasks such as named entity recognition (NER), chunking, word segmentation and part-of-speech (POS) tagging. It has been traditionally investigated using statistical approaches (Lafferty et al., 2001), where conditional random fields (CRF) (Lafferty et al., 2001) has been proven to be an effective framework, by taking discrete features as the representation of input sequence (Sathiya and Sellamanickam, 2007). With the advances of deep learning, neural sequence labeling models have achieved state-of-the-art results for many tasks (Peters et al., 2017).

For the purpose of this paper, we consider neural network solution for multilingual named entity recognition for Bulgarian, Czech, Polish and Russian languages for the BSNLP 2019 Shared Task (Piskorski et al., 2019). Our solution is based on BERT language model (Devlin et al., 2018), use bidirectional LSTM (Hochreiter and Schmidhuber, 1996), Multi-Head attention (Vaswani et al., 2017), NCRFpp (Yang and Zhang, 2018) (being neural network version of CRF++framework for sequence labelling) and Pooling Classifier (for language classification) on the top as additional information.

2 Task Description

2.1 Data Format

The data consists of raw documents and the annotations, separately provided by the organizers. Each annotation contains a set of extracted entities and their types without duplication. We convert each raw document and corresponding annotations to labeled sequence and predict named entity label for each token in the input sentence. The documents are categorized into topics. There are two topics in the dataset released first: named "brexit" and "asia_bibi".

2.2 Tasks

The BSNLP Shared Task has three parts (Piskorski et al., 2019):

1. Named Entity Mention Detection and Classification;

2. Name Lemmatization;

3. Cross-lingual entity Matching.

For more details about the dataset and the task refer to the description on the web page[1]. We focused on Named Entity Mention Detection (Named Entity Recognition) in this work.

3 System Description

We propose modeling the task as both sequence labeling and language classification jointly with a neural architecture to learn additional information about text. The model consists of one encoder, which on its own is build from the pretrained multilingual BERT model, followed by several trainable layers and two decoders. While the first decoder generates output tags, the second decoder

---

[1]Full BSNLP Shared Task description available at http://bsnlp.cs.helsinki.fi/shared_task.html.

Proceedings of the 7th Workshop on Balto-Slavic Natural Language Processing, pages 94–99,
Florence, Italy, 2 August 2019. ©2019 Association for Computational Linguistics

identifies the language of the input sentence[2]. The system architecture is presented in Figure 1 and consists of seven parts:

1. BERT Embedder as pretrained multilingual language model;

2. Weighted aggregation of BERT output;

3. Recurrent BiLSTM layer to be trained for the NER task;

4. Multi-Head attention to take shorter dependencies between words into account;

5. linear layer as the head of the encoder part;

6. NCRF++ inference layer for decoding, i.e. final sequence labelling;

7. Concatenation operation of Max Pooling, Average Pooling and last output of Multi-Head attention layer, later passed to linear layer for classification as a second decoder for language identification.

3.1 Neural Network Architecture

3.1.1 BERT Embedder

The BERT embeddings layer contains Google's original implementation of multilingual BERT language model. Each sentence is preprocessed as described in BERT paper (Devlin et al., 2018):

1. Process input text sequence to WordPiece embeddings (Wu and Mike Schuster, 2016) with a 30,000 token vocabulary and pad to 512 tokens.

2. Add first special BERT token marked "[CLS]".

3. Mark all tokens as members of part "A" of the input sequence.

But instead of BERT's original paper (Devlin et al., 2018) we keep "B" ("Begin") prefix for labels and do a prediction for "X" labels on training stage. BERT neural network is used only to embed input text and don't fine-tune on the training stage. We freeze all layers except dropout here, that decreases overfitting.

We take hidden outputs from all BERT layers as the output of this part of the neural network and pass to the next level of the neural network. So the shape of output is 12×768 for each token of 512 length's padded input sequence.

3.1.2 BERT Weighting

Here we sum all of BERT hidden outputs from previous part:

$$o_i = \gamma \times \sum_{i=0}^{m-1} b_i s_i \qquad (1)$$

where

- o_i is output vector of size 768;

- $m = 12$ is the number hidden layers in BERT;

- b_i is output from i BERT hidden layer;

- γ and s_i is trainable task specific parameters.

As we do not fine-tune BERT, we should adapt its outputs for our specific sequence labeling task. The suggested weighting approach is similar to ELMo (Peters et al., 2018), with a lower number of weighting vectors parameters s_i. This approach can help to learn importance of each BERT output layer for this task and and network doesn't lose too much information about text, that was stored in all BERT outputs.

3.1.3 Recurrent Part

This part contains two LSTM networks for forward and backward passes with 512 hidden units so that the output representation dim is 1024 for each token. We use a recurrent layer for learning dependencies between tokens in an input sequence (Hochreiter and Schmidhuber, 1996).

3.1.4 Multi-Head Attention

After applying the recurrent layer, we use Self-attention mechanism to learn any other dependencies in a sequence for each token. This can be denoted as $D(d_h|S)$, where D is some hidden dependency; d_h is the h head of attention, and S is all sequence. each head can learn its dependencies such as morphological, syntactic or semantic relationships between words (tokens). Presumably, dependencies may look as shown at Figure 2. Also, mechanism attention can compensate limitations of the recurrent layer when working with long sequences (Bahdanau et al., 2015). In our

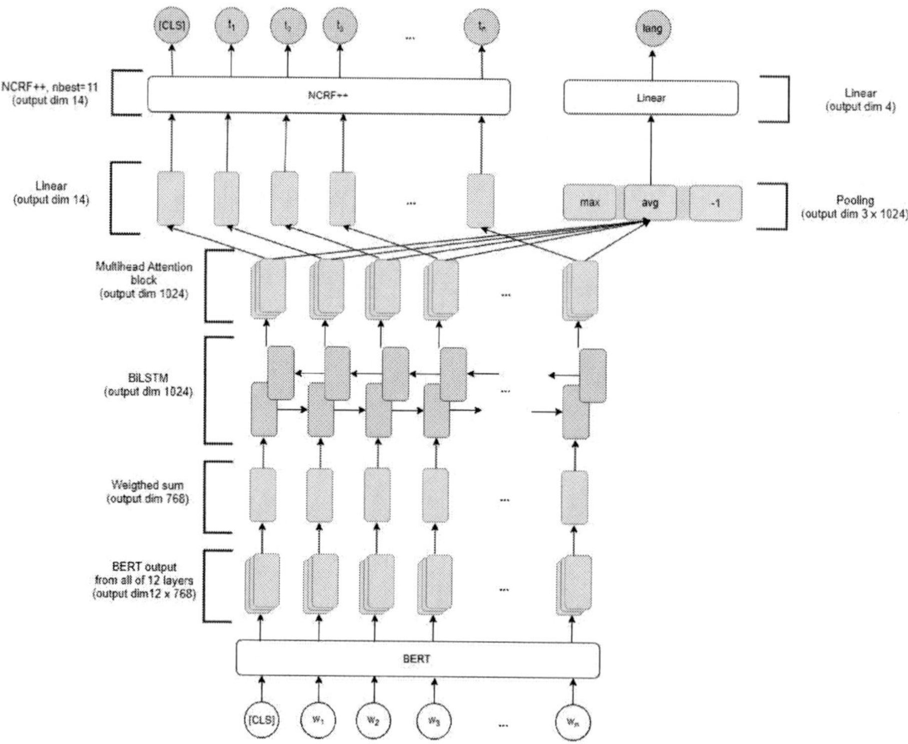

Figure 1: The system architecture

architecture, we use multihead-attention block as proposed in the paper "attention is all you need" (Vaswani et al., 2017). We took 6 heads and value and key dim 64.

3.1.5 Inference for NER Task

After the input sequence was encoded, we achieve the final representation of each token in a sequence. This representation is passed to Linear layer with $tanh$ activation function and gets a vector with 14 dim, that equals to the number of entities labels (include supporting labels "pad" and "[CLS]"). The inference layer takes the extracted token sequence representations as features and assigns labels to the token sequence. As the inference layer, we use Neural CRF++ layer instead of vanilla CRF. That captures label dependencies by adding transition scores between neighboring labels. NCRF++ supports CRF trained with the sentence-level maximum log-likelihood loss. During the decoding process, the Viterbi algorithm is used to search the label sequence with the highest probability. But also, NCRF++ extends the decoding algorithm with the support of $nbest$ output (Yang and Zhang, 2018). We chose the $nbest$ parameter equal to 11, because we have 11 meaning-ful labels. In this decision we followed the original article (Yang and Zhang, 2018).

3.1.6 Inference for Language Classification

We train our system for language classification. For the classification inference, we use Pooling Linear Classifier block as proposed in ULMFiT paper (Howard and Ruder, 2018). We pass output sequence representation H from Multihead-attention part to different Poolings and concat (as shown in Figure 1):

$$h_c = [h_0, maxpool(H), meanpool(H)] \quad (2)$$

where [] is concatenation;

h_0 is first output significant vector of Multihead-attention part (which does have "[CLS]" label).

The result of concat Pooling (3×1024) is passed to Linear layer, and that predicts probability for four language classes (Bulgarian, Czech, Polish and Russian).

3.2 Postprocessing Prediction

After getting labels for the sequence of WordPiece tokens, we should convert prediction to word level labels extraction named entities. Each WordPiece token in the word is matched with neural network label prediction. We use ensemble classifier on labels by count all predicted labels for one word except "X" and select label for a word with the higher number of votes.

For final prediction we unite token's sequences which have not "O" ("Other") label to spans and write to result of entities set.

4 Training the System

4.1 Data Conversion

On the training stage we divide the input data into two parts: the training set (named "brexit") and development set (named "asia_bibi"). Hence we train the system on one topic and evaluate the system on another topic. Because the input contains raw text and annotation, but BERT take words sequence as input, we convert data to word level IOB markup (Ramshaw and Marcus, 1995). After that, each word was tokenized by WordPiece tokenizer and word label matched with IOBX labels.

On the prediction stage result, labels were received by voice classifier. After this, we transform word predictions to spans markup. The results of develop evaluation stage described in Table 1.

After evaluation stage we train our network on all input data ("brexit" and "asia_bibi") to make final predictions on the blind test set.

4.2 Training Procedure

The proposed neural network was trained with joint loss:

$$\mathcal{L} = \mathcal{L}_{SL} + \mathcal{L}_{clf} \tag{3}$$

where $\mathcal{L}_{SL}$ is maximum log-likelihood loss (Yang and Zhang, 2018) for the sequence labeling task and $\mathcal{L}_{clf}$ is Cross Entropy Loss for the language classification.

We use Adam with a learning rate of $1e - 4$, $\beta_1 = 0.8$, $\beta_2 = 0.9$, $L2$ weight decay of 0.01, learning rate warm up, and linear decay of the learning rate. Also, gradient clipping was applied for weights with $clip = 1.0$.

Training of proposed neural network architecture was performed on one GPU with the batch size equal to 16, the number of epochs equal to 150, but stopped at epoch number 80 because the loss function has ceased to decrease. The model required only around 3 GB of memory instead of fine-tuning all BERT model, which would have required more than 8 GB GPU memory. All training procedure lasted around five hours on one GPU with the evaluation of development set on each epoch.

The final model was trained on unit of training and development datasets.

5 Results and Discussion

5.1 Evaluation Results

As baseline for BSNLP Shared Task we use a simple CRF tagger and obtain exact word level f1-score 0.372 on the development dataset.

Finally we use joint model for named entity recognition task and language classification task because the model without part of the classification gave a result by several percent less than proposed final model. This means that the joint model pays attention to a specific language morphology and some connections between words within one language.

label	precision	recall	f1-score
PER	0.733	0.725	0.729
PRO	0.384	0.547	0.451
EVT	0.385	0.370	0.377
LOC	0.648	0.872	0.744
ORG	0.550	0.630	0.587
avg/total	0.540	0.629	0.578

Table 1: Evaluation metrics on development dataset

For proposed neural network architecture the evaluation of the training stage was produced on development dataset. Table 1 shows span-level metrics precision, recall, and f1-measure. For development set, we obtained the following scores: language classification quality (f1-score): 0.998 and Multilingual Named Entity Recognition quality (f1-score): 0.70 for exact word level matching and 0.578 for exact full entities matching. Also we train model without language classification, which resulted in f1-score equal to 0.66 . This confirms the impact of language classification. Our model significantly outperforms the CRF baseline.

The evaluation of test dataset presented in Table 2 (relaxed partial matching) and Table 2 (relaxed exact matching) is measured by the BSNLP Shared Task organizers.

Relaxed partial matching

label	precision	recall	f1-score
PER	0.84955	0.87119	0.86023
LOC	0.77526	0.93197	0.84642
ORG	0.62642	0.87170	0.72898
PRO	0.42079	0.81416	0.55483
EVT	0.24074	0.15476	0.18841
All	0.90142	0.69917	0.78752

Relaxed exact matching

label	precision	recall	f1-score
PER	0.76835	0.74023	0.73317
LOC	0.87747	0.73014	0.79705
ORG	0.71390	0.52295	0.60369
PRO	0.34439	0.18506	0.24075
EVT	0.10714	0.16667	0.13043
All	0.56225	0.46901	0.50102

Table 2: Evaluation metrics on test dataset

5.2 Error Analysis

First of all, we face some errors with converting from origin data format (raw and annotations) to word markup and back to origin format after predictions were made. This problems stand for extra spaces, bad Unicode symbols and symbols, absent in WordPiece vocabulary. Other errors are caused by neural network prediction failures. The model turns to be overfitted on the negative label "O" so that there are many false positives in the prediction. Lastly, the infrequent labels "PRO" and "EVT" are often confused.

6 Related Work

The related work has several parts: firstly, our work follows the recent trend of using pretrained neural languages models, such as (Devlin et al., 2018; Peters et al., 2018; Howard and Ruder, 2018). The main difference between original BERT's approach for named entity recognition task (Devlin et al., 2018) we use its only as input embeddings of sequence without fine-tuning. From ELMo paper (Peters et al., 2018) we use weighting approach for different outputs from network and getting final representation of sequence. From ULMFiT work we took part which is related to the final decoding for classification (Pooling Classifier) without proposed language model (Howard and Ruder, 2018). Secondly we model the task of NER as a joint sequence labeling and classification task following other joint architec-

tures (Liu and Lane, 2016; Nguyen et al., 2016).

7 Conclusion and Future Work

We have proposed neural network architecture that solves Multilingual Named Entity Recognition without any additional labeled data for Bulgarian, Czech, Polish and Russian languages. This implementation allows to train the model even on a modern personal computer with GPU. This neural network architecture can be used for other tasks, that can be reformulated as a sequence labeling task for any other language.

As the next steps in the study of the underlying architecture, we can increase or decrease the number of units on each layer or remove the recurrent layer or multihead-attention layer. As improvements of the system, we can fine-tune BERT embeddings and put additional layers on top of BERT or pass other modern language models as an input.

Acknowledgments

The article was prepared within the framework of the HSE University Basic Research Program and funded by the Russian Academic Excellence Project "5-100". We are thankful to the Muppets and to the BSNLP shared task organizers.

References

Dzmitry Bahdanau, Kyunghyun Cho, and Yoshua Bengio. 2015. Neural Machine Translation by Jointly Learning to Align and Translate. *CoRR*, abs/1409.0473.

Jacob Devlin, Ming-Wei Chang, Kenton Lee, and Kristina Toutanova. 2018. Bert: Pre-training of Deep Bidirectional Transformers for Language Understanding. In *NAACL-HLT*.

Sepp Hochreiter and Jürgen Schmidhuber. 1996. Lstm can Solve Hard Long Time Lag Problems. In *NIPS*.

Jeremy Howard and Sebastian Ruder. 2018. Universal Language Model Fine-tuning for Text Classification. In *ACL*.

John D. Lafferty, Andrew McCallum, and Fernando Pereira. 2001. Conditional Random Fields: Probabilistic Models for Segmenting and Labeling Sequence Data. In *ICML*.

Bing Liu and Ian Lane. 2016. Attention-Based Recurrent Neural Network Models for Joint Intent Detection and Slot Filling. In *INTERSPEECH*.

Thien Huu Nguyen, Kyunghyun Cho, and Ralph Grishman. 2016. Joint event extraction via recurrent neural networks. In *Proceedings of the 2016 Conference of the North American Chapter of the Association for Computational Linguistics: Human Language Technologies*, page 00309, San Diego, California. Association for Computational Linguistics.

Matthew E. Peters, Waleed Ammar, Chandra Bhagavatula, and Russell Power. 2017. Semi-supervised sequence tagging with bidirectional language models. In *ACL*.

Matthew E. Peters, Mark Neumann, Mohit Iyyer, Matt Gardner, Christopher Clark, Kenton Lee, and Luke S. Zettlemoyer. 2018. Deep contextualized word representations. In *NAACL-HLT*.

Jakub Piskorski, Laska Laskova, Micha Marciczuk, Lidia Pivovarova, Pavel Pib, Josef Steinberger, and Roman Yangarber. 2019. The second cross-lingual challenge on recognition, classification, lemmatization, and linking of named entities across Slavic languages. In *Proceedings of the 7th Workshop on Balto-Slavic Natural Language Processing*, Florence, Italy. Association for Computational Linguistics.

Lance A. Ramshaw and Mitchell P. Marcus. 1995. Text Chunking using Transformation-Based Learning. *CoRR*, cmp-lg/9505040.

Keerthi Sathiya and Sundararajan Sellamanickam. 2007. *Crf versus svm-struct for sequence labeling*, volume 1. Yahoo Research Technical Report.

Ashish Vaswani, Noam Shazeer, Niki Parmar, Jakob Uszkoreit, Llion Jones, Aidan N. Gomez, Lukasz Kaiser, and Illia Polosukhin. 2017. Attention Is All You Need. In *NIPS*.

Yonghui Wu and Quoc VLe Mohammad Norouzi Wolfgang Macherey Maxim Krikun Yuan Cao Qin Gao Klaus Macherey Mike Schuster, Zhifeng Chen. 2016. *Googles neural machine translation system: Bridging the gap between human and machine translation*, volume arXiv:1609.08144.

Jie Yang and Yue Zhang. 2018. Ncrf++: An Open-source Neural Sequence Labeling Toolkit. In *ACL*.

JRC TMA-CC
Slavic Named Entity Recognition and Linking
Participation in the BSNLP-2019 shared task

Guillaume Jacquet   Jakub Piskorski   Hristo Tanev   Ralf Steinberger
Joint Research Centre
European Commission
Ispra, Italy
`{fname.lname}@ec.europa.eu`

Abstract

We report on the participation of the JRC *Text Mining and Analysis Competence Centre* (TMA-CC) in the BSNLP-2019 Shared Task, which focuses on named-entity recognition, lemmatisation and cross-lingual linking. We propose a hybrid system combining a rule-based approach and light ML techniques. We use multilingual lexical resources such as JRC-NAMES and BABELNET together with a named entity guesser to recognise names. In a second step, we combine known names with wild cards to increase recognition recall by also capturing inflection variants. In a third step, we increase precision by filtering these name candidates with automatically learnt inflection patterns derived from name occurrences in large news article collections. Our major requirement is to achieve high precision. We achieved an average of 65% F-measure with 93% precision on the four languages.

1   Introduction

Multilingual Named Entity Recognition (NER) and the grounding of names to real-world entities is an essential component of the JRC TMA-CC's[1] large-scale, multi-annual and highly multilingual media monitoring effort called *Europe Media Monitor - EMM*[2] (Steinberger et al., 2017).

EMM has been analysing online news articles since 2003, reaching a current average of 320K articles per day from about 12K news sources in up to 70 languages. EMM clusters related news, categorises them into thousands of categories, detects breaking news and tracks topics over short periods of time. For a subset of about two dozen languages, EMM recognises and disambiguates entity mentions. The EMM-NER component constitutes the backbone of our submissions to the BSNLP-2019 Shared Task (Piskorski et al., 2019).

2   Approach

We submitted four system instance results, all of which are based on our in-house NER system *NERONE* (Ehrmann et al., 2017; Steinberger et al., 2015), which we describe first.

NERONE identifies and disambiguates mentions of persons, organisations, locations, events and products by first looking up *known names* and by then guessing new names. The list of *known names* contains about 1.2 million names. 600 000 unique entities have an average of 2 variants, the biggest number of variants for one entity being 6 200. The guessing of new names is based on large lexical resources (1.5 million entries) and ca 200 language-agnostic recognition patterns using the finite-state formalism described in (Piskorski, 2007). NERONE continuously updates the list of *known names*. Newly guessed names can become part of the list of *known names* if they are considered reliable enough. Reliability is mostly based on the frequency of the newly guessed name, the number of languages where it appears, the number of sources where it appears. Once eligible it is automatically added as a new known name or merged as a new variant of an existing name, including across languages and scripts (Steinberger et al., 2011). On average, 150 new variants and new names are automatically added daily to the list of *known names*. This list of known names (JRC-NAMES), is distributed publicly, together with the name variants, the titles, the language and date when it was found (Ehrmann et al., 2017). Based on previous work focused on multi-word entities (Jacquet et al., 2019), we furthermore added 2.1 million names and variants of the relevant entity

---

[1] `https://ec.europa.eu/jrc/en/text-mining-and-analysis`
[2] `http://emm.newsbrief.eu`

Proceedings of the 7th Workshop on Balto-Slavic Natural Language Processing, pages 100–104,
Florence, Italy, 2 August 2019. ©2019 Association for Computational Linguistics

categories from BabelNet (Navigli and Ponzetto, 2012). In the disambiguation steps, names that are part of a larger name are ignored (e.g. *John F Kennedy Airport*) and location names are disregarded if a homographic entity name of another category exists (e.g. Мартин (*Martin*) which could be both a small city in Slovakia and a person name).

In the remaining part of this Section we describe the four approaches explored, all of which are built on top of *NERONE*, which is known to have high precision, but low recall. We modified it to extend the recall, knowing that the precision will fall (*NERONE* with wildcards), then tried different levels of filtering to optimise the balance between precision and recall.

It is important to emphasise at this point that the four NER approaches presented in this paper are JRC's contribution (as one of the co-organisers of the Shared Task) to the provision of 'good' baseline systems to compare against.

2.1 JRC-TMA-CC-1: *NERONE*

The JRC-TMA-CC-1 variant uses *NERONE* as described before. We only did a slight adaptation for the location recognition. As our list of known location names (LOC), derived from GeoNames[3] is very short for some languages, we merged the LOC lists for the Cyrillic script languages Russian, Bulgarian, Bosnian, Macedonian and Serbian and we did the same for the Latin script west Slavic languages Polish, Czech and Slovak. It corresponds to the update of 200 000 entries among the existing 1.3 million location name resource.

2.2 JRC-TMA-CC-2: *NERONE* + wildcards

In addition to the system used in JRC-TMA-CC-1, we added wildcards to each name part of all entity types except for the GeoNames-derived LOC lists. The objective is to increase Recall by also capturing morphological variants of the known names. During morphological inflection, suffixes can be added to the base form of the name (e.g. *Andrej Babiš* inflected as *Andrejem Babišem*), but it also happens that final letters get replaced (suffix replacement, e.g. *Garbiňe Muguruzaová* inflected as *Garbiňe Muguruzaovou*). We therefore removed the last two letters of each name part and added a wildcard (*Garbiňe Muguruzaová* would become *Garbi% Muguruzao%*). To avoid over-

---

[3] https://www.geonames.org/

generating wildcard patterns, we did not remove letters from name parts that are three letters or shorter and we only removed one letter in four-letter words. Note that we use the term 'suffix' not in the morphological sense, but simply to denote the final letters of a name string.

2.3 JRC-TMA-CC-3: *NERONE* + wildcards and suffix filtering

Due to the vast number of different names, of which some can also be a string subset of longer names, the wildcards do occasionally overgenerate, i.e. capture names that are not variants, but names in their own right (e.g. *Josef Mill* would create the wildcard pattern *Jos% Mil%* which would wrongly match *Josefa Miller* as a possible inflection of *Josef Mill*). Submission JRC-TMA-CC-3 is based on the previous method, but here we aim to reduce such false positives (increase Precision) by filtering the names matched with the wildcards against a list of the more frequent suffix replacement rules.

To create such suffix replacement rules, we first searched in an average of 2 million news articles per language[4] for all our known names with the wildcard described in JRC-TMA-CC-2 to gather possible inflections of names, resulting in variant frequency lists for each name (see Table 1 for examples of collected variants). We then applied the following algorithm:

1. We hypothesise that the main form according to BabelNet and JRC Names is the main form. We have found a good empirical evidence this is true.

2. Tokenise all the names

3. For each token from the main variant Tm find the corresponding token from one of the derivations Td.

4. Find the common parts between the token Tm and Td. For example (cf. first case in Table 1), the common part between *Kotleby* and *Kotleba* is *Kotleb*.

5. Find the difference between the two forms and produce a list of candidate suffix rules,

---

[4] EMM collects daily meta-data from thousands of news articles, including article URLs. Exploiting these URLs, we collected (for the still active URLs) one year of articles for each of the four analysed languages.

Known name	potential variant list	freq
Mariana Kotleby	*Mariana Kotleby*	82
	Marian Kotleba	64
	Mariana Kotlebu	23
	Marianem Kotlebou	22
Garbin Muguruza	*Garbiňe Muguruzaovou*	92
	Garbiňe Muguruzaová	44
	Garbiňe Muguruzaové	22
	Garbině Muguruzaovou	8
	Garbiňe Muguruzaovou	7
Andrej Babiš	*Andrej Babiš*	29934
	Andreje Babiše	20470
	Andrej Babi	5935
	Andreje Babie	4271
	Andrejem Babišem	3979
Harvey Weinstein	*Harveyho Weinsteina*	278
	Harvey Weinstein	162
	Harveymu Weinsteinovi	20
	Harvey Weinsteinem	10
	Harvey Weinsteinovi	10
Energetický a průmyslový holding	*Energetický a průmyslový holding*	169
	Energetického a průmyslového holdingu	155
	Energetickému a průmyslovému holdingu	14
	Energetickým a průmyslovým holdingem	6
	Energetickém a průmyslovém holdingu	5

Table 1: Example of variant lists extracted from news.

endings	inflections	ratio
-uza	uzaová	0.4000
	uzaovou	0.3000
	uzaové	0.2000
-za	z	0.1125
	ze	0.1029
	zem	0.0386
-a	u	0.0696
	em	0.0657
	y	0.0602
-rej	reje	0.2656
	rejem	0.0938
	reji	0.0938
-ey	eyho	0.1366
	eym	0.0478
	y	0.0260
-cky	cký	0.2083
	ckého	0.1667
	ckém	0.1667

Table 2: Example of inflection probabilities

in this last case the rules will look like $y \rightarrow a$; $by \rightarrow ba$; $eby \rightarrow eba$.

6. In the case when the first token is completely contained in the second one, like *Marian* and *Mariana*, we extract a rule by taking the last two letters from the main form and the last corresponding ending from the derivative form $an \rightarrow ana$.

7. The inflection rules are gathered and we calculate various statistics. For example, the conditional probability that the first part of the rule is transformed into the second part of the rule. The statistics were collected from the list of word variants

Table 2 shows some examples of inflection rules obtained with this algorithm. This list was then used to filter acceptable inflections according to the initial base form: only those suffix replacement rules that had a probability higher than 0.01 were considered valid suffixes. If a name inflection found belonged to the eliminated low-frequency suffix replacement rules, it was not considered.

2.4 JRC-TMA-CC-4: *NERONE* + wildcards and less strict suffix filtering

This variant is identical to JRC-TMA-CC-3 with a lower threshold for filtering set to 0.001.

3 Results

While the Shared Task was subdivided into three subtasks, namely, Entity Recognition, Normalisation and Linking, our contribution focused less on the normalisation subtask and more on recognition, with a priority on precision scores and on cross-lingual entity-linking. Table 3 shows the results obtained by the four systems we submitted. The scores reported only refer to F-measure scores. For each evaluation category and each language, the bold score corresponds to the highest obtained F-measure. As a first observation, according to the description of the four systems, we were expecting the JRC-TMA-CC-1 system to obtain high precision but low recall, the JRC-TMA-CC-2 system to obtain high recall but low precision, and JRC-TMA-CC-3 and JRC-TMA-CC-4 to filter the too noisy recognition from JRC-TMA-CC-2 and deliver good precision/recall balance, therefore better F-measure. This is what one could observe when evaluating on the training set for the four languages. On the test set, one can observe the same phenomenon for Polish and Bulgarian, both for the relaxed partial and strict recognition, however, it applies to a smaller extent for Russian on the *Nord-Stream* topic and Czech on the *Ryanair* topic. By checking the error logs, these differences appear to be due to mis-recognition of key entities for these specific topics. Additionally to the F-measure scores reported in Table 3, the high precision scores we obtained for all languages are worth mentioning . We obtained best precision ranking compare to the other shared task participants for all four languages. As an average for both topics, our JRC-TMA-CC-4 system obtained for Czech, Russian, Bulgarian and Polish a precision of, respectively, 94.4%, 90.2%, 95.4%, 93.7% (at a price of lower recall). This precision is also quite well-distributed across entity types. For

AVERAGE ON BOTH TOPICS			Language			
Phase	*Metric*	system	cs	ru	bg	pl
Recognition	Relaxed Partial	JRC-TMA-CC-1	**62.0**	73.6	73.2	56.13
		JRC-TMA-CC-2	61.6	72.0	72.4	54.8
		JRC-TMA-CC-3	58.0	**73.7**	73.8	50.9
		JRC-TMA-CC-4	58.0	73.5	**74.2**	**57.4**
	Relaxed Exact	JRC-TMA-CC-1	**55.6**	**68.7**	67.3	48.6
		JRC-TMA-CC-2	54.3	66.2	66.7	45.5
		JRC-TMA-CC-3	55.3	68.2	67.6	48.4
		JRC-TMA-CC-4	55.3	68.0	**67.9**	**49.6**
	Strict	JRC-TMA-CC-1	47.6	59.9	63.9	41.8
		JRC-TMA-CC-2	49.9	60.4	64.4	44.0
		JRC-TMA-CC-3	**50.0**	**60.6**	64.6	44.6
		JRC-TMA-CC-4	**50.0**	60.5	**65.2**	**45.9**
Entity linking	Single language	JRC-TMA-CC-1	29.8	41.8	51.8	21.9
		JRC-TMA-CC-2	**35.9**	**42.9**	51.5	**30.3**
		JRC-TMA-CC-3	33.5	41.9	51.5	25.8
		JRC-TMA-CC-4	33.9	41.8	**52.4**	28.2
	Cross-lingual	JRC-TMA-CC-1	24.7			
		JRC-TMA-CC-2	**29.7**			
		JRC-TMA-CC-3	26.4			
		JRC-TMA-CC-4	27.3			

Table 3: Evaluation results (F-scores) across all scenarios and languages on the test data.

PER, LOC, ORG, PRO and EVT, we respectively obtained 92.4%, 95.9%, 89.2%, 96.0% and 83.3%. The fact that we were able to improve our existing system with quite a simple adaptation is promising and encourages us to push further this process of name ending/inflection filtering. Concerning the entity-linking evaluation, Table 3 shows results for each single language and, more importantly, for cross-lingual linking. Despite the low recall of our four systems compare to other teams, our F-measure scores are ranked 2nd for both single language and cross-lingual linking. We will have to analyse the error logs in more detail to investigate possible improvements. Also, we observe that in almost all languages and topics, the best results are obtained by the JRC-TMA-CC-2 system, which is most likely correlated to a high recall.

4 Related Work

NER systems are often the first step in event detection, question answering, information retrieval, co-reference resolution, topic modelling, etc. The first NER task was organised by (Grishman and Sundheim, 1996) in the Sixth Message Understanding Conference. Early NER systems were based on handcrafted rules (Chiticariu et al., 2010), lexicons, orthographic features and ontologies. These systems were followed by NER systems based on feature-engineering and machine learning (Nadeau and Sekine, 2007).

There are not many systems for NER that address inflected languages like the Slavic ones. Among the others, (Piskorski et al., 2007) tackled the task of matching morphological variants of names in Polish text by optimising string similar-ity calculations for inflections. (Pajzs et al., 2014) experimented with name lemmatisation and inflection variant generation in the highly inflected and agglutinative language Hungarian. (Gareev et al., 2013) describes NER for the highly inflective Russian language. The first edition of the Shared Task on Slavic NER was organised in the context of BSNLP 2017 (Piskorski et al., 2017)

5 Conclusions and Future Work

We presented lightweight method to improve the performance of our in-house NER system NERONE for the recognition and linking of inflected named entities in inflected languages without delving into the morphological rules and proper name declension paradigms of each of the languages. We learnt potential name inflection patterns by searching for suffix variants of known names in large volumes of text. We then changed the known-name lookup part of NERONE by replacing the last letters of each name with wildcards to capture inflectional variants. We used the newly captured potential name inflections to reduce the number of wrong wildcard matches. As expected, we achieved good precision scores, 94.4%, 90.2%, 95.4%, 93.7% respectively for Czech, Russian, Bulgarian and Polish and unbalanced F-measures, from too low (58.0% and 57.4% for Czech and Polish) to reasonably good (73.5% and 74.2% for Russian and Bulgarian). One of the main drive of developing the described extension of NERONE was to contribute to the provision of 'good' baseline systems for the BSNLP-2019 Shared Task.

The proposed systems could be improved in many ways, including, i.a.: (a) expansion of the set of inflection patterns to guess *new* names, (b) integration of a classifier to distinguish the reading of entities that can designate different entity types (e.g. *BBC* as an organisation or as a product, (c) expansion of the lookup of geographical names, (d) integration of a mechanism to distinguish the Czech female gender marker *-ova* from case markers as it behaves differently: Forms such as *Merkelova* are the Czech nominative base form of the German Chancellor *Merkel* and inflections apply to *Merkelova* instead of to our name list's base form *Merkel*, (e) introduction of additional heuristics to narrow down the possible name mention matches, since the automatically generated groups of name inflection variants, from which we learn the inflection patterns, contain errors because the wildcards match too generously, and (f) updating and completing our list of geographical names as the coverage for different languages currently ranges from over 100,000 geographical names to below 3,000.

References

Laura Chiticariu, Rajasekar Krishnamurthy, Yunyao Li, Frederick Reiss, and Shivakumar Vaithyanathan. 2010. Domain adaptation of rule-based annotators for named-entity recognition tasks. In *Proceedings of the 2010 conference on empirical methods in natural language processing*, pages 1002–1012. Association for Computational Linguistics.

Maud Ehrmann, Guillaume Jacquet, and Ralf Steinberger. 2017. JRC-Names: Multilingual entity name variants and titles as linked data. *Semantic Web*, 8(2):283–295.

Rinat Gareev, Maksim Tkachenko, Valery Solovyev, Andrey Simanovsky, and Vladimir Ivanov. 2013. Introducing baselines for Russian named entity recognition. In *International Conference on Intelligent Text Processing and Computational Linguistics*, pages 329–342. Springer.

Ralf Grishman and Beth Sundheim. 1996. In *The 16th International Conference on Computational Linguistics*.

Guillaume Jacquet, Jakub Piskorski, and Sophie Chesney. 2019. Out-of-context fine-grained multi-word entity classification. In *Proceedings of the 34th ACM/SIGAPP Symposium On Applied Computing (SAC 2019)*.

David Nadeau and Satoshi Sekine. 2007. A survey of named entity recognition and classification. *Lingvisticae Investigationes*, 30(1):3–26.

Roberto Navigli and Simone Paolo Ponzetto. 2012. BabelNet: The automatic construction, evaluation and application of a wide-coverage multilingual semantic network. *Artificial Intelligence*, 193:217–250.

Júlia Pajzs, Ralf Steinberger, Maud Ehrmann, Mohamed Ebrahim, Leonida Della Rocca, Eszter Simon, and Tamás Váradi. 2014. Media monitoring and information extraction for the highly inflected agglutinative language Hungarian.

Jakub Piskorski. 2007. ExPRESS – Extraction Pattern Recognition Engine and Specification Suite. In *Proceedings of the International Workshop Finite-State Methods and Natural Language Processing 2007 (FSMNLP 2007)*.

Jakub Piskorski, Laska Laskova, Michał Marcińczuk, Lidia Pivovarova, Pavel Přibáň, Josef Steinberger, and Roman Yangarber. 2019. The second cross-lingual challenge on recognition, classification, lemmatization, and linking of named entities across Slavic languages. In *Proceedings of the 7th Workshop on Balto-Slavic Natural Language Processing*, Florence, Italy. Association for Computational Linguistics.

Jakub Piskorski, Lidia Pivovarova, Jan Šnajder, Josef Steinberger, and Roman Yangarber. 2017. The first cross-lingual challenge on recognition, normalization, and matching of named entities in Slavic languages. In *Proceedings of the 6th Workshop on Balto-Slavic Natural Language Processing*, pages 76–85, Valencia, Spain. Association for Computational Linguistics.

Jakub Piskorski, Marcin Sydow, and Karol Wieloch. 2007. Comparison of string distance metrics for lemmatisation of named entities in Polish. In *Language and Technology Conference*, pages 413–427. Springer.

Ralf Steinberger, Martin Atkinson, Teófilo Garcia, Erik Van der Goot, Jens Linge, Charles Macmillan, Hristo Tanev, Marco Verile, and Gerhard Wagner. 2017. EMM: Supporting the analyst by turning multilingual text into structured data. In *Transparenz aus Verantwortung: Neue Herausforderungen für die digitale Datenanalyse*. Erich Schmidt Verlag.

Ralf Steinberger, Guillaume Jacquet, and Leonida Della Rocca. 2015. Creation and use of multilingual named entity variant dictionaries. *Traduire aux confins du lexique: les nouveaux terrains de la terminologie*, 40:113.

Ralf Steinberger, Bruno Pouliquen, Mijail Kabadjov, and Erik van der Goot. 2011. JRC-Names: A Freely Available, Highly Multilingual Named Entity Resource. In *Proceedings of the 8th International Conference Recent Advances in Natural Language Processing (RANLP'2011)*, pages 104–110, Hissar, Bulgaria.

Building English-to-Serbian Machine Translation System
for IMDb Movie Reviews

Pintu Lohar, Maja Popović and Andy Way
ADAPT Centre
Dublin City University
Ireland
`name.surname@adaptcentre.ie`

Abstract

This paper reports the results of the first experiment dealing with the challenges of building a machine translation system for user-generated content involving a complex South Slavic language. We focus on translation of English IMDb user movie reviews into Serbian, in a low-resource scenario. We explore potentials and limits of (i) phrase-based and neural machine translation systems trained on out-of-domain clean parallel data from news articles (ii) creating additional synthetic in-domain parallel corpus by machine-translating the English IMDb corpus into Serbian. Our main findings are that morphology and syntax are better handled by the neural approach than by the phrase-based approach even in this low-resource mismatched domain scenario, however the situation is different for the lexical aspect, especially for person names. This finding also indicates that in general, machine translation of person names into Slavic languages (especially those which require/allow transcription) should be investigated more systematically.

1 Introduction

Social media platforms have become hugely popular web-sites where Internet users can communicate and spread information worldwide. Social media texts, such as user reviews and micro-blogs, are often short, informal, and noisy in terms of linguistic norms. Usually, this noise does not pose problems for human understanding, but it can be challenging for NLP applications such as sentiment analysis or machine translation (MT). Additional challenge for MT is sparseness of bilingual (translated) user-generated texts, especially for neural machine translation (NMT). The NMT approach has emerged in recent years and already replaced statistical phrase-based (PBMT) approach as state-of-the-art. However, NMT is even more sensitive to the low-resource settings and domain mismatch (Koehn and Knowles, 2017). Therefore, the challenge of translating user-generated texts is threefold, and if the target language is complex, then fourfold.

In this work, we focus on neural machine translation of English IMDb movie reviews into Serbian, a morpho-syntactically complex South Slavic language. To the best of our knowledge, this is the first experiment dealing with machine translation of user-generated content involving a South Slavic language. The main questions of our research described in this work are (i) What performance can be expected of an English-to-Serbian machine translation system trained on news articles and applied to movie reviews? (ii) Can this performance be improved by translating the monolingual English movie reviews into Serbian thus creating additional synthetic in-domain bilingual data? (iii) What are the main issues and what are the most important directions for the next experiments?

In order to answer these questions, we build a neural (NMT) machine system on the publicly available clean out-of-domain news corpus, and a phrase-based (PBMT) system trained on the same data in order to compare the two approaches in this specific scenario. After that, we use these two systems to generate synthetic Serbian movie reviews thus creating additional in-domain bilingual data. We then compare five different set-ups in terms of corpus statistics, overall automatic scores, and error analysis.

All our experiments were carried out on publicly available data sets. In order to encourage further research on the topic, all Serbian human translations of IMDb reviews produced for purposes of this research are made publicly available, too[1].

---

[1] https://github.com/m-popovic/imdb-corpus-for-MT

Proceedings of the 7th Workshop on Balto-Slavic Natural Language Processing, pages 105–113,
Florence, Italy, 2 August 2019. ©2019 Association for Computational Linguistics

2   Related Work

A considerable amount of work has been done on social media analysis, mostly on the sentiment analysis of user-generated texts, but many publications deal with different aspects of translation of user-generated content. Some papers investigate translating social media texts in order to map widely available English sentiment labels to a less supported target language and thus be able to perform the sentiment analysis in this language (Balahur and Turchi, 2012, 2014). Several researchers attempted to build parallel corpora for user-generated content in order to facilitate MT. For example, translation of Twitter microblog messages by using a translation-based cross-lingual information retrieval system is applied in (Jehl et al., 2012) on Arabic and English Twitter posts. (Ling et al., 2013) crawled a considerable amount of Chinese-English parallel segments from micro-blogs and released the data publicly. Another publicly available corpus, TweetMT (naki San Vicente et al., 2016), consists of Spanish, Basque, Galician, Catalan and Portuguese tweets and has been created by automatic collection and crowd-sourcing approaches. (Banerjee et al., 2012) investigated domain adaptation and reduction of out-of-vocabulary words for English-to-German and English-to-French translation of web forum content. Estimation of comprehensibility and fidelity of machine-translated user-generated content from English to French is investigated in (Rubino et al., 2013), whereas (Lohar et al., 2017) and (Lohar et al., 2018) explore maintaining sentiment polarity in German-to-English machine translation of Twitter posts.

Whereas South Slavic languages are generally less supported in the NLP, they have been investigated in terms of user-generated content. For example, sentiment classification of Croatian Game reviews and Tweets is investigated in (Rotim and Šnajder, 2017), and (Ljubešić et al., 2017) proposes adapting a standard-text Slovenian POS tagger to tweets, forum posts, and user comments on blog posts and news articles. These languages have been dealt with in machine translation research as well. (Maučec and Brest, 2017) gives an overview of Slavic languages and PBMT, and (Popović and Ljubešić, 2014) explores similarities and differences between Serbian and Croatian in terms of PBMT. Linguistic characteristics of South Slavic languages which are problematic for

PBMT were investigated in (Popović and Arčan, 2015), and (Popović, 2018) compares linguistically motivated issues for PBMT with those of the recently emerged NMT.

However, to the best of our knowledge, MT of user-generated texts involving South Slavic languages has not been investigated so far. In this work, we present the first results of translating English IMDb movie reviews into Serbian.

3   Data Sets

We carried out our experiments using the publicly available "Large Movie Review Dataset"[2](Maas et al., 2011) which contains $50,000$ IMDb user movie reviews in English. The data set is mainly intended for sentiment analysis research, so each review is associated with its binary sentiment polarity label "positive" or "negative". Negative reviews have a score ≤ 4 out of 10, positive reviews have a score ≥ 7 out of 10 and the reviews with more neutral ratings are not included. The overall distribution of labels is balanced, namely $25k$ positive and $25k$ negative reviews. In the entire collection, no more than 30 reviews are allowed for any particular movie.

For our experiments, we kept 200 reviews (100 positive and 100 negative) containing about $2,500$ sentences for testing purposes, and used the remaining $49,800$ reviews (about $500k$ sentences) for training. Human translation of the test set into Serbian, which is necessary for fast automatic evaluation of MT outputs, is currently in progress, and at the time of our first experiment described in this work, Serbian reference translations were available for 33 test reviews (17 negative and 16 positive) containing 485 sentences (208 negative and 277 positive).

For the baseline out-of-domain training, we used the South-east European Times (SEtimes) news corpus (Tyers and Alperen, 2010) consisting of about $200k$ parallel sentences from the news articles. In order to be able to compare the results with the in-domain scenario, the development set is extracted from the SETimes corpus, too.

4   Expanding English IMDb Reviews into a Bilingual Training Corpus

The Serbian language is generally not very well supported in terms of NLP resources. The English-Serbian publicly available parallel OPUS

---

[2]http://ai.stanford.edu/ amaas/data/sentiment/

data[3] consists mostly of subtitles, which are rather noisy. The only really clean parallel corpus there is "SEtimes", which is the reason why we used it for the baseline system in our first experiments – we wanted to avoid any effects of noisy data. To the best of our knowledge, there are no publicly available parallel corpora containing user-generated texts in Serbian.

Therefore, we created synthetic IMDb parallel corpus by translating English IMDb reviews into Serbian using our baseline systems. This technique is shown to be very helpful for NMT systems (Sennrich et al., 2016; Poncelas et al., 2018; Burlot and Yvon, 2018) and has become a common practice in the development of NMT systems. It is usually called "back-translation", because the monolingual in-domain data is normally written in the target language and then translated into the source language. In this way, the synthetic corpus consists of noisy source and clean natural target language texts. In our case, however, we are interested in translating into Serbian but we do not have any movie reviews in Serbian, only in English (the source language). Therefore, we actually applied the "forward-translation" technique, which is also shown to be helpful, albeit less than back-translation (Park et al., 2017; Burlot and Yvon, 2018).

In our case, we expected it to be even more suboptimal than for some other language pairs, because our target language is more complex than the source language in several aspects. The Serbian language, as other Slavic languages, is morphologically rich and has a rather free word order. Furthermore, unlike other Slavic languages, it is bi-alphabetical (with both Latin and Cyrillic scripts) so attention should be payed in order not to mix the two scripts in one corpus. Another possible inconsistency in corpora is different handling of person names – in Cyrillic, only transcription is possible, whereas in Latin both transcription as well as leaving the original are allowed. Apart from this, all person names are declined, as in other Slavic languages.

Usually, back- and/or forward-translation is performed by an NMT system in order to improve the performance of a baseline NMT system. Recently, a comparison between NMT and PBMT back-translation (Burlot and Yvon, 2018) shown that using a PBMT system for synthetic data can

lead to comparable improvement of the baseline NMT system with a lower training cost. Therefore, we decided to use and compare both approaches for improving our baseline NMT system.

5   Experimental Set-up

For our experiment, we have built one PBMT English-to-Serbian system using Moses toolkit (Koehn et al., 2007) and four English-to-Serbian NMT models using OpenNMT (Klein et al., 2017) in the following way:

- Train an out-of-domain PBMT system on the SEtimes corpus.

- Train a baseline out-of-domain NMT system on the SEtimes corpus.

- Translate the English IMDb training corpus into Serbian using the PBMT system, thus generating a synthetic parallel corpus $IMDb_{pbmt}$.

- Translate the English IMDb training corpus into Serbian using the baseline NMT system, thus generating a synthetic parallel corpus $IMDb_{nmt}$.

- Train a new NMT system on the SEtimes corpus enriched with the $IMDb_{pbmt}$ corpus.

- Train another NMT system using SEtimes corpus enriched with the $IMDb_{nmt}$ corpus.

- Train one more NMT system using SEtimes corpus enriched with both $IMDb_{pbmt}$ and $IMDb_{nmt}$ corpora ($IMDb_{joint}$).

Table 1 shows the statistics for each of the three training corpora (SEtimes, $IMDb_{pbmt}$ and $IMDb_{nmt}$), for the development set, as well as for the test set. First, it can be noticed that the IMDb training corpus contains more than twice segments and running words than the English part of the SEtimes corpus, and it has a much larger vocabulary. Another fact is that, due to the rich morphology, the Serbian SEtimes vocabulary is almost twice as large as the English one. Nevertheless, this is not the case for the synthetic IMDb data, where the Serbian vocabulary is only barely larger or even comparable to the English one. This confirms the intuition about sub-optimal forward translation mentioned in the previous section – machine translated data generally exhibit less lexical and syntactic variety than natural data (Burlot and Yvon,

---

train	reviews	segments	words (en)	voc (en)	words (sr)	voc (sr)
SEtimes (natural)	/	224167	4675549	81064	4439280	155447
IMDb (natural)	49800	536433	11313315	223972	/	/
IMDb$_{pbmt}$	49800	536433	/	/	12012734	236272
IMDb$_{nmt}$	49800	536433	/	/	11077566	195912

dev (SEtimes)	/	1000	20338	4757	19244	6806
OOV rate [%]		SEtimes	0.25	5.6	0.48	7.9
		IMDb	1.29	19.9	/	/
		IMDb$_{pbmt}$	/	/	2.21	29.0
		IMDb$_{nmt}$	/	/	2.18	29.0

test (IMDb)	33	485	8530	2548	7630	3220
OOV rate [%]		SEtimes	1.16	17.5	1.83	22.2
		IMDb	0.24	4.2	/	/
		IMDb$_{pbmt}$	/	/	2.39	27.4
		IMDb$_{nmt}$	/	/	2.76	32.3

Table 1: Corpus statistics

2018), and here we are additionally dealing with a scarce out-of-domain MT system translating into a more complex language.

For the development set, as intuitively expected, out-of-vocabulary rates are smaller for the in-domain SEtimes corpus, and for the less morphologically complex English language. As for the test set, the English part behaves in the same way, namely the OOV rates are smaller when compared to the in-domain IMDb training corpus. However, for the synthetic Serbian data, the OOV rates are comparable with those of the out-of-domain development corpus and much higher than for development corpus when compared to its in-domain the SEtimes corpus, which again illustrates the effects of sub-optimal synthetic data.

6 Results

6.1 Overall Automatic Evaluation

We first evaluated all translation outputs using the following overall automatic MT evaluation metrics: BLEU (Papineni et al., 2002), METEOR (Lavie and Denkowski, 2009), TER (Snover et al., 2006), chrF (Popović, 2015) and characTER (Wang et al., 2016). BLEU, METEOR and TER are word-level metrics whereas chrF and characTER are character-based metrics. BLEU, METEOR and chrF are based on precision and/or recall, whereas TER and characTER are based on edit distance. The results both for the development as well as for the test set can be seen in Table 2.

The results for the development set are as it could intuitively be expected: the best option is to use a NMT system trained on the in-domain data (baseline), and using any kind of additional out-of-domain data deteriorates all scores.

As for the test set, it could be expected that the scores will be worse than for the development set. However, several interesting tendencies can be observed. First of all, the baseline NMT system outperforms the baseline PBMT system despite the scarcity of the training corpus and domain mismatch (Koehn and Knowles, 2017), however only in terms of word-level scores – both character-level scores are better for the PBMT system. Furthermore, adding IMDb$_{pbmt}$ data deteriorates all word-level scores and improves both character-level scores. On the other hand, adding IMDb$_{nmt}$ data improves all baseline scores, but the improvements of the character-based scores are smaller than those yielded by adding the IMDb$_{pbmt}$ corpus. Finally, using all synthetic data IMDb$_{joint}$ improves all scores (except BLEU) over the baseline, however the improvements are smaller than the improvements of each individual synthetic data sets (IMDb$_{nmt}$ for word-level scores and IMDb$_{pbmt}$ for character-level scores).

6.2 Automatic Error Analysis

In order to better understand the character-metrics preference for the PBMT-based systems, we car-

(a) Overall automatic evaluation scores for the development set (SEtimes)

development set (SEtimes)		BLEU↑	METEOR↑	TER↓	chrF↑	chrTER↓
system	training corpus					
PBMT	SEtimes	33.1	29.4	48.9	61.2	41.5
NMT	SEtimes	**39.2**	**32.2**	**42.6**	**62.7**	**39.1**
	SEtimes+IMDb$_{pbmt}$	36.2	30.8	44.7	61.1	41.0
	SEtimes+IMDb$_{nmt}$	38.1	31.7	43.0	61.6	40.1
	SEtimes+IMDb$_{joint}$	35.1	30.2	45.5	59.8	41.9

(b) Overall automatic evaluation scores for the test set (IMDb)

test set (IMDb)		BLEU↑	METEOR↑	TER↓	chrF↑	chrTER↓
system	training corpus					
PBMT	SEtimes	10.8	18.6	69.1	40.5	56.3
NMT	SEtimes	13.7	19.2	65.8	37.4	61.4
	SEtimes+IMDb$_{pbmt}$	11.6	19.0	66.9	**40.7**	**55.3**
	SEtimes+IMDb$_{nmt}$	**14.7**	**20.4**	**63.2**	38.8	60.2
	SEtimes+IMDb$_{joint}$	13.3	19.7	64.8	40.6	55.5

Table 2: Overall word-level and character-level automatic evaluation scores for the development (SEtimes) and the test (IMDb) corpus.

ried out a more detailed evaluation in the form of error classification. Automatic error classification of all translation outputs is performed by the open source tool Hjerson (Popović, 2011). The tool is based on combination of edit distance, precision and recall, and distinguishes five error categories: inflectional error, word order, omission, addition and mistranslation. Following the set-up used for a large evaluation involving many language pairs and translation outputs in order to compare the PBMT and NMT approaches in (Toral and Sánchez-Cartagena, 2017), we group omissions, additions and mistranslations into a unique category called lexical errors. The results for both development and for the test set can be seen in Table 3 in the form of error rates (raw error count normalised over the total number of words in the translation output).

Again, the findings for the in-domain development set could be intuitively expected, and are in line with the findings of (Toral and Sánchez-Cartagena, 2017): the NMT system better handles grammatical features (morphology and word order) than the PBMT system, whereas there is no difference regarding lexical aspect.

The tendencies for the inflectional errors are same for the test set. The lowest inflectional error rate can be observed for the baseline NMT system, and it is slightly increased when the IMDb$_{nmt}$ corpus is added. Other three systems, involving

the PBMT approach, exhibit much more inflectional errors. For the other two error categories, the situation is slightly different. Word order is also better for the baseline NMT system than for the PBMT system, however adding the IMDb$_{nmt}$ corpus does not improve it whereas the IMDb$_{pbmt}$ corpus does. Possible reason is the free word order in the Serbian language, so that the system trained on IMDb$_{pbmt}$ data simply generated the word order closest to the one in the reference translation. As for the lexical errors, it can be seen that the lexical error rate is much higher for the baseline NMT system than for the baseline PBMT system, which corresponds to the domain-mismatch challenge for NMT (Koehn and Knowles, 2017). Furthermore, the highest reduction of this error type is achieved when the IMDb$_{pbmt}$ corpus is added.

6.3 Manual Inspection of Lexical Errors

In order to further explore the increase of the lexical errors in systems involving the NMT model, we carried out a qualitative manual inspection of three translation outputs: from the baseline NMT system, from the NMT system with additional IMDb$_{pbmt}$ corpus, and from the NMT system with additional IMDb$_{nmt}$ corpus.

We found out that in general, there are many person names (actors, directors, etc., as well as characters) in the IMDb corpus. As mentioned in Section 4, Serbian (Latin) allows both transcrip-

(a) Error rates (%) for the development set (SEtimes)

development set (SEtimes)				
system	training corpus	inflection	word order	lexical
PBMT	SEtimes	15.4	5.3	**36.1**
NMT	SEtimes	**11.8**	**4.0**	**36.1**
	SEtimes+IMDb$_{pbmt}$	12.5	4.4	37.2
	SEtimes+IMDb$_{nmt}$	11.8	4.1	36.6
	SEtimes+IMDb$_{joint}$	12.6	4.4	38.0

(b) Error rates (%) for the test set (IMDb)

test set (IMDb)				
system	training corpus	inflection	word order	lexical
PBMT	SEtimes	14.2	5.1	54.1
NMT	SEtimes	**10.0**	4.9	60.1
	SEtimes+IMDb$_{pbmt}$	14.4	**4.6**	**53.7**
	SEtimes+IMDb$_{nmt}$	10.4	5.0	57.3
	SEtimes+IMDb$_{joint}$	13.4	4.7	53.8

Table 3: Results of automatic error analysis including three error categories for the development (SEtimes) and test (IMDb) corpus.

tion as well as leaving the original names, but it should be consistent in a text. Whereas in the test reference translation the names were left in the original, neither of the MT systems handled the names in a consistent manner. Both PBMT and NMT-based systems generated originals, transcriptions and sometimes unnecessary translations of the names in a rather random way, and in addition, NMT-based systems often omitted or repeated (the parts of) the names.

This finding could explain both the increase of the lexical error rates as well as decrease of the character-level overall scores for the NMT-based systems. Several examples can be seen in Table 4, and for each example, the best version of the given name is shown in bold. The names on the left were problematic for the baseline NMT system and then improved (albeit not always in the perfect way) by adding the IMDb$_{pbmt}$ corpus, but not improved (or even worsened) by adding the IMDb$_{nmt}$ corpus. The names on the right were treated properly both by the baseline NMT system as well as by the IMDb$_{nmt}$ system, however the IMDb$_{pbmt}$ system transcribed the first name thus making it more distant from the reference, and unnecessarily translated the second name as though it were a common noun.

This finding, together with the facts described in Section 4, indicate that Serbian, as well as other Slavic person names and other name enti-

ties should be further investigated in the context of machine translation, not only for movie reviews or other types of user-generated context, but in general.

7 Summary and Outlook

In this work, we focused on the task of building an English-to-Serbian machine translation system for IMDb reviews. We first trained a phrase-based and a neural model on out-of-domain clean parallel data and used it as baselines. We then generated additional synthetic in-domain parallel data by translating the English IMDb reviews into Serbian using the two baseline machine translation systems. This "forward-translation" technique improved the baseline results, although "back-translation" (translating natural Serbian texts into English) would be more helpful. Further analysis shown that morphology and syntax are better handled by the neural approach than by the phrase-based approach, whereas the situation is different for the lexical aspect, especially for person names. This finding also indicates that in general, machine translation of person names into Slavic languages (especially those which require/allow transcription) should be investigated more systematically.

The most important directions for the future work on user-generated texts are finding appropriate Serbian texts (for example, movie review ar-

	IMDb$_{pbmt}$ is better	IMDb$_{nmt}$ is better
source	best Clark Kent	to watch Patrick Duffy
reference	najbolji **Clark Kent**	gledati **Patricka Duffyja**
SEtimes	best Kent	pratiti **Patrick Duffy**
SEtimes+IMDb$_{pbmt}$	najbolji **Klark Kentu**	da gledaju Patrik Dafi
SEtimes+IMDb$_{nmt}$	best Kent Kent	pratiti **Patrick Duffy**
source	the Richard Donner Cut	Kate Winslet (as Rose)
reference	verziju **Richarda Donnera**	Kate Winslet (kao **Rose**)
SEtimes	odlaska Richard Cut	Winslet (kao Jack)
SEtimes+IMDb$_{pbmt}$	**Ričard Donner** smanji	Kate Winslet (kao ruža)
SEtimes+IMDb$_{nmt}$	Richard Cut Cut	Kate Winslet (kao **Rose**)
source	Lester's Superman II	
reference	**Lesterov** Supermen II	
SEtimes	's Superman II	
SEtimes+IMDb$_{pbmt}$	**Lestera** u Superman II	
SEtimes+IMDb$_{nmt}$	's Superman II	
source	scriptwriter Tony Morphett	
reference	scenarista **Tony Morphett**	
SEtimes	scenarista Tony Tony	
SEtimes+IMDb$_{pbmt}$	scenarista **Toni Morphett**	
SEtimes+IMDb$_{nmt}$	scenarista Tony Tony	

Table 4: Examples of different name entities (person names)

ticles in the news) and using them for enlarging the in-domain part of the training corpus by back-translation, as well as enlarging out-of-domain data by cleaning the subtitles corpora, and by back-translating monolingual Serbian news articles. In addition, more IMDb reviews should be evaluated in future experiments. Apart from this, future work should involve other types of user-generated content, such as product or hotel reviews and micro-blog posts, as well as other (South) Slavic languages.

Acknowledgments

This research was supported by the ADAPT Centre for Digital Content Technology at Dublin City University, funded under the Science Foundation Ireland Research Centres Programme (Grant 13/RC/2106) and co-funded under the European Regional Development Fund.

References

Alexandra Balahur and Marco Turchi. 2012. Multilingual Sentiment Analysis using Machine Translation? In *Proceedings of the 3rd Workshop in Computational Approaches to Subjectivity and Sentiment Analysis*, pages 52–60, Jeju, Korea.

Alexandra Balahur and Marco Turchi. 2014. Comparative Experiments Using Supervised Learning and Machine Translation for Multilingual Sentiment Analysis. *Computer Speech and Language*, 28(1):56–75.

Pratyush Banerjee, Sudip Kumar Naskar, Johann Roturier, Andy Way, and Josef van Genabith. 2012. Domain Adaptation in SMT of User-Generated Forum Content Guided byOOV Word Reduction: Normalization and/or Supplementary Dat. In *Proceedings of the 16th Annual Conference of the European Association for Machine Translation (EAMT 2012)*, pages 169–176, Trento, Italy.

Franck Burlot and François Yvon. 2018. Using Monolingual Data in Neural Machine Translation: a Systematic Study. In *Proceedings of the 3rd Conference on Machine Translation (WMT 2018)*, pages 144–155, Belgium, Brussels.

Laura Jehl, Felix Hieber, and Stefan Riezler. 2012. Twitter Translation Using Translation-based Cross-lingual Retrieval. In *Proceedings of the 7th Workshop on Statistical Machine Translation (WMT 2012)*, pages 410–421.

Guillaume Klein, Yoon Kim, Yuntian Deng, Jean Senellart, and Alexander M. Rush. 2017. Opennmt: Open-source toolkit for neural machine translation. In *Proceedings of the 55th Annual Meeting of the Association for Computational Linguistics-System Demonstrations*, pages 67–72, Vancouver, Canada.

Philipp Koehn, Hieu Hoang, Alexandra Birch, Chris Callison-Burch, Marcello Federico, Nicola Bertoldi, Brooke Cowan, Wade Shen, Christine Moran, Richard Zens, Chris Dyer, Ondej Bojar, Alexandra Constantin, and Evan Herbst. 2007. Moses: Open source toolkit for SMT. In *Proceedings of 45th annual meeting of the ACL on interactive poster & demonstration sessions*, pages 177–180, Prague, Czech Republic.

Philipp Koehn and Rebecca Knowles. 2017. Six Challenges for Neural Machine Translation. In *Proceedings of the First Workshop on Neural Machine Translation*, pages 28–39, Vancouver.

Alon Lavie and Michael J. Denkowski. 2009. The METEOR Metric for Automatic Evaluation of Machine Translation. *Machine Translation*, 23(2-3):105–115.

Wang Ling, Guang Xiang, Chris Dyer, Alan Black, and Isabel Trancoso. 2013. Microblogs as Parallel Corpora. In *Proceedings of the 51st Annual Meeting of the Association for Computational Linguistics (ACL 2013)*, pages 176–186, Sofia, Bulgaria.

Nikola Ljubešić, Tomaž Erjavec, and Darja Fišer. 2017. Adapting a State-of-the-Art Tagger for South Slavic Languages to Non-Standard Text. In *Proceedings of the 6th Workshop on Balto-Slavic Natural Language Processing (BSNLP 2017)*, pages 60–68, Valencia, Spain.

Pintu Lohar, Haithem Afli, and Andy Way. 2017. Maintaining Sentiment Polarity of Translated User Generated Content. *The Prague Bulletin of Mathematical Linguistics*, 108(1):73–84.

Pintu Lohar, Haithem Afli, and Andy Way. 2018. Balancing Translation Quality and Sentiment Preservation. In *Proceedings of the 13th Conference of the Association for Machine Translation in the Americas (AMTA 2018)*, pages 81–88, Boston, MA.

Andrew L. Maas, Raymond E. Daly, Peter T. Pham, Dan Huang, Andrew Y. Ng, and Christopher Potts. 2011. Learning Word Vectors for Sentiment Analysis. In *Proceedings of the 49th Annual Meeting of the Association for Computational Linguistics and Human Language Technologies (ACL-HLT 2011)*, pages 142–150, Portland, Oregon, USA.

Mirjam Sepesy Maučec and Janez Brest. 2017. Slavic languages in phrase-based statistical machine translation: a survey. *Artificial Intelligence Review*, 51(1):77–117.

Kishore Papineni, Salim Roukos, Todd Ward, and Wie-Jing Zhu. 2002. BLEU: a Method for Automatic Evaluation of Machine Translation. In *Proceedings of the 40th Annual Meeting of the Association for Computational Linguistics (ACL 2002)*, pages 311–318, Philadelphia, PA.

Jaehong Park, Jongyoon Song, and Sungroh Yoon. 2017. Building a Neural Machine Translation System Using Only Synthetic Parallel Data. *CoRR*.

Alberto Poncelas, Dimitar Shterionov, Andy Way, Gideon Maillette de Buy Wenniger, and Peyman Passban. 2018. Investigating Back translation in Neural Machine Translation. In *Proceedings of the 21st Annual Conference of the European Association for Machine Translation (EAMT 2018)*, Alicante, Spain.

Maja Popović. 2011. Hjerson: An Open Source Tool for Automatic Error Classification of Machine Translation Output. *Prague Bulletin of Mathematical Linguistics*, 96:59–68.

Maja Popović. 2015. chrF: character n-gram F-score for automatic MT evaluation. In *Proceedings of the 10th Workshop on Statistical Machine Translation (WMT 2015)*, pages 392–395, Lisbon, Portugal.

Maja Popović. 2018. Language-related issues for NMT and PBMT for English–German and English–Serbian. *Machine Translation*, 32(3):237–253.

Maja Popović and Mihael Arčan. 2015. Identifying main obstacles for statistical machine translation of morphologically rich South Slavic languages. In *Proceedings of the 18th Annual Conference of the European Association for Machine Translation (EAMT 2015)*, pages 97–104, Antalya, Turkey.

Maja Popović and Nikola Ljubešić. 2014. Exploring cross-language statistical machine translation for closely related South Slavic languages. In *Proceedings of the EMNLP 2014 Workshop on Language Technology for Closely Related Languages and Language Variants*, pages 76–84, Doha, Qatar.

Leon Rotim and Jan Šnajder. 2017. Comparison of Short-Text Sentiment Analysis Methods for Croatian. In *Proceedings of the 6th Workshop on Balto-Slavic Natural Language Processing (BSNLP 2017)*, pages 69–75, Valencia, Spain.

Raphael Rubino, Jennifer Foster, Rasoul Samad Zadeh Kaljahi, Johann Roturier, and Fred Hollowood. 2013. Estimating the Quality of Translated User-Generated Content. In *Proceedings of 6th International Joint Conference on Natural Language Processing (IJCNLP 2013)*, pages 1167–1173, Nagoya, Japan.

Iñaki San Vicente, Iñaki Alegria, Cristina Espa na Bonet, Pablo Gamallo, Hugo Goncalo Oliveira, Eva Martinez Garcia, Antonio Toral, Arkaitz Zubiaga, and Nora Aranberri. 2016. TweetMT: A Parallel Microblog Corpus. In *Proceedings of the 10th International Conference on Language Resources and Evaluation (LREC 2016)*, Portorož, Slovenia.

Rico Sennrich, Barry Haddow, and Alexandra Birch. 2016. Improving Neural Machine Translation Models with Monolingual Data. In *Proceedings of the 54th Annual Meeting of the Association for Computational Linguistics (ACL 2016)*, pages 86–96, Berlin, Germany.

Matthew Snover, Bonnie J. Dorr, Richard M. Schwartz, and Linnea Micciulla. 2006. A Study of Translation Edit Rate with Targeted Human Annotation. In *Proceedings of the 7th Conference of Association for Machine Translation in the Americas (AMTA 2006)*, pages 223–231, Cambridge, MA.

Antonio Toral and Víctor Manuel Sánchez-Cartagena. 2017. A Multifaceted Evaluation of Neural versus Statistical Machine Translation for 9 Language Directions. In *Proceedings of the 15th Conference of the European Chapter of the Association for Computational Linguistics (EACL 2017)*, Valencia, Spain.

Francis M Tyers and Murat Serdar Alperen. 2010. South-east European Times: A parallel corpus of Balkan languages. In *Proceedings of the LREC Workshop on Exploitation of Multilingual Resources and Tools for Central and (South-) Eastern European Languages*, pages 49–53, Valetta, Malta.

Weiyue Wang, Jan-Thorsten Peter, Hendrik Rosendahl, and Hermann Ney. 2016. CharacTer: Translation Edit Rate on Character Level. In *Proceedings of the 1st Conference on Machine Translation (WMT 2016)*, pages 505–510, Berlin, Germany.

Improving Sentiment Classification in Slovak Language

Samuel Pecar, Marian Simko, Maria Bielikova
Slovak University of Technology in Bratislava
Faculty of Informatics and Information Technologies
Ilkovicova 2, 842 16 Bratislava, Slovakia
{samuel.pecar, marian.simko, maria.bielikova}@stuba.sk

Abstract

Using different neural network architectures is widely spread for many different NLP tasks. Unfortunately, most of the research is performed and evaluated only in English language and minor languages are often omitted. We believe using similar architectures for other languages can show interesting results. In this paper, we present our study on methods for improving sentiment classification in Slovak language. We performed several experiments for two different datasets, one containing customer reviews, the other one general Twitter posts. We show comparison of performance of different neural network architectures and also different word representations. We show that another improvement can be achieved by using a model ensemble. We performed experiments utilizing different methods of model ensemble. Our proposed models achieved better results than previous models for both datasets. Our experiments showed also other potential research areas.

1 Introduction and Related Works

Amount of text data produced by users in the world has grown rapidly in recent years. On the Web, users produce text using different platforms, such as social networks or portals aggregating customer reviews. Most of the produced text can be considered as opinionated. There is a significant need for utilization of natural language processing tasks, such as sentiment analysis or other connected tasks – emotion recognition, stance detection, etc.

Sentiment analysis can be viewed as one of the most common and widespread tasks in natural language processing. Recent advancements in neural networks allowed further research also for minor non-English languages. In recent years, there have been several studies researching sentiment classification of multiple Slavic languages,

such as Czech (Habernal et al., 2014; Steinberger et al., 2014), Croatian (Rotim and Šnajder, 2017), Lithuanian (Kapočiutė-Dzikienė et al., 2013), Russian (Chetviorkin and Loukachevitch, 2013), and Slovak (Krchnavy and Simko, 2017; Pecar et al., 2018). Interesting study was also proposed by Mozetič et al. (Mozetič et al., 2016), where authors studied the role of human annotators for sentiment classification and provided also datasets for sentiment analysis of Twitter posts for multiple languages including some Slavic languages.

Whereas state-of-the-art methods widely employ different neural model architectures, such as the attention mechanism (Wang et al., 2016) or model ensemble techniques (Araque et al., 2017), recent research in sentiment analysis in Slavic languages still employs more traditional machine learning methods, mostly Support Vector Machines (SVM). We suppose this can be cause due to low availability of larger annotated datasets for Slavic languages, ones that are quite common for English or other major languages.

We see as an essential for further improvement of sentiment classification employing different techniques of transfer learning, especially using different pre-trained word representations on large text corpora. In recent years, there have been introduced many new methods for word representations, such as ELMo (Peters et al., 2018), BERT (Devlin et al., 2018) or ULM-FIT (Howard and Ruder, 2018). Unfortunately, most of these pre-trained word representations are only available for English language and further training requires a significant amount of hardware resources and extensive text corpora. On the other hand, there have been recently introduced also word representations for other languages, such as pre-trained ELMo word representations (Che et al., 2018; Fares et al., 2017) or fastText (Grave et al.,

Proceedings of the 7th Workshop on Balto-Slavic Natural Language Processing, pages 114–119,
Florence, Italy, 2 August 2019. ©2019 Association for Computational Linguistics

2018) for many different languages.

In this paper, we discuss possible methods for improving sentiment classification for Slovak language by using state-of-the-art methods. Our main contribution is employment of different neural model architectures for sentiment classification in Slovak. We also provide a study on how each block of architecture can contribute to overall sentiment classification.

2 Model

We believe that application of different neural network architectures can bring significant improvements of results. For our study, we consider employing several such architectures. A general architecture is shown in Figure 1 (Pecar et al., 2019). As shown in the figure, we consider four main block of this architecture, which are either variable or permanent. The last layer (linear decoder) is followed by logarithmic soft-max activation function to obtain final model predictions.

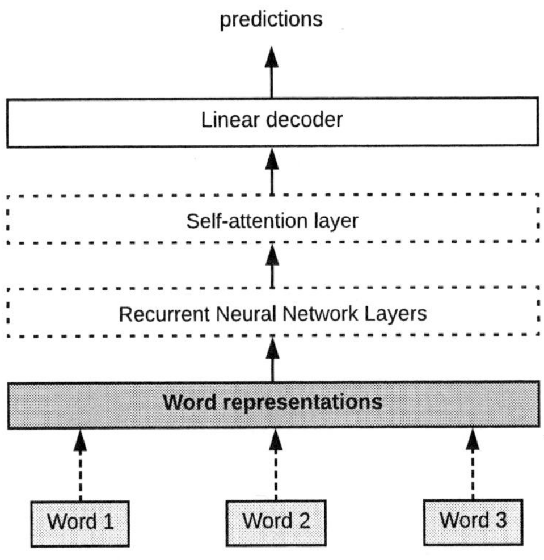

Figure 1: General neural model architecture

Word Representations

Word representations are an essential part of each neural network as embedding layer. We can consider this layer as permanent, since it is always present and we experiment only with different sizes of embedding layer and different forms of pre-trained embeddings. For this layer, we consider using standard embedding layer in the form of lookup table with dimension of 300. Different types of word representations have been recently widely used, such as ELMo (Peters et al., 2018) and BERT (Devlin et al., 2018). For our study, we used the pre-trained version of ELMo for Slovak language (Che et al., 2018), fastText for Slovak (Grave et al., 2018) and also pretrained word2vec for Slovak trained on prim dataset (Jazykovedný ústav Ľ. Štúra SAV, 2013).

Recurrent Neural Network Layers

We use different recurrent neural network architectures, where we consider using LSTM (Hochreiter and Schmidhuber, 1997) and Bi-LSTM (Schuster and Paliwal, 1997) with different number of stacked layers (one or two in our case). To simplify number of hyperparameters and types of architectures with different size, we consider using only size of 512.

Self-Attention Layer

To improve contribution of the most informative words, we also employ an attention mechanism. The attention mechanism assigns each word its annotation (informativeness) and the final representation is computed as weighted sum of all annotations from a sentence.

Linear Decoder

The linear decoder represents a standard linear layer, which tries to classify samples to classes. This layer can be considered as permanent, since it is always present and tries to classify samples into 2 or 3 classes depending on the target dataset.

Model Architectures

We consider several combination of described layers for evaluation of quality of neural networks for specific datasets. All architectures are shown in Table 1.

For purposes of our experiments we alternate four different word representations (randomly initialized embedding layer – LookUp, deep contextualized word representations – ELMo, fastText and word2vec). We combine different types and sizes of recurrent layers (1 LSTM, 1 Bi-LSTM) with or without use of the attention layer. For fastText and word2vec representations, we used only the last architecture employing one bidirectional LSTM with self-attention mechanism.

Model Ensemble

The last architecture we consider for improving quality of sentiment classification is using differ-

Model name	Word Representations	Recurrent Layer	Self-Attention
lookup-LSTM	LookUp	1 LSTM	None
lookup-BiLSTM	LookUp	1 Bi-LSTM	None
lookup-BiLSTM-att	LookUp	1 Bi-LSTM	Yes
ELMo-LSTM	ELMo	1 LSTM	None
ELMo-BiLSTM	ELMo	1 Bi-LSTM	None
ELMo-BiLSTM-att	ELMo	1 Bi-LSTM	Yes
w2v-BiLSTM-att	word2vec	1 Bi-LSTM	Yes
fast-BiLSTM-att	fastText	1 Bi-LSTM	Yes

Table 1: Different architectures used for experiments.

ent types of model ensemble. We consider using the same type of model for one model ensemble. Each model ensemble consists of three same models with different initialization and separate training. We also consider two types of ensemble, where models either vote for prediction or we average probabilities of model predictions.

3 Data and Evaluation

For evaluation of our models, we used two different datasets. The first dataset (*Reviews3*) consists of customer reviews of various services, which were manually labeled by 2 annotators. Since many reviews were only slightly positive or negative and agreement between annotators were not very high, we can categorize reviews into three different classes, where we consider positive, negative and neutral class (contains slightly positive or negative reviews). The second dataset (*Twitter*) consists of tweets in Slovak language (Mozetič et al., 2016), which were also labeled manually. Since some of the tweets from the original dataset did not exist anymore, we provide only evaluation on tweets available via standard Twitter API. The descriptive statistics of both datasets is shown in Table 2.

Dataset	Neg.	Neut.	Pos.	Total
Reviews3	431	2911	1978	5320
Twitter	12815	10817	27078	50710

Table 2: Statistics of used datasets.

To evaluate quality of our models we use F1 score. Since all datasets can be considered as highly unbalanced, we evaluate micro and macro F1 score separately.

One of the problems of the *Reviews3* dataset is its size. Since it contains approximately 5000 annotated reviews, we need to perform complete cross-validation, where the dataset is split in ratio 8:1:1 for train, valid and test set. For the *Twitter* dataset we split dataset in ratio 8:1:1 for train, valid and test set without any cross-validation. We also provide twitter ids for each set to preserve further reproducibility of experiments.

The only preprocessing used for our experiments is escaping punctuation to improve quality of tokenization of spaCy tokenizer in Slovak language. We also provide list of further hyper-parameters and techniques used for training our models: dropout after embedding layer 0.5; dropout after recurrent and attention layer 0.3, negative log likelihood loss, Adam optimizer.

4 Results

We performed many experiments using model architectures described in Section 2 for both datasets described in Section 3. We also compared our results with previously published results for the dataset *Reviews3* and also the dataset *Twitter*. Additionally, we also performed experiments using model ensemble for the dataset *Twitter*.

Model Results

In Table 3, we show results on the performance of the proposed models for sentiment classification for the dataset of customer reviews *Reviews3*. As we can observe, more robust models outperform smaller ones. Using deep contextualized word representations brings significant improvements of overall sentiment classification. We can also observe that a bidirectional recurrent network performs better than standard one-directional one. Using attention mechanism also brought further improvement. We also performed experiments using different pre-trained word representations with the most robust architecture. We can see that using word2vec and fastText did not bring any significant improvement for review dataset than using only randomly initialized embedding layer.

model	micro F1	macro F1
lookup-LSTM	0.7481	0.6960
lookup-BiLSTM	0.7687	0.7308
lookup-BiLSTM-att	0.7813	0.7337
ELMo-LSTM	0.8007	0.7613
ELMo-BiLSTM	0.8101	0.7681
ELMo-BiLSTM-att	0.8132	0.7693
w2v-BiLSTM-att	0.7838	0.7491
fast-BiLSTM-att	0.7819	0.7446

Table 3: Results of sentiment classification for dataset Reviews3.

In table 4, we show results on the performance of the proposed models for sentiment analysis for twitter domain (*Twitter*). We observe similar trends as for the domain of customer reviews. The most significant improvement brings using deep contextualized word representations. Similarly to the previous domain, employing bidirectional LSTM and attention mechanism improves the performance further. Unlike for dataset of customer reviews, using of fastText and word2vec representations brought improvement, which was significantly lower than using ELMo word representations.

model	micro F1	macro F1
lookup-LSTM	0.5804	0.5565
lookup-BiLSTM	0.5866	0.5614
lookup-BiLSTM-att	0.5967	0.5747
ELMo-LSTM	0.6594	0.6386
ELMo-BiLSTM	0.6671	0.6487
ELMo-BiLSTM-att	0.6978	0.6695
w2v-BiLSTM-att	0.6107	0.5908
fast-BiLSTM-att	0.6468	0.6188

Table 4: Results of sentiment classification for dataset Twitter.

Comparison with Previous Work

In Table 5, we show comparison against previously published works for sentiment classification for customer reviews. Both models used pretrained word2vec (Mikolov et al., 2013) word representations to improve quality of classification trained on prim dataset of the Slovak national cor-

pora (Jazykovedný ústav Ľ. Štúra SAV, 2013). The first model employs SVM (Krchnavy and Simko, 2017) for sentiment classification and the second one employs neural networks along with various form of text preprocessing (Pecar et al., 2018). Since the original papers do not consider macro F1 score for evaluation, we can compare our performance only in micro F1 score. Most of our models outperforms previously published models and our best models improve overall sentiment classification by more than 6 points.

model	micro F1	macro F1
ELMo-BiLSTM-att	0.8132	0.7693
SVM baseline	0.7512	-
NN baseline	0.7296	-

Table 5: Comparison of sentiment classification for dataset Reviews 3.

In Table 6, we show comparison with the original work of the authors of dataset (Mozetič et al., 2016). The authors performed evaluation with multiple machine learning algorithms and the best one was labeled as TwoPlaneSVMbin. We cannot compare our method with theirs completely, since we were not able to obtain all samples in their dataset (due to the twitter post unavailability), hence we used only a smaller portion. We performed also experiments with another method for improving overall quality of sentiment classification – model ensemble. We trained the same model multiple times (3 in this case) and performed two types of model ensemble. In both experiments, the ensembles performed better than any of the model.

model	micro F1	macro F1
ELMo-BiLSTM-att	0.6978	0.6636
voting 3	0.6994	0.6710
mean 3	0.7008	0.6728
TwoPlaneSVMbin	0.6840*	-

Table 6: Comparison of best performing model and different types of model ensemble for dataset Twitter. * - indicates differences in used dataset

Error Analysis

In figure 2, we provide also confusion matrix of our best performed model for Twitter dataset, since our model performed much worse for the Twitter dataset than the Review3 dataset.

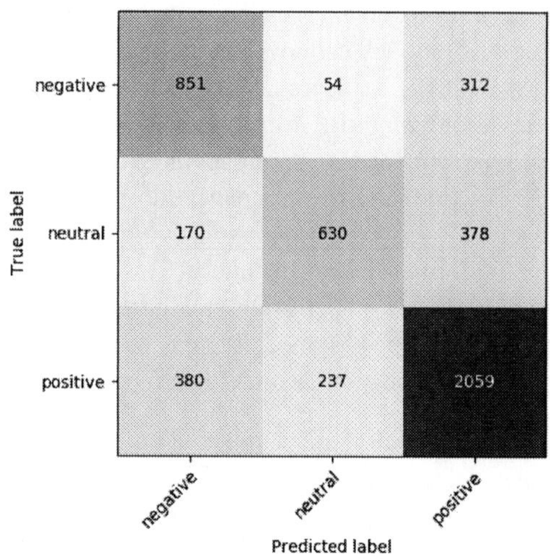

Figure 2: Confusion matrix for best performed model on Twitter dataset.

As we can observe, most mislabeled predictions are concerned with positive labels, where our model did not predict positive label or predicted it incorrectly. We performed also additional error analysis, where we looked for mislabeled tweets. After further analysis, we observed that many positively labeled tweets do not contain any sign of positive words and label was assigned due to additional information in link attached in tweet itself. This type of labeling dost not enable sentiment classification based only on textual data itself. Another observed problem could be considered labeling tweets based on real world context (e.g. political situation, twitter responses etc.), which was not provided. We suppose described problems caused significantly lower performance on Twitter dataset, since we tackled only problem of sentiment classification on texts themselves without utilizing any additional information. We believe there will be need for further manual evaluation to identify limits of human performance for this kind of dataset.

5 Conclusion

In our work, we tackled problem of sentiment classification for Slovak language, which suffers mainly from low resource datasets. We introduced several neural model architectures employing state-of-the-art techniques for sentiment analysis. As we showed, our models outperformed previously published models for sentiment classification in Slovak language. Our models performed significantly better especially for the dataset of customer reviews, where we achieved F1 score higher more than by 6 points. We suppose the main contribution to these results can be attributed to deep contextualized word representations – ELMo. Our results also showed there is only a little improvement of model performance utilizing bidirectional LSTM and attention mechanism. On the other hand, combination of those techniques along with used pre-trained word representations helps achieving significantly better results, especially for the dataset of customer reviews. The lower performance on twitter dataset could be due to nature of the dataset, where customer reviews tend to be mostly positive and negative and twitter post could be much more general in sentiment.

We suppose there is also a significant space for further improvement and application different methods, such as cross-lingual learning, where knowledge from multiple languages can be used to reduce the problem of lack of annotated resources (Pikuliak et al., 2019). Since we did not performed any significant fine-tuning and used only some of the standard setups, there can be a space to obtain even better results than we presented in this paper. Other point to consider can be training ELMo on much larger dataset, since authors of ELMo for many languages trained those representations only on the limited dataset. We provide also code for our experiments, which is available on GitHub [1].

Acknowledgments

This work was partially supported by the Slovak Research and Development Agency under the contracts No. APVV-17-0267 and No. APVV SK-IL-RD-18-0004, the Scientific Grant Agency of the Slovak Republic grants No. VG 1/0725/19 and No. VG 1/0667/18 and by the Cultural and Educational Grant Agency of the Slovak Republic, grant No. KEGA 028STU-4/2017.

References

Oscar Araque, Ignacio Corcuera-Platas, J. Fernando Sanchez-Rada, and Carlos A. Iglesias. 2017. Enhancing deep learning sentiment analysis with ensemble techniques in social applications. *Expert Systems with Applications*, 77:236 – 246.

Wanxiang Che, Yijia Liu, Yuxuan Wang, Bo Zheng, and Ting Liu. 2018. Towards better UD parsing:

---

[1] https://github.com/SamuelPecar/Slovak-sentiment-analysis

Deep contextualized word embeddings, ensemble, and treebank concatenation. In *Proceedings of the CoNLL 2018 Shared Task: Multilingual Parsing from Raw Text to Universal Dependencies*, pages 55–64, Brussels, Belgium. Association for Computational Linguistics.

Ilia Chetviorkin and Natalia Loukachevitch. 2013. Evaluating sentiment analysis systems in Russian. In *Proceedings of the 4th Biennial International Workshop on Balto-Slavic Natural Language Processing*, pages 12–17, Sofia, Bulgaria. Association for Computational Linguistics.

Jacob Devlin, Ming-Wei Chang, Kenton Lee, and Kristina Toutanova. 2018. Bert: Pre-training of deep bidirectional transformers for language understanding. *arXiv preprint arXiv:1810.04805*.

Murhaf Fares, Andrey Kutuzov, Stephan Oepen, and Erik Velldal. 2017. Word vectors, reuse, and replicability: Towards a community repository of large-text resources. In *Proceedings of the 21st Nordic Conference on Computational Linguistics*, pages 271–276, Gothenburg, Sweden. Association for Computational Linguistics.

Edouard Grave, Piotr Bojanowski, Prakhar Gupta, Armand Joulin, and Tomas Mikolov. 2018. Learning word vectors for 157 languages. In *Proceedings of the International Conference on Language Resources and Evaluation (LREC 2018)*.

Ivan Habernal, Tomáš Ptáček, and Josef Steinberger. 2014. Supervised sentiment analysis in czech social media. *Information Processing & Management*, 50(5):693–707.

Sepp Hochreiter and Jürgen Schmidhuber. 1997. Long short-term memory. *Neural computation*, 9(8):1735–1780.

Jeremy Howard and Sebastian Ruder. 2018. Universal language model fine-tuning for text classification. In *Proceedings of the 56th Annual Meeting of the Association for Computational Linguistics (Volume 1: Long Papers)*, pages 328–339, Melbourne, Australia. Association for Computational Linguistics.

Jazykovedný ústav Ľ. Štúra SAV. 2013. Slovenský národný korpus.

Jurgita Kapočiutė-Dzikienė, Algis Krupavičius, and Tomas Krilavičius. 2013. A comparison of approaches for sentiment classification on Lithuanian Internet comments. In *Proceedings of the 4th Biennial International Workshop on Balto-Slavic Natural Language Processing*, pages 2–11, Sofia, Bulgaria. Association for Computational Linguistics.

R. Krchnavy and M. Simko. 2017. Sentiment analysis of social network posts in slovak language. In *2017 12th International Workshop on Semantic and Social Media Adaptation and Personalization (SMAP)*, pages 20–25.

Tomas Mikolov, Kai Chen, Greg Corrado, and Jeffrey Dean. 2013. Efficient estimation of word representations in vector space. *arXiv preprint arXiv:1301.3781*.

Igor Mozetič, Miha Grčar, and Jasmina Smailović. 2016. Multilingual twitter sentiment classification: The role of human annotators. *PloS one*, 11(5):e0155036.

Samuel Pecar, Marian Simko, and Maria Bielikova. 2018. Sentiment analysis of customer reviews: Impact of text pre-processing. In *2018 World Symposium on Digital Intelligence for Systems and Machines (DISA)*, pages 251–256. IEEE.

Samuel Pecar, Marian Simko, and Maria Bielikova. 2019. NL-FIIT at SemEval-2019 task 9: Neural model ensemble for suggestion mining. In *Proceedings of the 13th International Workshop on Semantic Evaluation*, pages 1218–1223, Minneapolis, Minnesota, USA. Association for Computational Linguistics.

Matthew Peters, Mark Neumann, Mohit Iyyer, Matt Gardner, Christopher Clark, Kenton Lee, and Luke Zettlemoyer. 2018. Deep contextualized word representations. In *Proceedings of the 2018 Conference of the North American Chapter of the Association for Computational Linguistics: Human Language Technologies, Volume 1 (Long Papers)*, pages 2227–2237. Association for Computational Linguistics.

Matus Pikuliak, Marian Simko, and Maria Bielikova. 2019. Towards combining multitask and multilingual learning. In *SOFSEM 2019: Theory and Practice of Computer Science*, pages 435–446, Cham. Springer International Publishing.

Leon Rotim and Jan Šnajder. 2017. Comparison of short-text sentiment analysis methods for Croatian. In *Proceedings of the 6th Workshop on Balto-Slavic Natural Language Processing*, pages 69–75, Valencia, Spain. Association for Computational Linguistics.

Mike Schuster and Kuldip K Paliwal. 1997. Bidirectional recurrent neural networks. *IEEE Transactions on Signal Processing*, 45(11):2673–2681.

Josef Steinberger, Tomáš Brychcín, and Michal Konkol. 2014. Aspect-level sentiment analysis in czech. In *Proceedings of the 5th workshop on computational approaches to subjectivity, sentiment and social media analysis*, pages 24–30.

Yequan Wang, Minlie Huang, Xiaoyan Zhu, and Li Zhao. 2016. Attention-based LSTM for aspect-level sentiment classification. In *Proceedings of the 2016 Conference on Empirical Methods in Natural Language Processing*, pages 606–615, Austin, Texas. Association for Computational Linguistics.

Sentiment Analysis for Multilingual Corpora

Svitlana Galeshchuk
Governance Analytics,
PSL Research University /
University Paris Dauphine
Place du Marechal
de Lattre de Tassigny,
75016 Paris, France
s.galeshchuk@gmail.com

Julien Jourdan
PSL Research University /
University Paris Dauphine
Place du Marechal
de Lattre de Tassigny,
75016 Paris, France
julien.jourdan@dauphine.psl.eu

Ju Qiu
Governance Analytics,
PSL Research University /
University Paris Dauphine
Place du Marechal
de Lattre de Tassigny,
75016 Paris, France
ju.qiu@dauphine.psl.eu

Abstract

The paper presents a generic approach to the supervised sentiment analysis of social media content in foreign languages. The method proposes translating documents from the original language to English with Google's Neural Translation Model. The resulted texts are then converted to vectors by averaging the vectorial representation of words derived from a pre-trained Word2Vec English model. Testing the approach with several machine learning methods on Polish, Slovenian and Croatian Twitter corpora returns up to 86 % of classification accuracy on the out-of-sample data.

1 Introduction

Sentiment analysis is gaining prominence as a topic of research in different areas of application (journalism, political science, marketing, finance, etc.). In the last two decades, opinion-rich data sources are widely available because of web-resources and social networks. While lexicon-based frameworks have long been investigated for sentiment analysis, deep learning methods with a vectorial representation of words are proving to deliver promising results. The integration of two types of methods is widely investigated as well. Thus, the sentiment analysis approaches usually require either fine-grained lexicon of most frequent words along with their polarity scores or the dataset large enough for supervised training of deep learning network, sufficient computational memory, etc.

Moreover, most of the open-source datasets for training sentiment models comprise English-language texts. The lexicons are not always available for other languages, and it remains a time-consuming task to construct them. It motivates us to build on the existing approaches and test a rather general method to run a sentiment analysis for different languages without polarity dictionaries using relatively small datasets.

We address the challenges for sentiment analysis in Slavic languages by using the averaged vectors for each word in a document translated in English. The vectors derive from the Word2Vec model pre-trained on Google news.

Researchers tend to use the language-specific pre-trained Word2Vec models (e.g., Word2Vec model pre-trained on Wikipedia corpus in Greek, Swedish, etc.). On the contrary, *we propose benefiting from Google's Neural Translation Model translating the texts from other languages to English. Translated documents are then converted to the fixed-vectorial representation with Google Word2Vec model.*[1] *The supervised machine learning classifiers such as Gradient Boosting Trees, Random Forest, Support Vector Machines provide sufficiently high accuracy on the out-of-sample data converted to the aggregate vectors.*

The rest of the paper is structured as follows: Section 2 provides a brief review of related literature. Section 3 describes the methodology. Section 4 expands on data used. Section 5 presents the results from our experiments. Section 6 concludes with some observations on our findings and identifies directions of future research.

2 Related Work

This section elaborates on existing methods for sentiments analysis and the adjacent approaches to text data treatment that have helped us formulate the proposed process of sentiment analysis. Following Dashtipour et al. (2016), we divide sentiment analysis systems on lexicon-based, corpus-based and hybrid.

---

[1]https://drive.google.com/file/d/
0B7XkCwpI5KDYNlNUTTlSS21pQmM/edit

Proceedings of the 7th Workshop on Balto-Slavic Natural Language Processing, pages 120–125,
Florence, Italy, 2 August 2019. ©2019 Association for Computational Linguistics

2.1 Lexicon-Based Methods

Lexicon-based methods employ the dictionaries of pre-defined words with corresponding polarity scores. These scores define how positive the term is. Some approaches (e.g., Vader lexicon in Hutto and Gilbert (2014)) use the opinion of several experts and the final polarity measure equals the mean of the corresponding scores. A subset of the most popular and promising lexicon-based sentiment classifiers for English corpora has been reported in Levallois (2013). Concerning Slavic languages, Slovak lexicon translated from English and annotated with Bare-bones particle swarm optimization helps achieve 0.865 F1 score in sentiment classification reported in Krchnavy and Simko (2017). Gombar et al. (2017) construct Croatian domain-specific lexicon for domain-specific classification; Haniewicz et al. (2013) run sentiment analysis with polarity lexicon for reviews in Polish that renders up to 79% of accuracy. We will refer to these papers later in our study to corroborate our results by comparison with the existing methods.

The idea proposed in Wan (2009) shares some similarities with our method. Authors translate Chinese text in English and then employ lexicon-based ensemble method to classify texts on positive or negative. The reported accuracy is 85.3% though it requires Chinese and English lexicon and some additional calculation to create the ensemble method. However, word scoring in each constructed lexicon usually relies on human treatment and perception. The task is also labor-intensive, and it may be challenging to find fine-grained lexicons for some languages.

Moreover, a well-known drawback of lexicon-based method is the contextual ignorance as some terms may have different meanings in various documents. Besides, some documents (e.g., short texts as tweets) sometimes do not include any word from the lexicon. The introduction of word vectorial representation tend to address this disadvantage.

2.2 Corpus-based and Hybrid Methods with Vectorial Representation

Embedding approaches usually rely on the semantic vector spaces derived from the neural networks. Their application in supervised experimental setups for polarity analysis often demonstrates superior performance to the lexicon-based methods

(Le and Mikolov, 2014; Severyn and Moschitti, 2015). As the reference point in our study we use the papers of Giatsoglou et al. (2017) and Garten et al. (2018) where authors meticulously employ Sentence2Vec in their methodological settings. Giatsoglou et al. (2017) uses Sentence2Vec based on the Word2Vec model learned from the Wikipedia corpus in Greek. The performance is evaluated with the datasets of mobile phonesâĂŹ reviews in Greek. The model that exploits the vectors derived from the Wikipedia corpora+the reviews provides the highest accuracy of 70.89-82.40% on test samples. Author further try hybrid methods (lexicon- and embedding- driven) that deliver slightly better results. Rotim and Šnajder (2017) use similar approach for Croatian corpora obtaining 0.822 as F1 score for game reviews but the results are much worse for the Twitter dataset. In contrast to the authors, we do not train our Word2Vec model for the corpora in Slavic languages. Instead, we employ the pre-trained Google News Word2Vec model after translating texts to English. It makes our approach more universal and easier to apply to the foreign language corpora yielding satisfactory accuracy (see Results).

Garten et al. (2018) compute the cosine similarity between the aggregate vectorial representation of documents and the âĂIJnegativeâĂİ and âĂIJpositiveâĂİ dictionaries. Precision on the IMBD English reviews data varies between 0.70-0.75. Our findings show that the introduction of the polarity dictionaries delivers less accurate outputs than using Sentence2Vec. However, our set-up does not foresee unsupervised learning.

Feature-based approach for Czech language sentiment classification renders 0.69 as F1 measure in Habernal et al. (2013). The method has to be adjusted for other languages if used.

Zhang et al. (2017) report another approach for Twitter sentiment classification employing character-based Convolutional neural networks with different languages. The method transforms the characters in alphabetic order in UTF-8 codes facilitating sentence segmentation. The character embedding matrix is then used as an input for the convolutional neural network. We consider these findings as one of the benchmarks for comparison in our study.

3 Methodology

Recall from the previous sections that we tend to develop a sentiment analysis approach for multi-language use. Fig.1 depicts the proposed method.[2]

```
1.For   each    document   in    available
collection:
   Initialize text preprocessing2
   Translate to English
2. Load Google Word2Vec model
3. For each document in translated texts:
     For each word in document:
       If   word   is   in   Google   Word2Vec
vocabulary:
         Draw vector representation
     Compute  aggregated  representation  of
words in document
4. Generate the file with aggregated vector
representation for each document.
5. Initialize machine learning method.
```

Figure 1: Generic process of the multilingual sentiment classiffication

Word vectorial representation spurs the interest of many researchers in natural language processing due to its capacity to catch the meaning of terms depending on the context. Researchers and practitioners who use deep learning methods for sentiment analysis tend to learn the embedding from the available dataset or pre-trained word embedding models (i.e., Word2Vec, Glove). Each document is then represented as the stack of vectors. Document padding unifies the number of vectors that serve as the network input. It means that the network deals with [batchsize*size of vectorial stack*number of features] input data dimensions which may be computationally costly.

Instead, our model exploits vectorial representation of the words with a transfer learning approach: Google Word2Vec pre-trained model serves as a source of 300-dimensional dense vectors for each word in the text. Then the model computes an elementwise sum of the vectors divided by the number of terms in the text.

The use of Google Word2Vec model has several advantages over learning embeddings from the training data: (i) Google model has been pre-trained with the corpora of the news containing circa 100 billion words where each term has been used more than once and in different contexts. It

makes the model the state-of-the-art regarding the quality of vectors which plays a crucial role in our study as we use the translated text from Slavic languages to English; (ii) Google model comprises approximately 3 million words and phrases. This vocabulary covers the lion share of lexicon employed by web-resources and social networks users; (iii) we do not need to construct a large dataset to train our model as the vectors have already been pre-trained with a significant number of terms.

Google Translation. Machine translation does not always provide perfect accuracy from the linguistic point of view. However, the resulted translation with recently introduced GoogleâĂŹs Neural Machine Translation approach tends to deliver English text contextually similar to the input document (see Wu et al. (2016) for more details).

3.1 Machine Learning Methods Used

This subsection discusses the machine learning classifiers employed in a supervised learning approach to classify texts on positive or negative. The implementation details are stored in the Github repository.

Support Vector Machines Classification. This approach belongs to the family of versatile machine learning methods with high accuracy on non-large datasets. It tries to find the broadest possible margin between positive and negative classes. As in Giatsoglou et al. (2017) we use linear Support Vector Classifier (SVC) and Gaussian Radial Basis Function (RBF) in our set-up.

Random forest (RF) helps overcome the disadvantages of a single decision tree by summarizing and averaging predictions over the number of trees. It is an ensemble learning approach that uses the outputs of the individual predictors as votes. If the positive class gets more votes, the method will return the corresponding result.

Gradient Boosting Trees. In our set-up Gradient boosting (GBT) method represents an ensemble of classification decision trees. Each tree sequentially joins the ensemble correcting the antecedent by fitting its residual errors.

Deep Neural Networks (DNN) are versatile methods that address complex machine learning tasks. They are effective to capture non-linearities in the data and latent relationships between the variables. We build on state-of-art DNN architectures and recent findings on hyperparameters cali-

---

[2]We removed urls, emojis, digits and punctuation marks as text preprocessing

bration in our empirical search for the model with the best possible accuracy. The architecture of our DNN comprises 2 hidden layers with dropout rate of 0.2

3.2 Evaluation

For this classification problem, the quality of a model is measured by the proportion of correctly classified observations (accuracy). The receiver operating characteristic curve plots true positive rate against false positive rate for the test set. The area under the curve (AUC) represents another way to compare the classifiers.

4 Data

Multilanguage Corpora. We use the corpora in Polish, Slovenian and Croatian in our experimental set-up. Polish, Slovenian and Croatian languages belong to the Indo-European family as well as English. However, they are members of the Slavic branch that makes these languages share less close ties with English than, for example, French, Spanish or Italian would have.

We retrieve the dataset with texts and corresponding polarity scores for tweets in mentioned languages from the website of the European research infrastructure CLARIN. [3] Our dataset comprises 2794 tweets in Polish (1397 positive and 1397 negative), 4272 tweets in Slovenian (2312 positive and 1950 negative) and 3554 tweets in Croatian (2129 positive and 1425 negative).

Tweets may contain emojis and/or URLs. We removed them together with digits and punctuation marks as a part of the data preprocessing step. Later we employ Google Translator API via Python Library Google-api-translate to translate texts to English language. Google Translation Library is easy to use and it takes approximately 12 min to translate 1000 tweets. The corpora for Slovenian and Croatian languages are imbalanced. Hence, we use stratified split in the cross-validation settings that returns folds with the corresponding ratio of classes in training and test sets.

5 Results

After mentioned datasets have been translated to English, each tweet is converted to the vector creating the averaged representation of the document words. Data is split into training/testing sets as

80/20 respecting the ratio of positive and negative observations.

Table 1 presents the accuracy results for three datasets (Polish, Slovenian, Croatian). The overall accuracy of the best classifiers is more than 76% which may be seen as satisfactory taking into consideration state-of-the-art findings. The tree-based methods usually deliver marginally better accuracy to the SVC and DNN classifiers. The accuracy of more than 78% is higher than the one reported in Garten et al. (2018) where authors use both documents aggregate representation and pre-defined lexicon. Recall measure is lower for the negative class in case of the corpora in Croatian and Slovenian. The issue of the imbalanced data may explain it.

Data/cl.	RF	GBT	SVM	RBF	DNN
Polish	76.30	**78.46**	76.84	73.25	75.58
Slovenian	73.12	**76.10**	75.70	71.80	75.69
Croatian	**86.32**	86.26	85.17	86.14	85.58

Table 1: Accuracy with applied machine learning methods

Fig. 2, 3, 4. depict the ROC curve with the largest AUC for each datasets (2) RF for Polish, (3) GBR for Slovenian, (4) RF for Croatian. ROC curve detects tree-base methods outperform the rest of approaches for all datasets.

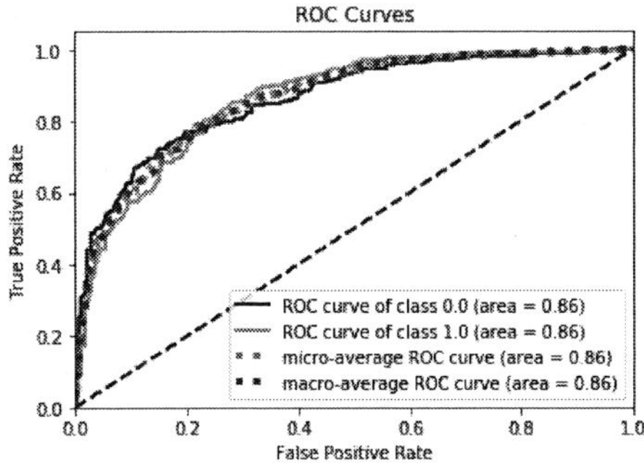

Figure 2: ROC curve with the largest AUC for Polish language

5.1 Comparison of Methods

In the previous sections we have described part of the exisiting state-of-the-art methods. This sub-section tries assessing the results obtained with our approach by comparison with mentioned studies. However, the direct juxtaposition is restricted as authors use different languages, corpora and

---

[3] https://www.clarin.si/repository/xmlui/

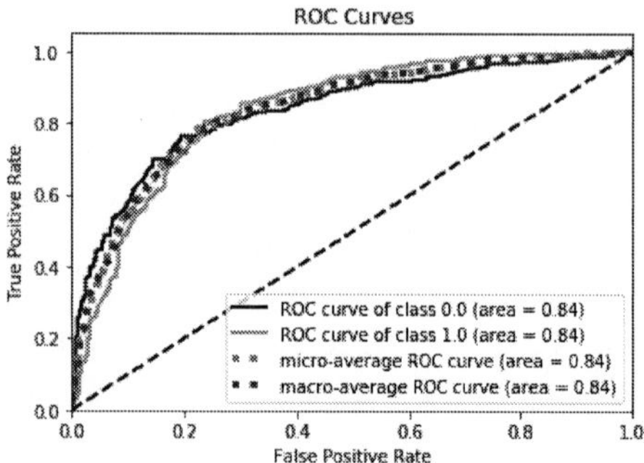

Figure 3: ROC curve with the largest AUC for Slovenian language

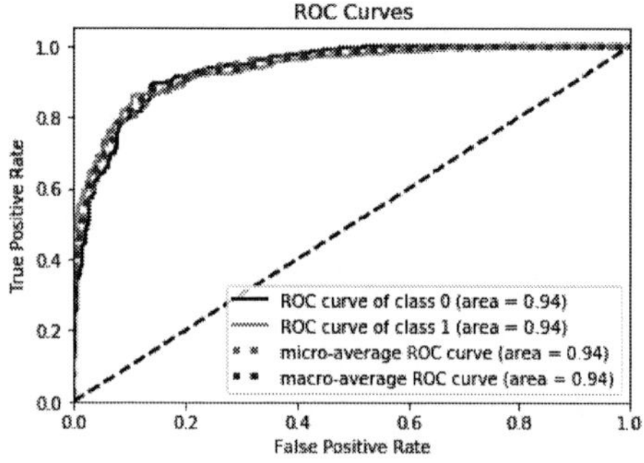

Figure 4: ROC curve with the largest AUC for Croatian language

scores to evaluate classifiers. Thus we choose the papers with developed methods in Polish, Slovenian and Croatian tested on social media or product review corpora to make the quantitative comparison as unbiased as possible. Table 2 reports the evaluation findings. The analysis proves that despite being generic our approach returns similar or better results for sentiment analysis in Polish, Slovenian and Croatian comparing to the other methods.

Author	Measure	Reported results	Results with developed method
POLISH LANGUAGE:			
Haniewicz et al. (2013)	Accuracy	circa 79.00	78.46
Zhang et al. (2017)	Accuracy	81.19	78.46
Buczynski and Wawer (2008)	Accuracy	77.05	78.46
SLOVENIAN LANGUAGE:			
Zhang et al. (2017)	Accuracy	78.07	76.10
Kadunc (2016)	Accuracy	76,20	76.10
CROATIAN LANGUAGE:			
Gombar et al. (2017)	F1 Score	0.66	0.86
Rotim and Šnajder (2017)	F1 Score	0.57	0.86
Agić et al. (2010)	F1 Score	0.63	0.86

Table 2: Comparison of Findings

6 Conclusion

The paper introduces and elaborates on the developed generic approach to sentiment analysis of multilingual corpora that encompasses translating texts to English, aggregating vectorial representation of translated words and eventually applying machine learning methods to classify documents on positive or negative. As pointed out earlier, the aim of the study is not to compete with the existing techics in terms of accuracy but to propose method that does not suffer from one-language applicability and is simple to implement. We build on the state-of-the-art and present a general set-up which may be used in supervised sentiment analysis for different Slavic languages. Testing the accuracy of our approach on a collection of tweets in three Slavic languages delivers comparable accuracy to the reported findings from recent papers on sentiment analysis for English and non-English corpora (see Related Work and Comparison of Methods). However, the difference in the classification accuracy for Polish, Slovenian and Croatian languages motivates us to test the method with other Slavic languages. These discrepancies may arrise from the quality of translation as well as from the imperfections in labeling the data. We are working on our own pre-labeled balanced dataset to further improve the approach.

Acknowledgments

We are grateful for the received support from the research initiative "Governance Analytics" funded by the PSL University under the program "Investissements Avenir" launched by the French Government and implemented by ANR with the references ANR-10-IDEX-0001-02 PSL Paris Sciences et Lettres (PSL). We would also like to thank the anonymous reviewers for their suggestions and comments.

References

Željko Agić, Nikola Ljubešić, and Marko Tadić. 2010. Towards sentiment analysis of financial texts in croatian. In *Proceedings of the Seventh International Conference on Language Resources and Evaluation*.

Aleksander Buczynski and Aleksander Wawer. 2008. Shallow parsing in sentiment analysis of product reviews. In *Proceedings of the Partial Parsing workshop at LREC*, volume 2008, pages 14–18.

Kia Dashtipour, Soujanya Poria, Amir Hussain, Erik Cambria, Ahmad YA Hawalah, Alexander Gelbukh, and Qiang Zhou. 2016. Multilingual sentiment analysis: state of the art and independent comparison of techniques. *Cognitive computation*, 8(4):757–771.

Justin Garten, Joe Hoover, Kate M Johnson, Reihane Boghrati, Carol Iskiwitch, and Morteza Dehghani. 2018. Dictionaries and distributions: Combining expert knowledge and large scale textual data content analysis. *Behavior research methods*, 50(1):344–361.

Maria Giatsoglou, Manolis G Vozalis, Konstantinos Diamantaras, Athena Vakali, George Sarigiannidis, and Konstantinos Ch Chatzisavvas. 2017. Sentiment analysis leveraging emotions and word embeddings. *Expert Systems with Applications*, 69:214–224.

Paula Gombar, Zoran Medić, Domagoj Alagić, and Jan Šnajder. 2017. Debunking sentiment lexicons: A case of domain-specific sentiment classification for croatian. In *Proceedings of the 6th Workshop on Balto-Slavic Natural Language Processing*, pages 54–59.

Ivan Habernal, Tomáš Ptáček, and Josef Steinberger. 2013. Sentiment analysis in czech social media using supervised machine learning. In *Proceedings of the 4th workshop on computational approaches to subjectivity, sentiment and social media analysis*, pages 65–74.

Konstanty Haniewicz, Wojciech Rutkowski, Magdalena Adamczyk, and Monika Kaczmarek. 2013. Towards the lexicon-based sentiment analysis of polish texts: Polarity lexicon. In *International Conference on Computational Collective Intelligence*, pages 286–295. Springer.

Clayton J Hutto and Eric Gilbert. 2014. Vader: A parsimonious rule-based model for sentiment analysis of social media text. In *Eighth international AAAI conference on weblogs and social media*.

Klemen Kadunc. 2016. Using machine learning for sentiment analysis of slovene web commentaries. *University of Ljubljana*.

Rastislav Krchnavy and Marian Simko. 2017. Sentiment analysis of social network posts in slovak language. In *2017 12th International Workshop on Semantic and Social Media Adaptation and Personalization (SMAP)*, pages 20–25. IEEE.

Quoc Le and Tomas Mikolov. 2014. Distributed representations of sentences and documents. In *International conference on machine learning*, pages 1188–1196.

Clement Levallois. 2013. Umigon: sentiment analysis for tweets based on terms lists and heuristics. In *Second Joint Conference on Lexical and Computational Semantics (* SEM), Volume 2: Proceedings of the Seventh International Workshop on Semantic Evaluation (SemEval 2013)*, volume 2, pages 414–417.

Leon Rotim and Jan Šnajder. 2017. Comparison of short-text sentiment analysis methods for croatian. In *Proceedings of the 6th Workshop on Balto-Slavic Natural Language Processing*, pages 69–75.

Aliaksei Severyn and Alessandro Moschitti. 2015. Twitter sentiment analysis with deep convolutional neural networks. In *Proceedings of the 38th International ACM SIGIR Conference on Research and Development in Information Retrieval*, pages 959–962. ACM.

Xiaojun Wan. 2009. Co-training for cross-lingual sentiment classification. In *Proceedings of the Joint Conference of the 47th Annual Meeting of the ACL and the 4th International Joint Conference on Natural Language Processing of the AFNLP: Volume 1-volume 1*, pages 235–243. Association for Computational Linguistics.

Yonghui Wu, Mike Schuster, Zhifeng Chen, Quoc V Le, Mohammad Norouzi, Wolfgang Macherey, Maxim Krikun, Yuan Cao, Qin Gao, Klaus Macherey, et al. 2016. Google's neural machine translation system: Bridging the gap between human and machine translation. *arXiv preprint arXiv:1609.08144*.

Shiwei Zhang, Xiuzhen Zhang, and Jeffrey Chan. 2017. A word-character convolutional neural network for language-agnostic twitter sentiment analysis. In *Proceedings of the 22nd Australasian Document Computing Symposium*, page 12. ACM.

Author Index